Software Quality Engineering

A Total Technical and Management Approach

Prentice Hall Series in Software Engineering
Randall W. Jensen, editor

Deutsch, *Software Verification and Validation: Realistic Project Approaches*
Deutsch and Willis, *Software Quality Engineering: A Total Technical and Management Approach*
Jensen and Tonies, *Software Engineering*
Peters, *Advanced Structured Analysis and Design*

Software Quality Engineering

A Total Technical and Management Approach

Michael S. Deutsch
Ronald R. Willis
Hughes Aircraft Company

Prentice Hall
Englewood Cliffs, NJ 07632

Library of Congress Cataloging-in-Publication Data

DEUTSCH, MICHAEL S.
  Software quality engineering.

  (Prentice Hall series in software engineering)
  Includes index.
    1. Computer software—Quality control. I. Willis,
Ronald R. II. Title.
QA76.76.Q35D48 1988   005   87-25712
ISBN 0-13-823204-0

The publisher offers discounts on this book when ordered
in bulk quantities. For more information, write:

> Special Sales/College Marketing
> Prentice Hall
> College Technical and Reference Division
> Englewood Cliffs, NJ 07632

Editorial/production supervision: Ann L. Mohan
Cover design: Edsal Enterprises

 © 1988 by Prentice-Hall, Inc.
A Division of Simon & Schuster
Englewood Cliffs, NJ 07632

Printed in the United States of America

10 9 8 7 6 5 4 3 2

ISBN 0-13-823204-0

Prentice-Hall International (UK) Limited, *London*
Prentice-Hall of Australia Pty. Limited, *Sydney*
Prentice-Hall Canada Inc., *Toronto*
Prentice-Hall Hispanoamericana, S.A., *Mexico*
Prentice-Hall of India Private Limited, *New Delhi*
Prentice-Hall of Japan, Inc., *Tokyo*
Simon & Schuster Asia Pte. Ltd., *Singapore*
Editora Prentice-Hall do Brasil, Ltda., *Rio de Janeiro*

Contents

CHAPTER 2

OVERVIEW OF THE BOOK 22

Part II

Engineering In Quality 43

CHAPTER 3

UNDERSTANDING SOFTWARE QUALITY 45

CHAPTER 4

SPECIFYING SOFTWARE QUALITY REQUIREMENTS 78

Preface

Software intensive systems and the problems they solve today are increasingly complex. The successful specification, design, development, installation, and support of these systems present an enormous intellectual challenge. We have begun to synthesize software development techniques into an engineering discipline that addresses this challenge. However, to date we have not mastered the skills needed to develop high-quality software systems. Some of the reasons are as follows:

- "High quality" has not been defined very well and may be viewed differently by the developer, customer, and user.

- Whenever "quality" *is* defined, the definitions are not meaningful to engineers.

- Quality thrusts in present practices are mainly concentrated in a review-oriented quality assurance framework that is semidetached from the engineering activities.

- Quality in the face of large complex system problems can become diffused and unmanageable.

- It has been very difficult to plan for quality because of the immaturity of the discipline.

This book is directed toward filling these gaps. We treat quality from a total technical and management viewpoint. We couple the more mature review, verification, and test technologies with specifiable quality factors that can be engineered. This entails defining quality in engineerable terms and then building a total quality planning framework that makes it possible to achieve a high-quality product even within a complex system development environment. We explain how quality is specified, and explore how this specification is translated into engineerable activities, how these activities are applied, and how to follow up and measure the resulting quality.

This book defines what high-quality software is, how to plan for it, and how to achieve it. This knowledge provides the manager with the tools needed to consciously select levels of desired quality and trade off effort and schedule against these levels. In short, a discipline is delineated that marries modern software engineering technology with the traditional rigor of quality assurance process methods; this discipline is *software quality engineering*.

The book is organized into four semi-independent parts:

- Part I, "Quality Concepts," deals with our quality approach at a summary or survey level. It includes an overview chapter that gives a synopsis of the full content of the book. This chapter can be used to prioritize further reading or to identify sections to peruse further.
- Part II, "Engineering In Quality," describes the overall approach to specifying software quality, achieving quality, and mapping a quality specification into an engineerable set of activities.
- Part III, "Using Verification and Validation to Review Out Defects and Test Out Errors," describes the major engineering activities used to cross-check the quality specification technique explained in Part II. The emphasis is on validating the system at the requirements and design stage. This validation is then coherently extended into a discussion of basic testing concepts, planning and controlling a test activity, and integration-level testing.
- Part IV, "Management Aspects of Software Quality," analyzes the economics of software quality and provides a guide to organizing the project to achieve quality.

The book is written in the form of an indexing scheme. It presents a number of discrete levels of quality and then points the reader to the technologies required to achieve a selected quality level. We have tried to target the content of the book to as wide an audience as possible. Specifically, we believe the following parties will find this book useful:

Software Engineers. Software engineers at all levels can benefit from guidance that will help them achieve desired levels of software quality. It fills a gap for them, that of trying to achieve high-quality software but not knowing what that means during the daily decision-making process. Engineers want to achieve quality in their work but need help in narrowing the distance between general concepts and specific practical methods to implement quality.

Software Managers. Software managers and program managers will need to enhance their grasp of the new challenge of planning for software quality requirements within real-world cost and schedule boundaries. The book serves as a planning tool for these managers.

System Engineers. To a large extent, system engineers will have to understand what software engineers mean when they say "quality" and learn how system-level design decisions can affect software quality.

Procuring Agencies. Those who purchase or contract for software will have to decide what level of quality is important to their system, trade off cost versus quality, and evaluate the quality of the delivered product. To the procuring agency, the book serves as a data base for quality specifications.

The book is presented somewhat in the fashion of a selectable shopping list (level of quality desired versus technique required), in order to help a wide spectrum of readers from major Department of Defense contractors to small commercial software shops achieve quality products within their individual constraints.

Part I

Quality Concepts

The Building Blocks of Software Quality

The real meat of this book is in Chapter 3 and beyond. But those chapters rely on a certain viewpoint and basic understanding of software quality. The purpose of this chapter is to persuade you to take on the required viewpoint and, if necessary, to raise your level of understanding.

1.1
Why Have Software Quality?

The title of this book contains the word ''engineering.'' This word denotes a disciplined, methodical approach to achieving software quality. The word was chosen for a purpose: to illuminate the recent advances in our understanding of the attributes of software quality and how we can methodically build those attributes into software. Before explaining how to go about achieving software quality through engineering, however, it is necessary to understand why software quality is desirable.

1.1.1 WHY A BOOK ON SOFTWARE QUALITY ENGINEERING?

This book brings together in one place all of the recent advances in the state of the art of software quality engineering. Some examples of these recent advances are detailed in the following publications:

- Rome Air Development Center, "Specification of Software Quality Attributes," RADC-TR-85-37 (Griffiss Air Force Base, NY: 1985).
- Robert Dunn, *Software Defect Removal* (New York: McGraw-Hill, 1984).
- "A Standard for Software Quality Metrics," IEEE Draft Standard P1061, (1986).
- A. Avizienis, "The N-Version Approach to Fault-Tolerant Software," *IEEE Transactions on Software Engineering*, vol. SE-11, no. 12, pp. 1491–1501.

The book couples these advances with traditional, proven techniques such as design and code reviews, testing techniques, independent verification and validation (IV&V), and quality assurance.

Finally, the book discusses the establishment of order and discipline (i.e., engineering) in the use of these software quality techniques through proper planning, personal assignments, quality and cost trade-offs, training, and judicious selection from the myriad of technologies available to help design in software quality.

1.1.2 WHAT IS "HIGH QUALITY"?

To understand what the phrase "high quality" means for software depends on your viewpoint. In fact, there are salespeople in our midst who take advantage of the ambiguity of the phrase and, having attracted our attention with it, proceed to sell us some product only remotely connected with software and quality. Rarely do they define what high quality is or how to specify it in some verifiable manner.

The definition of "high quality" is one of the problems we are trying to solve. In this book, we will define the term in a verifiable manner and show how the definition can be tailored to meet your specific needs.

1.1.3 HOW DOES A SOFTWARE DESIGNER MEET RELIABILITY REQUIREMENTS?

The user of a software product views quality much differently than the builder of the software product. For example, users want reliability, as measured by *mean time between failures* (MTBF), but designers think in terms such as modularity. Moreover, the term "MTBF" is often misapplied: users ask what the MTBF of a structure chart is (see Figure 1–1) when the question really doesn't make sense. MTBF is an attribute of executable code, not of a chart that hangs on a wall. And yet it should make sense

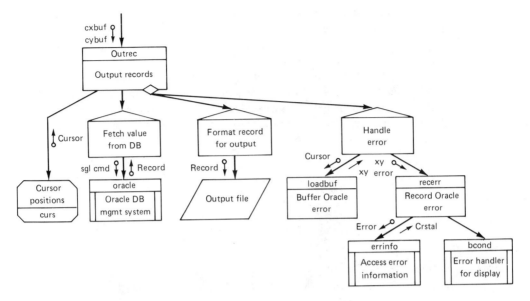

Figure 1-1 Does this software design have an MTBF > 200 Hours?

because we want engineers to design users' requests for quality into the software during the design process.

In this book we bridge the gap between the user's viewpoint and the designer's viewpoint, showing how to choose design-based quality attributes that satisfy user-based quality needs.

1.1.4 IS AN INCREASE IN RELIABILITY THE ANSWER?

A popular viewpoint about software quality concerns the detection and removal of errors from executing code. Typically, the occurrence of an error is recorded in terms of the time of the occurrence, the type of error involved, and the effect the error has on the system. The data points from several errors are then used to assess or predict the reliability of the software, and it is hoped that an upward trend will be revealed.

Does this upward trend denote high quality? Yes and no: yes, high quality software should be reliable and should show an improvement in reliability over time; but no, an increase in reliability is only one of many necessary attributes of high-quality software.

1.1.5 DO WE UNDERSTAND THE ROLE OF SOFTWARE?

To define high quality as it relates to software, we must understand the term "software." "Is it the holes in punched cards?" the system packager asked when assessing the shipping weight of the software!

Although the joke is old, have you ever heard of a good definition of software—a definition that is not constrained to someone's restricted viewpoint (e.g., a configuration identification number to a configuration manager) and yet that is clear enough so that the existence of software may be verified?

As Figure 1-2 illustrates, the role of software is to provide functionality to a computer system for a user. As the user perceives it, the software and hardware are bundled together into one indistinguishable box that provides some desirable automation capability to help that person do a job. This is a traditional problem . . . to define what software is in the mind of the person who is using it.

Figure 1-2 The role of software is to provide functionality to the computer user.

1.2
Whose Opinion Counts?

There are many different opinions about what attributes are important to achieving high quality, about the approach to achieving such quality in software, and about the level of quality to be achieved. Whose opinion counts?

1.2.1 DO WE TRY TO SATISFY THE USER, BUYER, DEVELOPER, OR MAINTAINER OF SOFTWARE?

Like beauty, quality is in the eye of the beholder. For software, there are four kinds of beholder, whose perceptions of quality can be summarized as follows:

- End User .... Helps me do my job better, faster, easier
- Buyer .... Meets the specifications
- Developer .... Few defects, error free at delivery
- Maintainer .... Understandable, testable, modifiable

Each of these has a different perception of what's important in terms of software quality. Then what do we do? Do we emphasize one to the exclusion of the others? Do we compromise to satisfy all of them? Is it possible to satisfy all of them without compromise?

1.2.2 WHICH APPROACH IS BEST?

Some of the more popular approaches to achieving software quality today are through the following techniques:

- Software quality assurance
- Independent verification and validation
- Government audits
- Quality metrics
- Modern development methodologies
- Use of the programming language Ada
- Software quality evaluation tools
- Software quality standardization
- Trend data analysis
- Reliability growth modeling
- Design/code inspection

So whom do we believe? Which one of the opinions is correct? Is any of them correct?

It turns out that all of the opinions are pieces of the same puzzle. Software quality engineering is the combination of all of these different approaches plus the decision-making rules for selecting just the right blend to achieve just the right result.

1.2.3 IS THERE A COMPROMISE: MANAGEMENT VS. ENGINEERING

Generally speaking, business management is driven by schedule, budget, and profit whereas engineering is driven by the quality of the product. The fear is that, if given free reign, engineers would continue to iterate designs until some level of exceptional quality was achieved, but at the expense of the delivery date and profit.

Is there a compromise between schedule and quality? Can a level of acceptable quality be achieved and still meet delivery dates and budgetary goals? The answer to these questions is an unqualified maybe!

Recent advances in software quality engineering reduce the effort and time required to achieve a level of quality acceptable to both the developer and the buyer. On the other hand, these same advances make quality so visible and easily understood that there may be more demands for quality than before (e.g., an item's being error free at delivery may not be enough anymore).

Contrary to popular belief, quality is not free. Engineering high-quality software requires investment—investment in the early stages of requirements and design to avoid later problems, and investment in design and code reviews to shake out errors that could plague the testing effort. Now it may be that the total cost to management of a quality product is less in the end than that of a lesser quality product (in fact, we believe it is), but when faced with the schedule and cost investment recommendation by engineering, will management accept the risk? *Is there a compromise?*

1.3
You Can't Achieve Quality Unless You Specify It!

This imperative regarding software quality is so important that it deserves the banner in Figure 1–3 to spell it out in big, bold letters. (Feel free to cut it out and paste it on your

YOU CAN'T ACHIEVE QUALITY. . . UNLESS YOU SPECIFY IT!

Figure 1-3.

wall!) Everyone has an opinion of what high quality is, and most opinions are different. It goes without saying, then, that no matter how good a job you think you have done, someone will find some quality defect in your work. Therefore, in order to achieve high-quality software, we must specify what we mean by high quality and then implement that specification. In other words,

High quality = Meeting the quality specification

That is to say, if we can stop all the handwaving for a minute and concentrate on defining in precise, measurable terms exactly what we mean when we say "high quality," then, and only then, will we be able to achieve it. Achieving high quality means to implement the quality requirements . . . no more, and no less.

1.4
The Apples and Oranges of Software Quality

We now turn to several aspects of software quality that are related and often misunderstood.

1.4.1 SOFTWARE QUALITY ENGINEERING VS. SOFTWARE QUALITY ASSURANCE

Software quality assurance (SQA) is a technique to help achieve quality. Generally, SQA fits in between the buyer and the developer, seeking to assure that what was contracted for is actually being accomplished. In addition, SQA attempts to identify and eliminate the causes of poor quality.

As Figure 1–4 depicts, SQA is operative outside the software engineering activities; indeed, one of the government requirements for effective SQA is that it be "independent" of the developing organization. As such, SQA is not involved with, but audits, the engineering process.

Figure 1-4 Software quality engineering is a part of engineering and quality assurance.

Software quality engineering, on the other hand, is part of the engineering process. Straddling both software engineering and software quality assurance, it is the achievement of quality through functioning as an integral part of the engineering process and through collaborating with SQA in identifying and removing quality bottlenecks. Succinctly stated, it is the work performed by software engineers to engineer quality into the product, while SQA is the auditing of the processes and products of engineers to validate that quality has indeed been engineered into the product.

A proposed new function, software technical assurance (STA), to support quality engineering, and the division of responsibilities between STA and SQA, are discussed in Chapter 15.

1.4.2 RELIABILITY IS A PROPER SUBSET OF SOFTWARE QUALITY

Oftentimes, software reliability is equated with software quality. However, reliability is a proper subset of software quality, as depicted in Figure 1–5.

According to IEEE standard 982, the reliability of a piece of software is the probability that a failure which causes deviation from required output by more than specified tolerances, in a specified environment, does not occur during a specified exposure period. (Paraphrasing, reliability is measured by how often software fails.) Software quality, on the other hand, is the aggregate of all those attributes which, when possessed by the software, will enable the software to perform its specified use. Among these attributes

Figure 1-5 Software reliability is a subset of software quality.

is reliability, as well as the other popular "ilities" (e.g., portability and maintainability) discussed later in Section 1.5.

1.4.3 PRODUCT QUALITY VS. PROCESS QUALITY

In talking about software quality, we must make sure that we distinguish between software product quality and software process quality . . . truly the apples and oranges of software quality.

Figure 1–6 helps to clarify the difference between the two types of quality. When we talk about software product quality, we are describing the attributes of the products resulting from software development. Product quality would then include, for example, the clarity of design documents, the traceability of designs, the reliability of code, and the coverage of tests.

When we talk about software process quality, we are describing the attributes of software development itself. Software development results from the interaction between

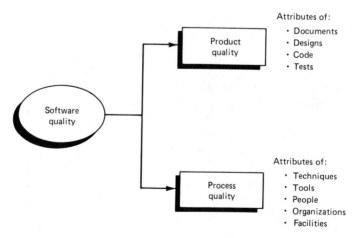

Figure 1-6 Differentiating product quality from process quality.

the five software engineering environment elements: techniques, tools, people, organization, and facilities. Process quality would then include, for example, the rigor of a technique, the productivity of a tool, the ability of a person, the communicativeness of an organization, and the availability of a facility.

Historically, in "immature" technologies one first concentrates on improving process quality to achieve better products. This is because saying that a technology is immature is another way of saying that we don't yet understand why people like the product produced by that technology. Software engineering has been this way for some time; ergo the reason there has been so much emphasis on techniques, tools, and facilities.

As we gain understanding of what software really is, we become better able to define the attributes of software that are desirable. For example, in Constantine's original work leading to his paper on structured design in 1974 ("Structured Design," *IBM System Journal*, vol. 4, no. 2 (1974), pp. 115–139), he looked for the characteristics shared by software systems that were easily maintained, and then designed a technique that would produce such characteristics. More recent work by Boeing and General Electric Corporations (see RADC-TR-85-37, *Specification of Software Quality Attributes*, February, 1985) has led to the expanded list of characteristics discussed in Section 1.5 as the "ilities."

So why all this fuss about the difference between process and product quality? First, many who talk about software quality don't clarify whether they are talking about product or process quality; and what they are talking about isn't clear unless you are looking for the distinction. Second, it is the opinion of the authors of this text that we should first specify the desirable attributes of the software product, and then choose techniques and tools that produce these attributes . . . not vice versa.

1.4.4 PRODUCTIVITY VS. QUALITY

Software productivity is the rate of producing software products. It is oftentimes measured in lines of code per man-month (LOC/MM). As a society, we must continually attempt to improve productivity because of the conflict between an increasing demand for software and a (relatively) decreasing supply of programmers.

A common question is, Will productivity get better or worse if we produce higher quality products? In other words, what is the relationship between the rate of production (or cost) and the quality of the product? Some of the main points, pro and con, are as follows:

Productivity Increases with Improved Quality

- Better quality results in less rework, which in turn reduces the total cost of development since rework costs approximate 50 percent of the total cost.

- Testing efforts are decreased because of fewer errors.

- Better quality means catching errors earlier; the earlier an error is caught, the cheaper it is to fix.

Productivity Decreases with Improved Quality

- Better quality requires investment, which isn't recouped until after delivery; so productivity associated with maintenance increases at the expense of a decrease in productivity associated with development.

- Design reviews improve quality but reduce productivity, because of the difference in people (review) costs compared with computer (test) costs.

- Quality-improvement techniques generally lead to more quality than is needed, thus reducing productivity (i.e., building more than is required).

In Chapter 14, we analyze the economics of quality-improvement guidelines for trading off costs against level of quality. This is as close as we come to resolving the difficult, emotional issue involved.

1.4.5 FUNCTIONAL VS. PERFORMANCE VS. QUALITY REQUIREMENTS

How often has it been said that something "can't be a quality requirement because it is a functional requirement"? So what? What rule says that a requirement can't be both a functional requirement and a quality requirement? Indeed, what prevents a requirement from being both a quality and a performance requirement?

Figure 1–7 depicts the relationship between three different types of software

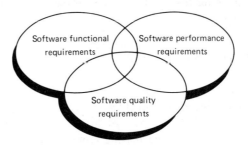

Figure 1-7.

requirements. The areas of intersection of the sets show that requirement types can have requirements in common. Some examples of these requirements are as follows.

FUNCTIONAL: Update file

FUNCTIONAL/QUALITY: Protect from unauthorized file updates

QUALITY: Separate critical files

QUALITY/PERFORMANCE: Organize files for minimum search time

PERFORMANCE: Less than two seconds per file update

So why is this topic worth talking about? Well, recall that you can't achieve quality unless you specify it. Therefore, to become expert in recognizing quality, you must become expert in specifying quality in a requirements specification, and understanding what a quality requirement is and is not is a necessary part of this expertise.

1.4.6 CODE VS. DESIGN VS. DOCUMENTATION QUALITY

To talk about software product quality entails specifying the attributes of code quality, design quality, and documentation quality. These are all different in some respects and the same in others.

A "high-quality" document is one that is

- understandable, consistent, and complete
- easy to use and accessible
- an accurate representation of the design and code
- and so on

A "high-quality" design is one that is

- understandable, consistent, and complete
- modular, simple, and traceable
- technically adequate
- and so on

"High-quality" code is code that is

- understandable, consistent, and complete
- efficient, fault tolerant, and traceable
- separately compilable
- and so on

Actually, there are more products than designs, code, and documents (e.g., tests, reports, and services) that need to be considered in the whole effort to specify quality. In this book, however, we will focus primarily on design and code quality.

1.4.7 DYNAMIC VS. STATIC QUALITY ATTRIBUTES

Software quality attributes can be classified as either dynamic or static. The distinction is in how one tests to validate that the attribute exists in the product.

Dynamic quality attributes are validated by examining the dynamic behavior of software while it is executing. The following are dynamic attributes:

- Mean time between failure
- Failure recovery time
- Percent of available resources used

Static quality attributes are validated by inspecting nonexecuting software products. The following are static attributes:

- Modularity
- Simplicity
- Completeness

Some attributes fall into both classes; that is, they are validated by both inspection and testing. An example of this type of attribute is machine independence, verified by inspection to ensure that knowledge of the machine is not encoded into data statements, and verified by execution on different types of machine.

1.5
The "Ilities" of Software Quality

The "ilities" of software quality, so called because most end in the suffix "ility," are commonly agreed-upon user needs. They are at the core of most, if not all, treatments of software quality.

Recall that, depending on your viewpoint, quality will have a different definition. The definitional focus of the "ilities" is the end user of software, that is, the person who uses or maintains the software, not the person who builds or buys the software. Therefore, the definitions of the "ilities" deal with the functionality provided by the software.

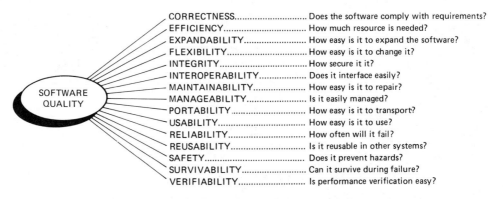

CORRECTNESS	Does the software comply with requirements?
EFFICIENCY	How much resource is needed?
EXPANDABILITY	How easy is it to expand the software?
FLEXIBILITY	How easy is it to change it?
INTEGRITY	How secure it it?
INTEROPERABILITY	Does it interface easily?
MAINTAINABILITY	How easy is it to repair?
MANAGEABILITY	Is it easily managed?
PORTABILITY	How easy is it to transport?
USABILITY	How easy is it to use?
RELIABILITY	How often will it fail?
REUSABILITY	Is it reusable in other systems?
SAFETY	Does it prevent hazards?
SURVIVABILITY	Can it survive during failure?
VERIFIABILITY	Is performance verification easy?

Figure 1-8 The "ilities" of software quality.

Fifteen software "ilities" are shown in Figure 1-8, together with the end user's concern from which they are derived. They are one of the foundations of software quality engineering.

From now on, we will refer to the "ilities" as software quality factors. They will be discussed and defined at length in Chapter 3. As an exercise, you might relate the list to software that you have had experience with that users ranked highly, and other software that users did not rank very highly.

1.6
Reviewing and Testing Are Not Enough
to Achieve Software Quality

It used to be that having been thoroughly tested was a mark of quality. Then inspection and testing were required. Today even more is needed.

1.6.1 THREE BASIC WAYS TO ACHIEVE SOFTWARE QUALITY

Three basic ways to achieve software quality are illustrated in Figure 1-9.

Testing for errors is the oldest of the three methods and one that all programmers are familiar with. To test software means to execute the software under simulated conditions to see whether or not it fails (that is, terminates as a result of an error). Because testing depends on a program's execution, it occurs after the software has been specified, designed, and coded. Although testing is a critical step in achieving software quality, it is not enough: software that is not maintainable will not improve merely as a result of more testing.

Reviewing for defects is a method that became popular in the 1970s. To review software means to subject designs and source code to manual inspection for compliance with standards and specifications. A noncompliant feature found during an inspection is a defect. Reviews are conducted on designs after the design is complete, and on code after programming is complete. Again, although review is a critical step in achieving software quality, it is not enough: certain levels of reliability cannot be achieved merely as a result of more review.

Engineering quality into the software is the most recent addition to the family of approaches to achieving software quality. To engineer in quality means to add quality to software during the engineering process. To achieve this, engineers and programmers must be conscious of quality requirements at the same time they are building in the functional requirements. Quality requirements thus take on the same relationship to the product as do functional requirements.

Engineering in quality should be where we place our emphasis. If done well, that is, if we add quality to the product as we build it, then the need for reviewing and testing is greatly reduced. Unfortunately, the terms "defect" and "error" in the techniques seduce us into thinking of achieving quality as a kind of clean-up operation after poor

Figure 1-9 Achieving software quality.

quality has already found its way into the software. Engineering in quality focuses in on the necessity for producing quality *during the design process itself.*

Although engineering in quality is fundamental, no quality program can be complete without reviewing and testing. (Humans will never be perfect.) There are levels of quality that can only be attained through inspection by our peers or through execution of the software in its actual computer environment.

1.6.2 THE SOFTWARE QUALITY LIFE CYCLE

The three ways to achieve quality just discussed are shown interacting with each other in Figure 1-10. This is the viewpoint of the software development life cycle of a person concerned with quality. It is also the basic structure of this book—the way we have organized the discussion of software quality engineering.

The first step in our life cycle model is to engineer a solution. This activity transforms functional and quality software requirements into software designs and code, and is constrained by cost and schedule. Software engineering techniques and tools are used as mechanisms to accomplish it. In engineering a solution we seek to engineer in quality by using techniques and tools that result in designs and code that have the required qualities as attributes.

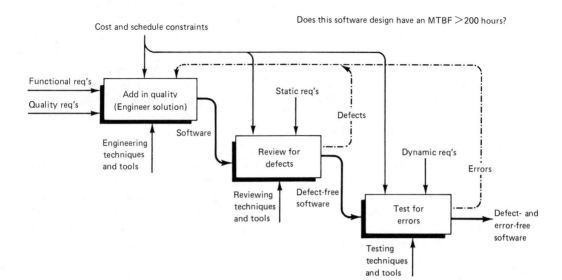

Figure 1-10 Software quality life-cycle.

The second step in the life cycle model is to review the resulting design and code. This activity transforms software designs and code into two products: software defects and defect-free software. Design and code defects become controls on the engineering activity to redesign or recode the solution (that is, engineering rework made necessary by noncompliant features). Review techniques and tools are used as mechanisms to accomplish the review activity.

The last activity in the life cycle model is to test the resulting code. This activity transforms defect-free code into two products: software errors and defect- and error-free code. Coding errors become controls on the engineering activity to redesign or recode the solution (again, engineering rework made necessary by noncompliant features). Testing techniques and tools are used to accomplish the testing activity.

The life cycle model not only serves as a framework for a discussion of software quality engineering, but it also points out why a quality system may or may not be efficient. Three throttles or controls, which can become bottlenecks, on the efficiency of the quality system are:

- Budgetary and scheduling controls on the activities
- Effectiveness of the techniques and tools
- Volume of rework

Inadequate budgets and unrealistic schedules can choke a quality program. Have you ever seen a project run by crisis management that also had an effective quality program? Probably not, because people who are reacting to crises only have time to "get the job out the door." They don't have enough time to add quality to the product, or time for thorough review, or time for exhaustive testing. Furthermore, crises change management priorities: the filled-in milestone becomes the only important goal, while quality becomes one of those "cans that are kicked ahead."

Techniques and tools are the mechanisms for performing the engineering, reviewing, and testing activities. Engineering techniques and tools are good if they result in a high percentage of the required quality attributes (i.e., they result in the "ilities," together with few defects and errors). Reviewing techniques and tools are good if they lead to the discovery of a large percentage of the actual defects. Testing techniques and tools are good if they lead to the discovery of a large percentage of the actual errors.

The volume of flow occurring over the defect and error feedback loops is also a critical throttle to the quality system efficiency. Obviously, the higher the traffic over these feedback loops, the more rework that is necessary, and therefore, the lower the efficiency of the system. The effectiveness of the engineering techniques and tools, together with other factors such as personnel skill, organizational policy, and resource availability, are major controls on this flow.

1.7
Total Quality Planning

Total quality planning is the consideration of all activities necessary to achieve software quality. Too often, plans overemphasize some subset of all that needs to be done at the expense of neglecting other, equally important activities. Total quality planning works on the principle that the chain is no stronger than its weakest link.

A total quality plan is organized into the following major areas, discussed in turn subsequently:

Total Quality Plan

PREPARATION	Putting into place that which is necessary to engineer in quality
SPECIFICATION	Making quality engineerable
EVALUATION	Validating that quality was in fact engineered in

1.7.1 PREPARATION

Preparation means getting ready to do a job before the job starts; that is, preparation is never having to catch up. The preparation part of the total quality plan deals with preparing people, organizations, and the software engineering environment, and ensuring that the software requirements are producible. Preparation should result in the following before the job starts:

SKILLED PEOPLE
REALISTIC PLANS

EFFECTIVE METHODOLOGY
PRODUCIBLE REQUIREMENTS

The cornerstone of quality is skilled and motivated people. If you are a software manager, you cannot overemphasize the effort you put into preparing people to be skilled. The total quality plan must include preparations to:

- Hire good people.
- Train people in the use of the methodology.
- Match people's talents with job needs.
- Motivate people toward quality goals.

As mentioned, unrealistic plans can choke the efficiency of a quality system. Realistic planning takes time and effort, but if done correctly, achieving quality in software is possible. Realistic plans are those that

- Are based on what *can* be done, not what needs to be done.
- Are based on realism, not optimism.
- Are based on a practical understanding of the job.
- Include sufficient time for iteratively reviewing and reworking.
- Are in use (as opposed to being ignored).

Having an effective methodology means providing effective tools and techniques for the engineering, reviewing, and testing activities. As discussed, effective techniques and tools not only make quality achievable, but also make the quality system more efficient. Preparation for effective methodology means accomplishing the following before the job starts:

- Selecting the techniques and tools based on the level of quality required (see Chapter 5).
- Implementing the tools (i.e., readying them for use).
- Writing instructions, (i.e., training materials) for use of the techniques and tools.
- Conducting trial runs of the software to "shake out" the bugs.

Lastly, preparation must include a review of the software requirements to determine whether they are producible. Requirements can be unproducible if they are (1) technically infeasible, or (2) more work than budgeted for. The following table lists the attributes of good software requirements.

Attributes of a good requirements product	Attributes of requirements that are producible
Modifiable	Consistent
Complies with contract	Appropriate detail
Structured	Understandable
Good design	Not design restrictive
Complete	Testable
Traceable	Feasible
Portable	No unfinished holes
Necessary and sufficient to perform the job	Manageable
Technologically sound	

1.7.2 SPECIFICATION

As mentioned earlier, you can't achieve quality unless you specify it. Therefore, a significant part of the total quality plan must include activities dedicated to the specification of required software quality attributes. The specification process can be broken down as follows:

Specification

GATHER QUALITY NEEDS

DEVELOP COMPLETE SET OF REQUIREMENTS

ENSURE MEASURABILITY AND TESTABILITY

Gathering quality needs means understanding and capturing the user's unique needs with respect to software quality. Developing a complete set of software quality requirements means converting those needs to specifications of quality. Ensuring the measurability and testability of the requirements means making the requirements objective (not subjective) and understandable to the engineers who are responsible for implementing them. Techniques for accomplishing these specification goals are discussed in detail in Chapter 4.

1.7.3 EVALUATION

The purpose of evaluation is to *validate that quality has in fact been engineered into the software.* The emphasis is on *demonstrating good quality*, not finding poor quality. Evaluation should include consideration of the following:

Review Out Defects

INTERNAL REVIEWS

REVIEWS OF DOCUMENTATION

FORMAL REVIEWS

Test Out Errors

UNIT TEST

CSC TEST

CSCI TEST

Review techniques and tools are discussed in Part IV of the text; testing is the subject of Part V.

_____Chapter 2_____

Overview of the Book

_____

This chapter provides a summary of the key concepts and methodologies presented in detail in the body of the book. The three-tier quality model introduced in Chapter 1, consisting of three major activities—engineering in quality, reviewing out defects, and testing out errors—is explored further. Methods for engineering in quality are summarized in Section 2.1, and verification and validation techniques are outlined in Section 2.2. The managerial aspects of software quality are summarized in Section 2.3.

The chapter can serve as a somewhat fleshed-out introduction to software quality engineering. Alternatively, the reader might elect to use it as a survey to identify those portions of the book to be looked into further or to arrange subsequent readings hierarchically.

2.1
Engineering in Quality

What is good quality, and how do we engineer it into software? Based on what we know today, there are 27 types of quality that engineers can imbue into software during the design and programming process:

1. Precision in calculations and outputs (accuracy)

2. Nondisruptive failure recovery (anomaly management)

3. Ease of expansion in functionality and data (augmentability)

4. Ability to decouple from the execution environment (autonomy)

5. Use of standards to achieve interoperability (commonality)

6. Necessity and sufficiency to perform the task (completeness)

7. Use of standards to achieve uniformity (consistency)

8. Geographical separation of functions and data (distributivity)

9. Access to complete, understandable information (quality in documentation)

10. Economical use of communication resources (communication efficiency)

11. Economical use of processing resources (processor efficiency)

12. Economical use of storage resources (storage efficiency)

13. Wide range of applicability of a function (functional scope)

14. Wide range of applicability of a unit (generality)

15. Ability to decouple from the support environment (independence)

16. Orderliness of design and implementation (modularity)

17. Ease of operating the software (operability)

18. Avoidance of hazardous conditions (safety management)

19. Design and source code understandability (self-descriptiveness)

20. Straightforward implementation of functions (simplicity)

21. Functional support for the management of changes (support)

22. Controlled access to functions and data (system accessibility)

23. Simultaneous harmonious operability of two or more systems (system compatibility)

24. Ability of code to relate to requirements and vice versa (traceability)

25. Provisions for how to learn to use the software (training)

26. Logical features (functions, memory, etc.) in the physical implementation (virtuality)

27. Insight into validity and progress of development (visibility)

But good quality is not defined by engineers, it is simply fitness for use. Good quality is measured by the person who *uses* the software, so the true test for its presence is performed after the software has been delivered and installed. There are at least 15 types of fitness for use:

1. What was produced is what was specified, and vice versa. (correctness)

2. The number of resources required for the execution of the software is affordable. (efficiency)

3. The software was built to be open ended, making it easy to modify it to add new capabilities. (expandability)

4. The software is adaptable to a wide range of different environments and needs to be expanded only as a last resort. (flexibility)

5. The user is reasonably certain that the software or data is not being tampered with or stolen. (integrity)

6. The software produces or uses results that comply with industry standards. (interoperability)

7. Productivity during the maintenance life cycle is high and covers error detection through each new release. (maintainability)

8. The support environment is complete and easy to use (manageability)

9. The software may be used with several operating systems and on various computers. (portability)

10. It is easier to use the software than not to use it. (usability)

11. The mean time between failures is acceptable. (reliability)

12. A large library of software building blocks exists. (reusability)

13. The software can be trusted not to endanger life or property (safety)

14. Essential functions are still available even though some part of the system is down. (survivability)

15. Productivity is high during software certification. (verifiability)

We can kill two birds with one stone if we can achieve the 15 fitness-for-use attributes by engineering in the previous 27 types of quality during the design and programming process. Table 2–1, based on Rome Air Development Study RADC-TR-85-37, shows how each fitness-for-use attribute is covered by one or more of the engineering attributes.

The qualities in the table define the boundaries of what might be required of any given software product. Of course, not all systems require all of these qualities. For example, if the end user has no security problems, then integrity and hence, system accessibility, is not a concern. Or if the user does not maintain the software, then maintainability (and hence, completeness, consistency, modularity, self-descriptiveness, traceability, and visibility) is no great concern. The point is, we must zero in on an agreed-upon definition of what "high quality" means for each software product. We don't want to underspecify it of course, but neither do we want to overspecify what is required for software quality.

Which brings us back to the important point made in Chapter 1: *You can't achieve quality unless you specify it!* So the next step in quality engineering function is to specify the software quality requirements. The three major activities for this process are:

Analyze the end user's need for quality

Convert quality needs to requirements

Document and get agreement on the quality requirements

For the first step, we collect and organize the specific needs for quality that the

TABLE 2–1

Fitness-for-Use Attributes (columns) × **Engineering Attributes** (rows)

Engineering Attributes	Correctness	Efficiency	Expandability	Flexibility	Integrity	Interoperability	Maintainability	Manageability	Portability	Reliability	Reusability	Safety	Survivability	Usability	Verifiability
Accuracy										*			*		
Anomaly Management										*		*	*		
Augmentability			*												
Autonomy													*		
Commonality						*									
Completeness	*						*								
Consistency	*						*								
Distributivity												*	*		
Quality of Documentation							*			*					
Efficiency of Communication		*													
Efficiency of Processing		*													
Efficiency of Storage		*													
Functional Scope						*					*				
Generality			*	*							*				
Independence						*			*		*				
Modularity			*	*		*	*		*		*				*
Operability												*			
Safety Management															
Self-descriptiveness			*	*			*		*		*				*
Simplicity			*	*			*			*	*				*
Support								*	*		*				*
System Accessibility					*										
System Compatibility						*									
Traceability	*						*								*
Training														*	
Virtuality			*												
Visibility						*									*

intended user has. Then we determine the level of quality required (e.g., excellent, good, average, or not an issue) in each of the 15 fitness-for-use factors. The latter requires that we trade off level of quality when it conflicts with factors like cost and schedule.

Next, to convert the quality needs to requirements, we establish a requirements data base. Then each vague, subjective need is converted into one or more testable, objective requirements. Each of these is then reviewed to ensure that it meets the standard of high quality. This superset of requirements is then allocated to the various software configuration items which divide the system up into major software components.

The last step is to document the results of the software quality requirements analysis and to use this documentation as a mechanism for agreement with the customer. The resulting specification may be written into a contract defining the quality desired.

Given the attributes of quality defined in the requirements specifications, how do we achieve the said requirements? In general, there are eight methods for doing so:

1. Use of design and programming standards
2. Allocating quality requirements to design components
3. Straightforward implementation of the requirements
4. Design iteration
5. Use of modern design and programming techniques
6. Use of automated tools
7. Influencing external system design decisions
8. Use of special-quality engineering techniques.

Each of these plays a part in the overall implementation of software quality during the design and programming processes. Figure 2–1 illustrates how none is sufficient on its own to implement all of the 27 quality criteria. Thus, judicious selection and tailoring of the eight quality-achieving techniques are needed to achieve the required level of quality specified in the contract.

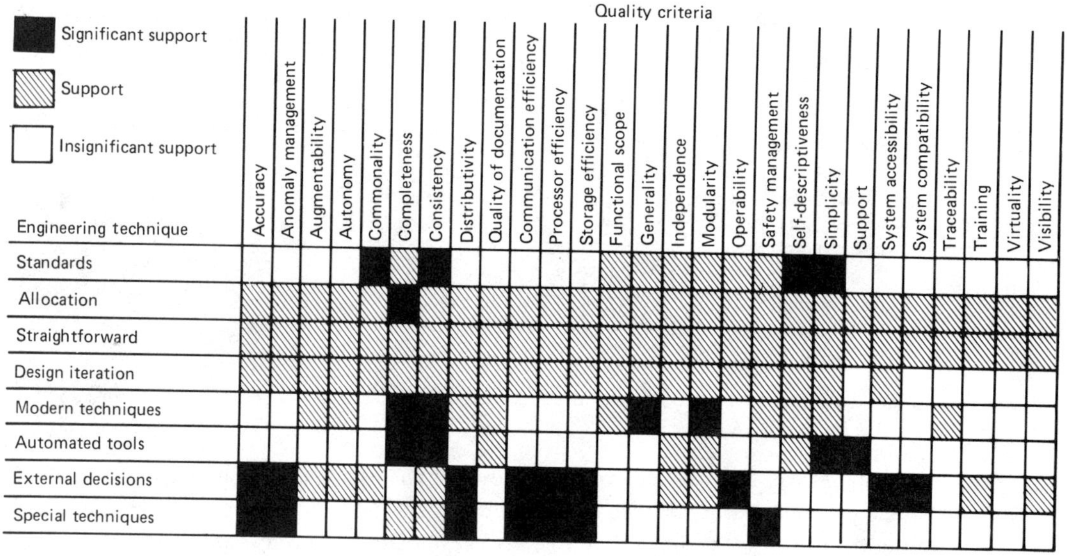

Legend:
- ■ Significant support
- ▨ Support
- ☐ Insignificant support

Quality criteria (columns): Accuracy, Anomaly management, Augmentability, Autonomy, Commonality, Completeness, Consistency, Distributivity, Quality of documentation, Communication efficiency, Processor efficiency, Storage efficiency, Functional scope, Generality, Independence, Modularity, Operability, Safety management, Self-descriptiveness, Simplicity, Support, System accessibility, System compatibility, Traceability, Training, Virtuality, Visibility

Engineering technique (rows): Standards, Allocation, Straightforward, Design iteration, Modern techniques, Automated tools, External decisions, Special techniques

Figure 2-1 Engineering techniques vs. quality criteria.

2.2
Using Verification and Validation to Review-out
Defects and Test-out Errors

The activities of verification and validation determine whether the software performs its intended functions and assure that the intended quality has been achieved. Verification and validation are achieved by the following combination of reviews and testing:

- Design reviews, walkthroughs, and inspections
- Requirements and design validation
- Independent verification and validation
- Testing concepts
- Control of software testing and integration

2.2.1   DESIGN REVIEWS, WALKTHROUGHS, AND INSPECTIONS

Reviews are the "first line of defense" for identifying defects in the engineering product. Four generic reviews are summarized here: (1) formal design reviews, (2) the internal review cycle, (3) walkthroughs, and (4) inspections.

Formal design reviews occur at the conclusion of each development cycle phase. The objective of a formal design review is to provide visibility so that management can determine whether the status of the product merits proceeding on to the next phase of development. A formal design review is a postprocess activity performed after the process of design material creation has been completed. The modern concept of a design review holds that responsibility for the design is shared among the developer, customer, and user.

The mechanics of a design review include the following steps: (1) The developer prepares a package of products to be reviewed and submits them to the customer several weeks before the actual review. (2) The developer prepares a design review presentation. (3) The actual review is conducted in a seminar that centers on presentations made by the developer. The major outputs of the design review are reports that document defects found during the review.

Formal design reviews have a couple of weaknesses connected with their rigid formats: (1) They lack the give and take necessary to effectively challenge the technical basis for the design. (2) They are not an effective forum for detailed quality evaluations. Less formal review techniques are needed to offset these weaknesses.

The *internal review cycle* is the oldest and most fundamental of review techniques. The originator of a product, perhaps a document, releases a draft version of that product to interested reviewers for examination. Comments are then fed back to the originator, who factors them into the next draft version of the product, and so on. The review cycle is likely to provide a more detailed review than the formal design review, but it requires a single party, the originator, to evaluate and act on possible contradictory comments.

The *internal walkthrough* is based on collective review and decision making. It involves the author of a product presenting the salient aspects of the product to a reviewing team of peers. This process furnishes feedback to the author within a time frame during which revisions are possible and inexpensive.

A moderator controls the discussion, maintains a focus on review of the product, and specifically avoids consideration of corrective action for any defects found. Correction is the job of the author. Defects discovered by the walkthroughs are formally recorded, and the author is obligated to address the problems found. If the problems are particularly numerous and/or severe, a follow-up walkthrough is conducted.

The *software inspection* is a rigorous in-process review method for detecting errors at their sources. Although similar to the walkthrough, the increased formality of the inspection provides more repeatable results, and corporate historical records of previous error patterns point to likely sources of errors.

The inspection team consists of three to eight participants. Each inspector plays a particular role, including that of moderator, designer, implementer, tester, or system engineer. The inspection process has five steps: (1) the overview meeting, (2) an individual preparation period, (3) the inspection meeting, (4) a rework period, and (5) a follow-up that verifies the network.

Errors discovered are rigorously recorded on forms and categorized. The statistics are accumulated into a data base and trends are analyzed, yielding the corporate historical records just mentioned.

Table 2–2 provides guidelines for the use of the preceding review techniques as a function of the four quality levels: not an issue, average, good, and excellent. The review processes intensify as the desired level of quality increases. The review techniques are explored in considerably more detail in Chapter 7.

TABLE 2-2 REVIEW ACTIVITIES VS. QUALITY LEVEL

Quality level	Reviews
Not an issue	• Internal review cycle • Internal walkthroughs
Average	• Internal review cycle • Inspections • Formal design review subset
Good	• Internal review cycle • Inspections • Formal design reviews (full set)
Excellent	• Internal review cycle • Inspections • Formal design reviews • Independent verification and validation reviews

2.2.2 VALIDATING REQUIREMENTS AND DESIGN

Clearly, it is a cost-effective goal to achieve confidence in the statement of requirements before proceeding with the design, implementation, and installation of a software system. Accordingly, a considerable portion of the schedule and budget on large, complex projects is consumed in understanding and refining the statement of the problem that is being solved. Intrinsically, system definition and development is partially a trial-and-error process. Nonetheless, while some iteration is inevitable, the process can be controlled through validation of the requirements and design.

Requirements validation and analysis was largely overlooked until the mid-1970s, when, within a period of less than five years, a number of advances in requirements technology emerged. (See also Chapter 8.) Highly significant among these advances was the concept of the *thread*. A thread is a path through a system that connects an external event or stimulus to an output event or response. A major promulgator of the threads technique was Computer Sciences Corporation, which used a graphics tool called the System Verification Diagram (SVD).

The SVD is primarily a manual technique that is intended to focus our consciousness on the content of functional requirements. It represents these requirements graphically as a sequence of stimulus-response elements. The form of a representative SVD is shown in Figure 2–2.

Each stimulus-response element is associated with specific requirements from the specification. In the diagram, each element is labeled with the requirement number or paragraph references. The stimulus consists of an input event and any associated conditional qualifiers of the state of the system at that point. The response is symmetrically composed of output events plus conditional qualifiers occurring as a result of the input event. An example of the generation of a thread from requirements is displayed in Figure 2–3, in which an input event is shown that entails a new hostile track detection and a conditional qualifier to the effect that the track files are not full, combining material from paragraphs 3.7.1.1.4 and 3.7.3.1.5 of the specification to form the stimulus of this thread. The response is also derived from information offered by these two paragraphs. The threads representing the requirements specification are concatenated with arrows which denote the flow of the thread sequence to form the SVD.

An effect that enhances the validation of the requirements occurs as a result of the structure of the SVD procedure. The process of constructing the SVD causes the requirements to be viewed in a parallel manner because of the graphic medium. Simply reading the text of the specification would allow only a serial assimilation of the information. The net effect is that inconsistencies, redundancies, and omissions are revealed in the SVD that would otherwise have gone undetected.

To illustrate a requirements flaw that would be exposed by this tool, consider again the hostile track thread of Figure 2–3. The conditional qualifier of the stimulus is that the track files are not full. It is natural to expect the requirements analyst to create a parallel thread consisting of the same input event and a corollary qualifier—that the track files are full. The identification of this thread is illustrated in Figure 2–4. What is the flaw here? Inspection of paragraphs 3.7.1.1.4 and 3.7.3.1.5 provides no indication of

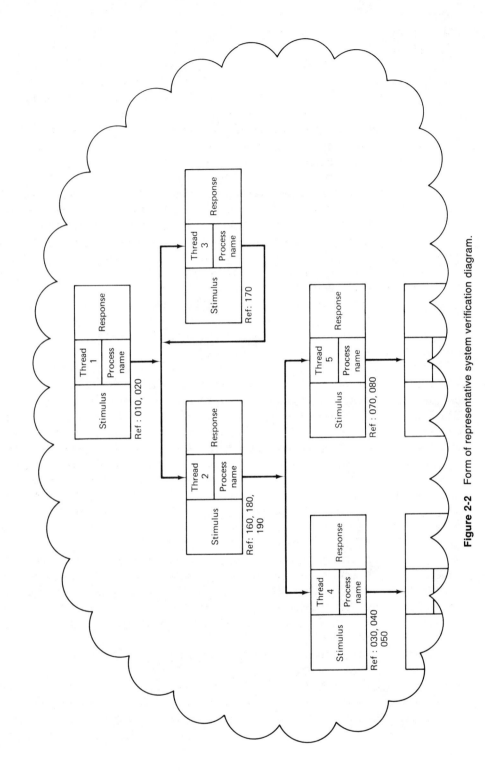

Figure 2-2 Form of representative system verification diagram.

         Part I   Quality Concepts

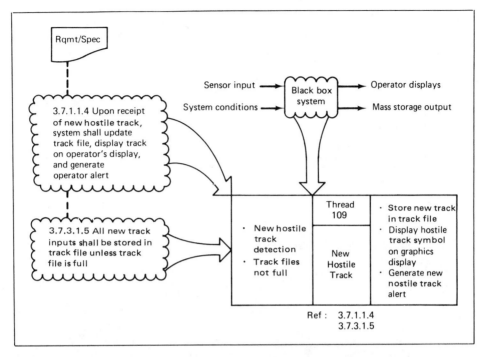

Figure 2-3 Identifying a thread from the requirements. (Robert Carey and Marc Bendic, "The Control of a Software Test Process," *Proceedings of the Computer Software and Applications Conference 1977* [New York, NY: IEEE, Inc.], IEEE Catalog No. 77CH 1291-4C; © 1977 IEEE.

what the system reaction should be to a new hostile track with the condition that the track files are full. In other words, the response to this stimulus cannot be signified on the SVD at this time. Further clarification is required, however, as this would seem to be a very important issue regarding the system in question. Perhaps the new track should be dropped, or perhaps it should displace an existing track of lesser importance. The requirements specification must be revised to clear up this omission.

Requirements and design validation activities that should be applied to each discrete level of quality—not an issue, average, good, and excellent—are summarized in Table 2–3. There are basically three "tracks" of activities: (1) functional requirements and design validation, (2) performance validation using modeling or simulation, and (3) prototyping. Each track is described further in Chapter 8.

2.2.3 INDEPENDENT VERIFICATION AND VALIDATION

Independent verification and validation (IV&V) is employed when added insurance is required for the functioning and performance of the system. The concept employs an independent agent other than the developer who applies reviews and/or testing to further assess the product of the developer.

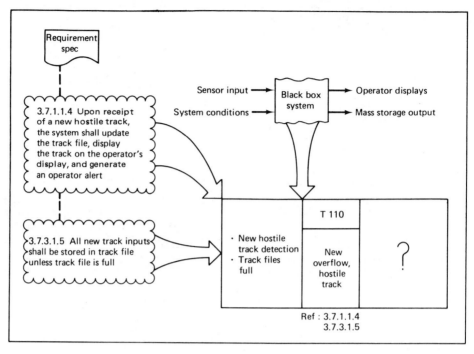

Figure 2-4 Identifying a requirement flaw.

TABLE 2-3 REQUIREMENTS/DESIGN
VALIDATION ACTIVITIES BY QUALITY LEVEL

Quality level	Requirements/design validation activities
Not an issue	• Informal/verbal traceability analysis • Algorithm modeling
Average	• Traditional requirements/design traceability (documented) • "Pencil/paper" performance modeling
Good	• Stimulus/response analysis with system verification diagram • Moderate system performance simulation • Input scenario simulation for test cases • Prototype critical areas
Excellent	• Detailed stimulus/response analysis • Detailed system performance simulation • Detailed input scenario simulation for test cases • Prototype more critical areas

The objective of IV&V is not necessarily to avoid all errors, but rather to eliminate, to a high degree of certainty, those errors that can result in catastrophic results. Such results might entail the loss of life, failure of the mission, or less compelling repercussions such as damage to equipment or significant economic loss. IV&V should be conducted with disinterest in the outcome of the evaluation, i.e., the agent performing the validation should have no stake in the results and should be free of influence from those who do.

A good IV&V contractor should

1. Have significant experience.
2. Have a base of personnel skilled in IV&V.
3. Hold a repertoire of qualified and transferable tools.
4. Not be a threat to the development contractor.

In regard to the last item, there should be absolutely no reason for the IV&V contractor to make the developer appear inept.

As in the previous discussions of quality technology, the IV&V activities are categorized in terms of the four levels of quality: not an issue, average, good, and excellent. The IV&V effort associated with each of these levels is outlined in broad general terms as follows:

- Not an issue—no IV&V effort.
- Average—system engineering support to customer for constructive critique of developer's products, including identification and recommendation of solutions to problems.
- Good—more extensive effort over development cycle with emphasis on analysis and testing of critical areas.
- Excellent—full life cycle parallel analysis, including system-level testing and integration.

A detailed explanation of these activities by level of quality is presented in Chapter 9.

2.2.4 TESTING CONCEPTS

Testing is defined as the controlled execution of the software product in order to expose errors. When, according to preestablished criteria, the number and severity of errors fall below a specified threshold, it is concluded that proper operation of the software has been demonstrated.

The ideal goal of testing is to test a software system by using a set of all possible inputs. However, this is impractical and economically infeasible for all but the most trivial of systems. The practical strategy involves the selection of a subset of the possible inputs that can establish a statistically significant high probability of correctness of the system within economic constraints. The major testing problem then becomes the issue of trying to accommodate opposing goals: we would like to test the system with as many test cases as possible, but at the same time we wish to minimize the number of test cases because of the effort involved in designing and generating test cases. Test engineering, then, remains perhaps more of an art than a science.

The selection of the subset of the possible test inputs is accomplished by partitioning testing into a number of domains and levels, each with a different set of goals. Each level of testing addresses the software at a different level of completeness or integration, culminating in testing of the entire integrated system. Each level has distinct testing goals. To the first order, two kinds of testing are performed: unit-level testing and integration-level testing. Unit-level testing involves execution of a single software component or a small number of components and emphasizes the demonstration of functions, coverage of the internal structure of the software, and demonstration of individual algorithm accuracies. Integration-level testing emphasizes the execution of interfaces between the units and the execution of the software to show compliance with computational performance requirements.

A more comprehensive set of test levels and domains is explored in Chapter 11.

The level of required quality will directly influence the intensity, focus, and organizational responsibilities of the testing approach for a particular system. General guidelines are as follows

Quality Level	Testing Approach
Not an Issue	Testing at this level is entirely programmer performed, with few written plans. Systems are small and simple enough to permit this informality.
Average	The main contrast between this and the previous level of testing involves the use of an independent organization for integration and system testing. Testing is based upon formal written plans and procedures.
Good	More structure is introduced into the testing for this level of quality. Threads and builds, to be discussed in the next section, partition the system into more manageable, functionally oriented segments and focus the testing on the concept of the operation of the system as a whole. A modest amount of anomaly testing and stress testing, which determines the response of the system to overload situations, is also performed.
Excellent	Testing at this level entails approximately the same approach as at the previous level, but is more comprehensive. More extensive stress and anomaly testing is performed, and the goal is usually to test the entire path structure at the unit testing level.

It should be noted that excellent quality is usually required only for portions of systems, so that the testing approach need not be totally homogeneous.

2.2.5 CONTROL OF SOFTWARE TESTING AND INTEGRATION

This subsection describes a method of software test and integration that segments a complex software development into more manageable functional elements and maintains a strong visible connection between testing and requirements. Consider again the SVD outlined in subsection 2.2.2 and further illustrated in Figure 2–5. Each stimulus-response element of the SVD can be mapped into the design to identify the specific software modules which, when executed, perform the function of that element. A relationship will then exist at a detailed level between the functional requirements (the stimulus-response elements) and the design (the modules). We call this relationship a *thread*; it is the primary means by which the software development can be accurately defined and closely controlled.

Detailed testing and integration planning can begin when the software architecture defining the structure of the modules is available. In systems sponsored by the Department of Defense, this normally occurs around the time of the preliminary design review. In this concept, software testing and development are intertwined; they do not occur separately and sequentially. The SVD has segmented the system into demonstrable functions (the threads), the development of which is temporally ordered. The modules associated with each thread are then coded and tested in a corresponding order. The threads are synthesized into higher order sections called *builds*, each of which incrementally demonstrates a significant partial functional capability of the system.

The results of the planning effort are displayed on a *build plan*. The build plan provides an overall view, temporally ordered, of the sequence of testing and integration events, including

- The sequence of the builds
- The relationship of the builds to each other
- The allocation of threads to builds
- The sequence of the threads

A sample build plan from a recent software system is exhibited in Figure 2–6. Each build adds new threads to the system and usually contains the cumulative capabilities of previous builds. Each build demonstration integrates and tests the new capabilities, and performs a regression test on the capabilities accumulated from previous builds. The final acceptance test of the total system is a naturally culminating event of this succession. Because threads, by their very nature, represent useful operational functions, functionality is demonstrated from the very beginning of the development with a high degree of visibility.

The benefits of the thread testing and integration approach are that it

- Allows testing and analysis in digestible quantities.
- Provides early demonstration of key functional capabilities.
- Defines the module development sequence and serves as a basis for allocating personnel.

The details of the thread testing technique are explained in Chapter 12.

36

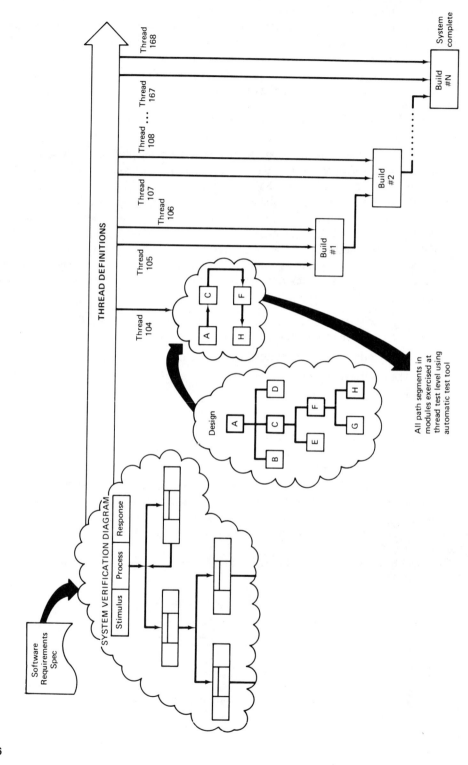

Figure 2-5 Software test and integration procedure visibly connected to requirements.

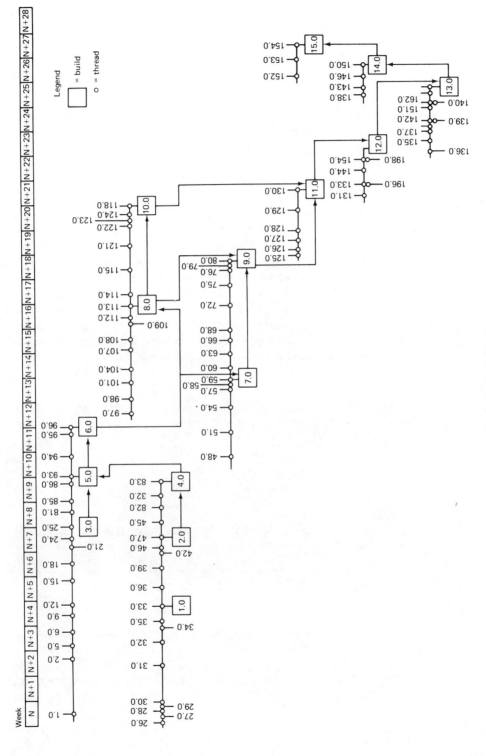

Figure 2-6 Example build plan.

2.3
Software Quality Management

2.3.1 ANALYZING THE ECONOMICS OF QUALITY

A major ingredient of the quality engineering process is the early consideration of quality versus cost. This involves the selection of quality factors, criteria, and levels, and their associated costs. Thus, quality requirements should be specified with a conscious recognition of the corresponding costs and the schedule. The point of departure for this summary economic analysis is the quality engineering scenario of engineering quality in, reviewing out defects, and testing out errors. The activities associated with these scenarios are mapped into an augmented version of the *Jensen Model*, a parametric software cost-estimating model.

In this model, relative costs and schedules are estimated for each of the four quality levels and the figures are referenced to the level at which quality is not an issue. The augmented Jensen Model relative costs for each of the four quality levels are displayed on Table 2–4. The components of the net cost consist of engineering, reviewing, testing, and IV&V activities. Shown for the engineering activities is both a theoretical, unconstrained range of costs, and a realistic range. IV&V costs represent a possible envelope of 25 to 100 percent of the product submitted to IV&V. The details of these cases are described in Chapter 14. The relative costs over the four levels of quality span the range of slightly greater than two to one.

TABLE 2–4 SUPPLEMENTED JENSEN MODEL RELATIVE COSTS

Quality Level	Engineering Activities	Review/Test	IV&V	Net
Nonissue	0.55 to 1.00	1.00	1.00	0.55 to 1.00
	0.68 to 1.00	1.00	1.00	0.68 to 1.00
Average	0.55 to 0.82	1.31	1.03 to 1.10	0.74 to 1.18
	0.68 to 0.82	1.31	1.03 to 1.10	0.92 to 1.18
Good	0.55 to 0.68	1.56	1.06 to 1.25	0.91 to 1.33
	0.68	1.56	1.06 to 1.25	1.12 to 1.33
Excellent	0.55	1.98	1.15 to 1.60	1.25 to 1.74
	0.68	1.98	1.15 to 1.60	1.55 to 2.15

Unconstrained   Realistic

The schedule variation over the range of quality is charted in Table 2–5. The analysis shows that, over the four levels of quality, the relative schedule will increase up to 30 percent.

The details of these analyses, plus a further analysis of life cycle costs, are presented in Chapter 14.

TABLE 2-5 RELATIVE SCHEDULE ANALYSIS

Quality Level	Relative Jensen Schedule
Nonissue	0.88 to 1.00
Average	0.97 to 1.06
Good	1.04 to 1.10
Excellent	1.16 to 1.30

2.3.2 MANAGEMENT ASPECTS OF SOFTWARE QUALITY ENGINEERING

As with any complex activity, software quality engineering must be planned, organized, monitored, and constantly readjusted to be successful. The following are some key points to keep in mind in managing for software quality:

- Engineers are the only ones who can add quality to software.
- Quality is defined by documented software quality requirements.
- The goal is not to motivate, but to educate.

Some of the things that are required for software quality management are as follows:

Quality requirements
Effective Plans
People
Organization
Reviews
Standards
Procedures
Training
Testing
Facilities
Tools
Measurement and Feedback
Subcontractor Control

No one person or organization is responsible for quality. Rather, everyone is responsible in some way or another. There are at least seven functions that act in concert to achieve software quality:

Software Engineering

Software Line Management

Testing

Software Technical Assurance

Software Quality Assurance

Configuration Control

Independent Verification and Validation (IV&V)

All of these except for software technical assurance (STA) are traditional, yet important roles in software engineering. STA is responsible, not for achieving quality, but instead for acting as a catalyst for engineers who are attempting to achieve quality. STA helps engineers perform quality-enhancing activities through the development of comprehensible quality specifications, quality planning, training, and coaching, and in general, through allowing engineers to design in quality.

The objective of measuring software product quality is to determine the extent to which a software product exhibits software quality requirements. To measure the software product quality involves holding the applicable requirements up against the product to see how many of them have been implemented in it. A measure of the progress of achieving quality can be determined by dividing the number of unimplemented quality requirements by the total number of quality requirements.

The objective of software process quality measurement is to detect roadblocks in the software development environment that interfere with achieving software product quality. There are many metrics suggested later in this book; the following illustrates the importance of rework as an indicator of poor quality (it emphasizes the saying, "Do it right the first time.")

$$QE = \text{Quality Effectiveness} = 1 - \frac{\text{Rework Effort}}{\text{Total Effort}}$$

A more detailed exploration of the management aspects of software quality is contained in Chapter 15.

2.3.3 UTILIZING TEAM TECHNIQUES

The organization of personnel into small teams permits the concentration of collective mental resources on the product being developed. This collaboration is intended to produce a higher quality product with the same labor as would be expended by each person acting individually. An intense effort by a highly cooperative and dedicated small group of people with strong leadership constitutes the main characteristics of the team approach. The degree to which these attributes can be pragmatically achieved is highly dependent upon the availability of skilled people.

Two key features that distinguish team practices from those of individuals in the conventional organization are:

- Continuous verification and validation of software
- Better integration of individual efforts

These features come about largely as a result of a continuous communication pattern.

The initial formal team concept is IBM's chief programmer team. Since the inception of this team and the approach it represented in the early 1970s, other team concepts have emerged. Practically any task can be organized as a team activity. The following teams have appeared in actual practice:

- The chief programmer team
- The dual-person design team
- The thread integration team
- Test teams

The structure and dynamics of each of these teams are detailed in Chapter 16.

Part II

Engineering in Quality

Chapter 3

Understanding Software Quality

In this chapter we consider how software quality can be defined as a set of software attributes that can be designed in during engineering. The key points to recognize are as follows:

- The basis for software quality is the user's need for certain software characteristics after the software is put into use, e.g., its fitness for the intended use.
- Software engineering techniques can be used to design in certain software attributes during development.
- The software engineering attributes can be mapped onto the user's needs in order to bridge the gap between what is needed and what can be designed in during development.

3.1
What Is Software?

We can't begin to itemize user needs for software quality without first understanding what software is as perceived by the user.

First, let's agree on who the user is. The software user is any person who comes in contact with the software product. The user may come in contact with the product in any of the following ways:

- By using the functionality resulting from execution of the software.
- By reading documents that describe the design or use of the software.
- By changing code or data that make up programs.
- By managing the administrative aspects of software.

By using the functionality of software, the user perceives the software as an electronic tool. The software helps this user perform a task by automating what would otherwise be done manually. For example, a spreadsheet automates record keeping and arithmetic, a word processor automates document storage and text formatting, and a command and control system automates information collection, decision making, and command communication.

By reading documentation, the user perceives software as a source of knowledge. For example, a user's guide helps the user understand how to use the functionality of the software, and a design document aids in understanding what the architecture of the implemented code is.

By changing code, the user perceives the software as organized programming language statements. Software then becomes a product with a problem the user must contend with: to fix an error, to adapt the code to a new environment, or to add a new function to the code. Therefore, the programming language statements need to be understood, analyzed, modified, tested, and installed.

By managing software, the user perceives the software as a part in a parts list or as a line item in a schedule. From this point of view, software is characterized by aspects of identification, packaging, storage, transport, separable work units, work effort estimates, and status. Since this perception of software is no different from the way hardware is viewed, we will forego considering it in this text.

From the preceding examination, we can say that as perceived by the user,

---

Software is . . .

the functionality of a computer system
the knowledge in software documentation
the code and data that make up programs

3.2
The User's Need for Software Quality

Software quality is based on user needs. Essentially, these needs can be broken down as shown in Figure 3–1.

Operational needs deal with the use of the software to perform the tasks it was

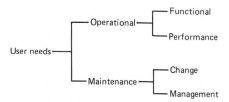

Figure 3-1 Software user needs.

intended to perform. Maintenance needs deal with modifying the software in one way or another to aid the user.

Within the operational needs, functionality deals with what the software does while executing and performance deals with how well it does it. For example, the functionality of communication software refers to the ability the software has to transmit and receive interprocessor messages, whereas the performance of communication software refers to the rate at which messages can be transmitted and received using it.

Within the maintenance needs, change deals with modifying the software to either correct errors (corrective change), adapt code to new environments (adaptive change), or add new functionality (perfective change). Management needs deal with planning for change, controlling versions of the software, testing, and installation.

Table 3–1 presents 15 quality factors (the ''ilities'' referred to in Chapter 1) and shows their relationship to the user's need for quality.

TABLE 3-1

User's Need	User's Concern	Quality Factor
FUNCTIONAL	How secure is it?	INTEGRITY
	How often will it fail?	RELIABILITY
	Can it survive during failure?	SURVIVABILITY
	How easy is it to use?	USABILITY
PERFORMANCE	How much is needed in the way of resources?	EFFICIENCY
	Does it comply with requirements?	CORRECTNESS
	Does it prevent hazards?	SAFETY
	Does it interface easily?	INTEROPERABILITY
CHANGE	How easy is it to repair?	MAINTAINABILITY
	How easy is it to expand?	EXPANDABILITY
	How easy is it to change?	FLEXIBILITY
	How easy is it to transport?	PORTABILITY
	Is it reusable in other systems?	REUSABILITY
MANAGEMENT	Is performance verification easy?	VERIFIABILITY
	Is the software easily managed?	MANAGEABILITY

3.2.1 QUALITY FACTORS DEFINED

The following list defines the 15 quality factors given in Table 3–1.

Correctness   deals with the extent to which the software design and implementation conform to the stated requirements. For example, whether all specified functions are implemented, whether the design is documented according to standards, and whether the performance of the software is within budgetary constraints are all correctness concerns. Fitness for use regarding correctness means that what was produced is what was specified, and vice versa.

Efficiency   deals with the resources needed to provide the required functionality. Among the different resources are the processor, random-access memory (RAM), disks, and communication lines. Fitness for use regarding efficiency means that the resources required for the execution of the software are affordable.

Expandability   deals with the perfective aspects of software maintenance, that is, increasing the software's functionality or performance to meet new needs. It might include adding a new type of deduction to an existing payroll program or adding an interface to a new sensor in a command and control information system. Fitness for use regarding expandability means that the software was built to be open ended, making it easy to modify it to add new capabilities.

Flexibility   deals with the adaptive aspects of software maintenance, that is, modifying the software to work in different environments. It includes a word processor's ability to adapt to different kinds of printers and an air traffic control system's ability to adapt to different airport configurations. Fitness for use regarding flexibility means that the software is readily adaptable, via a user interface or change of data, to a wide range of different environments without immediately resorting to expandability-type changes.

Integrity   deals with security against either overt or covert access to the programs or data bases. Fitness for use regarding integrity means that the user is reasonably certain that software and data are not being tampered with or stolen.

Interoperability   deals with how easy it is to couple the software with software in other systems or applications. For example, some spreadsheet software packages are integrable into a chart-drawing package, and some data bases may be combined into a single management information system. Fitness for use regarding interoperability means that the software produces or uses results that comply with industry standards.

Maintainability   deals with the ease of finding and fixing errors. (Note that according to this definition, maintainability does not entail adaptive or perfective maintenance; for these, see flexibility and expandability.) Since so much effort and time are spent in the maintenance phase of a software's life cycle, maintainability is a very important quality factor. Fitness for use regarding maintainability means that the software is productive during the maintenance life cycle, covering error detection through the issue of a new release.

Manageability deals with the administrative aspects of modification to the software. It includes tools to support changes such as configuration control systems and source code libraries, and media control, such as tape or disk handling. Fitness for use regarding manageability means that the support environment is complete and easy to use.

Portability deals with transporting the software to execute on a host processor or operating system different from the one for which it was designed. It includes recompiling a Fortran program on a different computer and changing the operating system of an existing computer. Fitness for use regarding portability means that the software may be used on several different operating systems or computers.

Usability deals with the initial effort required to learn, and the recurring effort to use, the functionality of the software. Usability can be enhanced or degraded by the naturalness of the user interface, the readability of documentation, and the number of keystrokes required for a given command. Fitness for use regarding usability means, more or less, that the software is easier to use than not to use.

Reliability deals with the rate of failures in the software that render it unusable. Some common failures are that the software is not accurate enough, that it gives incorrect results, that the response time is too slow, or that the software "hangs up" (stops without recovery). Fitness for use regarding reliability means that there is an acceptably long time between failures (e.g., one failure per year).

Reusability deals with the use of portions of the software for other applications. It includes the use of mathematical libraries in both statistical and scientific applications and the use of target-tracking algorithms in both civil air traffic control and military air defense applications. Fitness for use regarding reusability means that there is a large library of standard building blocks available to the software.

Safety deals with the absence of unsafe software conditions. An unsafe software condition could lead to a hazard—that is, loss of life or liability, or damage to property. Fitness for use regarding safety means that the software can be trusted.

Survivability deals with the continuity of reliable software execution (albeit, perhaps, with degraded functionality) in the presence of a system failure. Fitness for use regarding survivability means that the user can still use essential functions even though some part of the system is down. (E.g., a spreadsheet still calculates even though the printer is broken.)

Verifiability deals with how easy it is to verify that the software is working correctly. It includes the presence or absence of automatic self-testing and a library of standard test programs. Fitness for use regarding verifiability means that it is simple to certify that the software is correct.

3.3
Engineerable Quality Attributes

We next turn to attributes of quality that software engineers can deal with and implement during the design and development process. Each of the 27 software quality criteria listed in Table 3–2 is defined in terms of the characteristics that the software exhibits if it has been designed and constructed to meet that criterion. Furthermore, some considerations that a designer or programmer may use during development to achieve the said characteristics of the criterion are also given. (These considerations must be traded off as suggested in Chapter 5 because of conflicting relationships—not all considerations can be achieved on one software project.)

For each criterion, the difference between good and not so good quality for that criterion is illustrated. (The good quality is always on the right.) The illustrations are meant to create a model in the reader's mind for understanding the aim of the criterion. As such, they should not be viewed as the only way to implement the criterion or as a complete implementation of the criterion. A variety of design representations is used to get across the point that good software quality is independent of any particular representation or language.

Note that the term 'software' in the following definitions includes reference to all products of the software development process—in particular, code, design documentation, test software, test procedures, test results, support software, and user manuals.

3.3.1 ACCURACY

Software is accurate if it produces results that are within required accuracy tolerances (e.g., + or − 0.001 ft). To be accurate, mathematical libraries, numerical techniques, numerical conversions, and the like must preserve the number of bits of precision during calculations.

TABLE 3-2

SOFTWARE QUALITY CRITERIA

Accuracy	Achieving required precision in calculations and outputs	Generality	Range of applicability of a unit
Anomaly management	Nondisruptive failure recovery	Independence	Degree of decoupling from support environment
Augmentability	Ease of expansion in functionality and data	Modularity	Orderliness of design and implementation
		Operability	Ease of operating the software
Autonomy	Degree of decoupling from execution environment	Safety management	Software design to avoid hazards
		Self-descriptiveness	Understandability of design and source code
Commonality	Use of standards to achieve interoperability	Simplicity	Straightforward implementation of functions
Completeness	All software is necessary and sufficient	Support	Functionality supporting the management of changes
Consistency	Use of standards to achieve uniformity		
Distributivity	Geographical separation of functions and data	System accessibility	Controlled access to software and data
Document quality	Access to complete understandable information	System compatibility	Ability of two or more systems to work in harmony
		Traceability	Ease of relating code to requirements and vice versa
Efficiency of communication	Economic use of communication resources	Training	Provisions to learn how to use the software
Efficiency of processing	Economic use of processing resources	Virtuality	Logical implementation to represent physical components
Efficiency of storage	Economic use of storage resources	Visibility	Insight into validity and progress of development
Functional scope	Range of applicability of a function		

Accuracy₁

```
X,Y    REAL*4      type LOCATION is delta 0.00001 range 0.0 .. 100.0
                   X,Y LOCATION
```

Figure 3-2 Adding accuracy to a software design.

The following are some suggestions for achieving accuracy during software development:

- Select mathematical libraries to achieve the precision requirements.
- Use numerical analysis to design precise algorithms.
- Minimize the number of different data representations.
- Minimize the number of data representation conversions.
- Use prototyping or models to verify algorithm stability.
- Select computer hardware that is able to achieve the required precision.

Figure 3–2 shows two designs, the first without an explicit consideration of accuracy and the second with an explicit specification of accuracy designed in. The latter is more accurate because it explicitly constrains the precision and documents those constraints in the code.

3.3.2 ANOMALY MANAGEMENT

The software manages anomalous (error) conditions well if it can detect and gracefully recover from such conditions rather than disrupting processing or halting. In essence, the software should be designed for survivability when faced with software or hardware failures. Anomaly management includes detection and containment of, and recovery from, improper input data, computational failures, hardware faults, device failures, and communication errors. Real-time reconfiguration is one technique that can be used for recovery.

The following are some suggestions for achieving required levels of anomaly management during software development:

- Specify what ''valid'' means for all external inputs.
- Check input values for range and reasonableness.
- Use alternative means to continue execution in the presence of errors.
- Provide exception processing for all system-detected errors.
- Design in testing (rather than relying on test programs).
- Periodically check interfacing systems.
- Provide common error recovery services.
- Use error-checking information in communications messages.
- Check loop and case statement parameters before using these structures.
- Provide for alternate communication routing in case of failure of the main path.

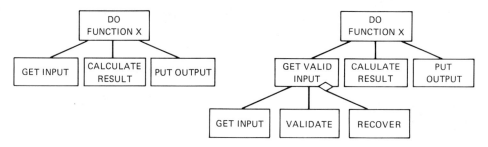

Figure 3-3 Adding anomaly management to a software design.

- Restore data-base integrity as part of the recovery.
- Reconnect recovered devices and systems without interruption.
- Design to avoid single points of failure.
- Partition tasks by execution priority.

Figure 3–3 shows two designs, the first without any consideration of anomaly management and the second with anomaly management designed in. In the first design, an invalid input would cause unpredictable results. In the second case invalid inputs are corralled before they cause trouble allowing graceful recovery to take place.

3.3.3 AUGMENTABILITY

The software is augmentable if it is easy to add new functional capability or new data to it, that is, if it is easy to expand its capabilities without major redesign or modification. A software designer trying to achieve augmentability should always presume that the current capabilities will be expanded in the future and try to avoid constructs that limit this expansion or try to add constructs that make the expansion easier. Augmentation can occur in the areas of data storage expansion, computational extension, channel extension, or design extension.

The following are some suggestions for achieving required levels of augmentability during software development:

- Partition the software to be logically complete and self-contained.
- Meet or exceed spare resource requirements.
- Implement performance requirements as adaptable parameters.
- Design a data base to accommodate expansion and change.
- Isolate software and hardware interfaces.
- Use commercial or reusable software wherever possible.
- Reference data base items symbolically.

Figure 3–4 shows two designs, the first without any consideration of augmentability and the second with augmentability designed in. In the first, specific knowledge of devices has been encoded into the data structure design, whereas in the second specific

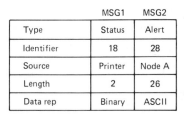

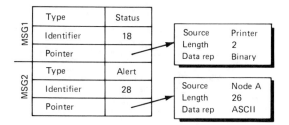

Figure 3-4 Adding augmentability to a software design.

device implementation has been separated from the main structure to accommodate expansion and change.

3.3.4 AUTONOMY

Software is autonomous when, in the event of failure of interfacing components, services, or devices, it can be automatically reconfigured and continue execution; that is, it is decoupled from its execution environment. Autonomy also includes the capability to test for conditions that could cause reconfiguration.

The following are some suggestions for achieving required levels of autonomy during software development:

- Minimize the use of operating system services.
- Minimize the complexity between interfacing software.
- Avoid encoding knowledge about devices or operating systems in an application.
- Isolate hardware and device protocol processing.
- Add executive self-test services for the operating system and hardware.

Figure 3–5 shows two designs, the first without any consideration of autonomy and the second with autonomy designed in. In the first, the TRACK function is not reconfigurable in the event of radar failure because knowledge of a specific device has been encoded into its functionality. In the second, the TRACK function has been designed to process device-independent target reports and can be reconfigured to continue execution using data from other sources.

Figure 3-5 Adding autonomy to a software design.

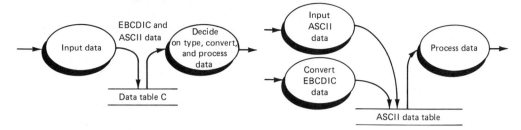

Figure 3-6 Adding commonality to a software design.

3.3.5 COMMONALITY

Software exhibits the characteristic of commonality when it uses established standards for data representation, for interfaces to communcation networks, and for interface with the user. In attempting to achieve commonality, the designer should start the design by collecting all established standards for data communication interfaces (e.g., IEEE standards based on the OSI model), data representation (e.g., ASCII), and user interfaces (e.g., function key standards) and design the software with these standards as constraints.

The following are some suggestions for achieving required levels of commonality during software development:

- Use one standard interface protocol.
- Use one software component for interface protocol handling.
- Use one standard data representation.
- Use one component for data representation translation.
- Do not constrain algorithms to work only on fresh data.
- Develop a user's manual as part of the design process.
- Use common formats for external messages.
- Establish a common vocabulary between the interfacing systems.

Figure 3–6 shows two designs, the first without any consideration of commonality and the second with commonality designed in. The first design requires a consideration of data representation types within application programs, making those programs less interoperable. In the second design, various data representation types are converted to a system-wide common type (ASCII in this case) upon input; this allows all application processing to be based on a common data representation type.

3.3.6 COMPLETENESS

Software is complete when every data item, function, interface, decision branch, line of code, etc., is necessary to accomplish the required capability (i.e., there is no superfluous code) and when there are sufficient data items, functions, etc., to implement all

```
case YEAR of                      case YEAR of
    1900 . . 1950: begin . . . end;     1900 . . 1950: begin . . . end;
    1950 . . 2000: begin . . . end;     1950 . . 2000: begin . . . end;
end;                                  else begin . . . end;
                                  end;
```

Figure 3-7 Adding completeness to a software design.

of the required capabilities. In other words, all and only the actual program code is required to implement the requirements.

The following are some suggestions for achieving required levels of completeness during software development:

- Allocate all software requirements to design components.
- Avoid data items that are not referenced.
- Define all options for decision points.
- Avoid unused parameters in procedure argument lists.
- Comment on the meaning and format of all data items.
- Clearly define all inputs, processing, and outputs.
- Avoid unreachable code.

Figure 3–7 shows two designs, the first without any consideration of completeness and the second with completeness designed in. In the first, processing based on calendar years outside the range 1900 . . . 2000 has not been defined. Even though values outside this range may be "impossible," the design is not complete because there is no specification of what should occur in case such a value is present. The second design contains such a specification, making it more complete.

3.3.7 CONSISTENCY

Software is consistent when the same standards are used throughout the design and implementation, for example, when one can be assured that the data name "x" in one unit refers to the same global item "x" referred to elsewhere. To achieve consistency, it is necessary to establish standards before the design and implementation effort begins and to ensure that the standards are uniformly enforced.

The following are some suggestions for achieving required levels of consistency during software development:

- Standardize the data representation format.
- Standardize the design representation.
- Standardize data and function naming.
- Standardize global data definition and use.
- Standardize interunit communication protocols.

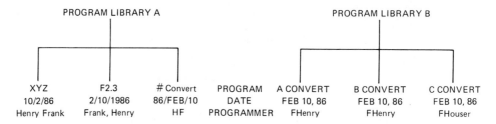

Figure 3-8 Adding consistency to a software design.

- Standardize input/output (I/O) protocol and formats.
- Standardize error-handling functions and protocols.
- Use a single, unique name for each data item and function.
- Ensure consistency of multiple versions of data bases.

Figure 3–8 shows two designs, the first without any consideration of consistency and the second with consistency designed in. The first program library is filled with inconsistencies indicating that standards were not used for program naming, dates, and even programmers' names. The second program library is uniform and unambiguous in nature.

3.3.8 DISTRIBUTIVITY

Software is distributed if its subparts are located on different processing or storage devices. The goal is to minimize the operational effect of failures, that is, to avoid single points of failure that can bring the whole system down. Thus, allocation or replication of functions and data on different devices will result in execution alternatives in case of a failure on a single device.

The following are some suggestions for achieving required levels of distributivity during software development:

- Graphically portray the complete design.
- Replicate critical components on two or more devices.
- Distribute the control of critical components.
- Do not allocate parts of a function to different devices.
- Do not allocate parts of a logical file to different devices.
- Make files accessible from all processing elements.
- Provide alternate routing in case of processor failure.

Figure 3–9 shows two designs, the first without any consideration of distributivity and the second with distributivity designed in. In the first, data (C-DATA) critical to the correct operation of the system are stored on a single disk device. If that device fails, the whole system fails with it. In the second design, the critical data has been replicated on two devices so that upon failure of the primary device, the system may recover and continue processing.

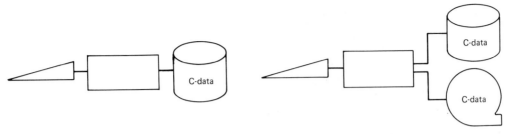

Figure 3-9 Adding distributivity to a software design.

3.3.9 QUALITY OF DOCUMENTATION

Software is well documented if a person can easily access information about the software design and capabilities and the information is understandable and complete. For example, it should be easy to trace from an error condition to the failed component, and then it should be easy to understand the design of the component and to be able to fix it. It should also be easy to look up information on how to use the software capabilities.

The following are some suggestions for achieving well-documented software during software development:

- Free documents from access control.
- Make information in a document understandable to the reader.
- Clearly depict control and data flow in designs.
- Provide an indexing scheme for quick access to subject matter.
- Separate documents on the basis of software functionality.
- Describe the software operational capabilities completely.
- Provide comprehensive descriptions of algorithms.
- Include code listings in documentation.

Figure 3–10 shows two designs, the first without any consideration of quality of documentation and the second with quality of documentation designed in. In the latter, the manual shown uses tabs to help the software user find information easily. Such a feature indicates concern for the end use during the process of designing the document.

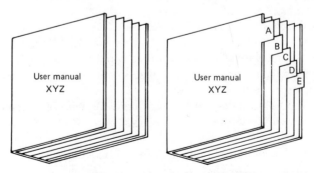

Figure 3-10 Adding documentation quality.

3.3.10 EFFICIENCY OF COMMUNICATION

Software communicates efficiently if it uses no more communication line bandwidth than is necessary to perform the required function, that is, if it minimizes the number of bits per second across a communication line (a network or telecommunication line).

The following are some suggestions for achieving required levels of communication efficiency during software development:

- Meet or exceed spare performance requirements for communication equipment.
- Use the shortest path between two communicating components.
- Use data compression for communication messages.
- Use error correction instead of resending messages.

Figure 3–11 shows two designs, the first without any consideration of communication efficiency and the second with communication efficiency designed in. The first design requires 2,000 bytes to be transferred across the communication network for each 2,000-byte buffer, regardless of the contents of the buffer. The second design includes data compression and decompression functions. The result is a reduction in the number of bytes traversing the communication network (1,000 versus 2,000).

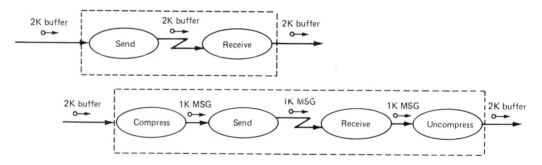

Figure 3-11 Adding efficiency of communication to a software design.

3.3.11 EFFICIENCY OF PROCESSING

Software processes efficiently if it uses no more processor bandwidth than is necessary to perform the required functions, that is, if it minimizes the number of instructions per second executed by a processor.

The following are some suggestions for achieving required levels of processing efficiency during software development:

- Meet or exceed spare performance requirements for processor equipment.
- Use an optimizing compiler or assembly language if necessary.

- Design data storage for efficient processing.
- Initialize data at the point of declaration of the data.
- Avoid memory overlays.
- Avoid non-loop-dependent statements in loops.
- Avoid recalculating the same expression in more than one statement.
- Avoid data packing and unpacking in a loop.
- Avoid different-size data items in the same expression.
- Avoid mixed data types in the same expression.
- Minimize the number of data items modified in each unit.

Figure 3–12 shows two designs, the first without any consideration of processing efficiency and the second with processing efficiency designed in. In the first design, the calculation ''2 * PI'' is performed during every iteration of the loop, but is not loop dependent. In the second, the same calculation is performed only once, prior to entering the loop. Both designs yield the same result, but the latter uses less processor resources.

```
for I: = FIRST to LAST do          TWOPI: = 2*PI
    SUM: = SUM + 2*PI*X(I)         for I: = FIRST to LAST do
end;                                   SUM: = SUM + TWOPI*X(I)
                                   end;
```

Figure 3-12   Adding efficiency of processing to a software design.

3.3.12   EFFICIENCY OF STORAGE

Software stores data or instructions efficiently if it uses no more RAM or disk memory than is necessary to perform the required functions, that is, if it minimizes the number of bytes of storage.

The following are some suggestions for achieving required levels of storage efficiency during software development:

- Meet or exceed spare performance requirements for storage equipment.
- Use virtual storage management.
- Use dynamic memory allocation.
- Use an optimizing compiler or assembly language if necessary.
- Avoid redundant storage of files and libraries.
- Separate software to efficiently use memory segments.
- Pack all data items.

Figure 3–13 shows two designs, the first without any consideration of storage efficiency and the second with storage efficiency designed in. The first design uses full

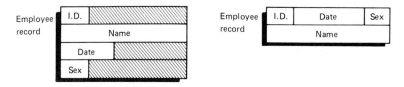

Figure 3-13   Adding efficiency of storage to a software design.

memory words to store data that occupy less than a full word. In the second design, the same data get packed into the memory words, thus saving storage resources.

3.3.13   FUNCTIONAL SCOPE

Software has good functional scope if its functions have a wide range of applicability, that is, if the functions are reusable in other similar applications or systems, or at other sites.

The following are some suggestions for achieving required levels of functional scope during software development:

- Avoid redundancy management for replicated functions.
- Avoid synchronization for replicated functions.
- Maximize software reuse in similar functions.
- Design in multisite commonality with site-specific adaptability.
- Document I/O as to its specific meaning and limitations.
- Specify the exact format of function I/O.
- Describe the unit's function in the unit prologue.

Figure 3–14 shows two designs, the first without any consideration of functional

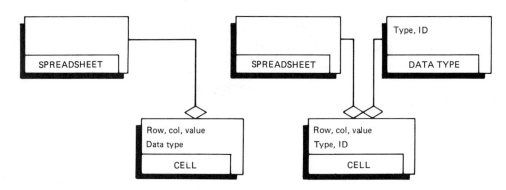

Figure 3-14   Adding functional scope to a software design.

scope and the second with functional scope designed in. In the first, the entity-relation-attribute (ERA) data design embeds site-specific data-type attributes in the definition of spreadsheet cells. In the second, the data design is expanded to separate out data-type information so that site- (processor) specific data-type attributes can be more easily adapted to other applications.

3.3.14 GENERALITY

Units of software are general if they provide a service for more than one function, that is, if they are called by two or more software components. In attempting to achieve generality, the designer should think about building a primitive function that can be of service for many uses. In many cases this can be accomplished by moving constraints such as the data item size and type from within the unit to the parameters in the unit interface.

The following are some suggestions for achieving required levels of generality during software development:

- Use object managers wherever possible.
- Avoid mixing input, processing, and output in one unit.
- Parametrize limits on input data structure size.
- Parametrize limits on input data item values.

Figure 3–15 shows two designs, the first without any consideration of generality and the second with generality designed in. The first design is an object manager of a single object type (A). The second is more general because it is an object and type manager providing common service for a variety of object types.

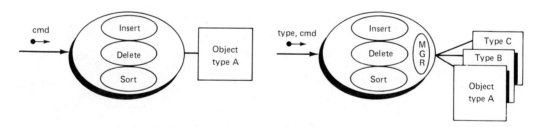

Figure 3-15 Adding generality to a software design.

3.3.15 INDEPENDENCE

Application software that is independent does not contain any references to its environment; that is, the software can be lifted and reused in other environments with little or no modification. For example, the software is independent if there are no references to uniqueness of the computing system, operating system, utilities, I/O routines, libraries, data-base system, microcode, computer architecture, or system algorithms.

The following are some suggestions for achieving required levels of independence during software development:

- Use a programming language (version) that is commonly available.
- Avoid nonstandard constructs of the programming language.
- Avoid the use of utilities that are unique to any system.
- Minimize the number of units doing external I/O.
- Avoid expressions dependent on word or character size.
- Avoid machine-dependent data item representations.
- Separate adaptation data from fixed data.
- Avoid the use of assembly or machine languages.

Figure 3–16 shows two designs, the first without any consideration of independence and the second with independence designed in. In the first, the design of GET COMMAND and GET RESPONSE is dependent on the particular computer environment (the keyboard here) because each command interfaces directly with the device in question. Device changes will then cause changes in both programs. The second design has isolated the two programs from the keyboard. Instead, they interface with a virtual device and are, therefore, independent of their environment.

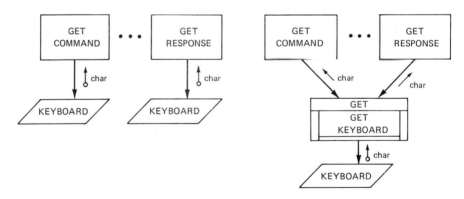

Figure 3-16 Adding independence to a software design.

3.3.16 MODULARITY

Software is modular if it is designed and implemented with all of the modern techniques that lead to an orderly, cohesive component structure with optimum coupling. Modularity is a conglomeration of various techniques, goals, and attributes that have been proven to lead to highly maintainable software. The key element in achieving modularity is the use of a structured design technique that will result in an organized, well-defined structure of components.

The following are some suggestions for achieving required levels of modularity during software development:

- Use a structured design technique.
- Use only structured programming language constructs.
- Use a structured testing technique.
- Represent designs in formally defined, unambiguous syntax.
- Design units that have a single processing objective.
- Maximize the cohesion of units.
- Minimize the complexity and volume in unit coupling.
- Avoid control variables used as formal parameters.
- Avoid data input via global data items or I/O statements.
- Return control and all output data to the calling unit.
- Make local data and code inaccessible outside the local unit.
- Make each unit separately compilable.
- Make each unit have an average of less than 100 source lines of code (SLOC).
- Separate each unit into a specification, declaration, and execution part.

Figure 3–17 shows two designs, the first without any consideration of modularity and the second with modularity designed in. The first design has grouped many different kinds of functions into one unit. By contrast, the second design has a single, clearly defined objective, is structured and understandable, and has neatly confined separate functions to separate units.

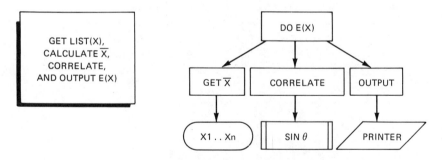

Figure 3-17 Adding modularity to a software design.

3.3.17 OPERABILITY

Software is operable if it is easy to use, that is, if it includes, among other things, an understandable user interface, a minimum number of keystrokes for the most often performed job, and selectable options to adapt the software to a specific user, and if it keeps the user informed of conditions over which he or she has control. Operability also includes the masking of system implementation details so that performing some job is natural from the user's perspective.

The following are some suggestions for achieving required levels of operability during software development:

- Minimize the number of required operations for the typical job.
- Log operator interactions.
- Report violations of access to the operator.
- Make resource status information available.
- Allow for reallocation of functions and data to resources.
- Allow for data manipulation regardless of location.
- Make system implementation details transparent.
- Provide the ability to pause, input data, and then continue.
- Allow for user review of input data prior to execution.
- Allow for user-selectable input media.
- Allow for user-selectable output media, formats, and amounts.
- Provide unique, descriptive labels for output data items.
- Use meaningful units of measure for output data items.
- Make error messages clear to the user.
- Have error messages specify the required user response.
- Minimize the number of different message and response formats.
- Use default values for required user inputs.

Figure 3–18 shows two designs, the first without any consideration of operability and the second with operability designed in. In the first design, the user interface uses keyboard-typed commands and cryptic syntax that has little relation to the natural way a user would perform the job without the computer. By contrast, the second user interface uses visual feedback, has a natural correspondence to a desktop, uses an input device not requiring mastery of a keyboard, and always displays the options a user can take at any point in the job.

3.3.18 SAFETY MANAGEMENT

Software is safe if it avoids unsafe conditions, i.e., those conditions that could lead to loss of life, property damage, or liability. Units of software (either functions or data) that participate in avoiding unsafe conditions are termed *critical*.

Software has good safety management when critical units are designed and implemented to avoid unsafe conditions. Avoiding unsafe conditions is achieved through separation of these critical units from noncritical units, by testing for unsafe conditions, and by fail-safe recovery from unsafe conditions when they occur. (Note that the term

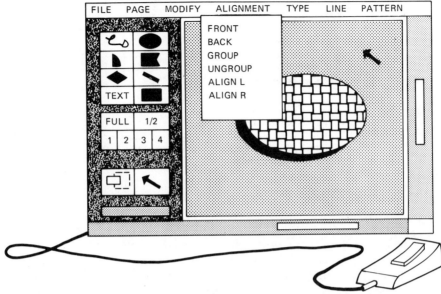

```
c > COPY C:\SYSTEM\MYFOLDER.DAT
    A:\SAVE\NEWDATA.TXT
```

Figure 3-18   Adding operability to a software design.

"critical," when used in other quality criteria (e.g., accuracy and anomaly management) often denotes safety requirements as well.)

The following are some suggestions for achieving required levels of safety management during software development:

- Separate critical functions and data from noncritical ones.
- Use the highest quality of unit interface (data coupling) between critical units.
- Separate error recovery code lexically from normal code in critical units.
- Separate critical functions and data likely to change.
- Establish and follow coding standards for critical units.
- Schedule the execution of critical units in a deterministic manner.
- Specify unsafe conditions and build in tests for them.
- Implement fail-safe recovery from detected unsafe conditions.

Figure 3–19 shows two designs, the first without any consideration of safety management and the second with safety management designed in. The first design uses a round-robin program dispatcher (first program 1, then program 2, etc.). This design can lead to a hazard if some processing load anomaly prevents the round-robin scheduler from scheduling a critical program on time. By contrast, the second design dispatches programs in a time-oriented manner. This design will be more deterministic and thereby safer than the round-robin scheduler.

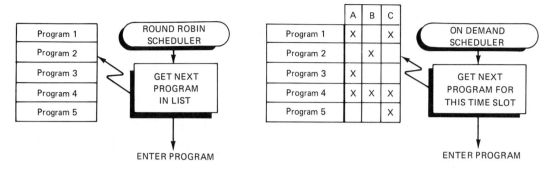

Figure 3-19 Adding safety management to a software design.

3.3.19 SELF-DESCRIPTIVENESS

Software is self-descriptive if a reader of the design or source code can easily understand how a function has been implemented, that is, if the software is a self-documented description of itself. Self-descriptiveness deals with the quantity of comments included in the code, with their effectiveness, and with programming or design language descriptiveness.

The following are some suggestions for achieving required levels of self-descriptiveness during software development:

- Document the results of decisions in design representations.
- Identify external interfaces in design representations.
- Establish standards for writing unit prologues, commenting, and structuring code.
- Follow established unit standards.
- Establish and follow standards for global data commenting.
- Provide comments for all decision points and transfers of control.
- Provide comments for all machine-dependent code.
- Use a higher order language (HOL) wherever possible.
- Provide comments for all nonstandard HOL statements.
- Provide comments for all data item attributes (e.g., range and accuracy).
- Provide comments on the ranges of values and defaults for all unit inputs.
- Logically block and indent code.
- Do not overload the meanings of keywords in the programming language.
- Describe the purpose or intent of the code in code comments.
- Describe the properties of data items in the names of the data item.

Figure 3–20 shows two designs, the first without any consideration of self-descriptiveness and the second with self-descriptiveness designed in. The first data record on

```
type                          type
I = 1 . . 31;                 DAYSOFMONTH = 1 . . 31;
K = record;                   DATE = record;
L : I; M : 1 . . 12; J : 0 . . 100;       DAY:      DAYSOFMONTH:
end;                          MONTH: (JAN . . DEC);
                              YEAR:   1900 . . 2000;
                              end;
```

Figure 3-20 Adding self-descriptiveness to a software design.

the left is cryptic, too terse, too compact, and obviously not written to be understood by a human. The second record results in exactly the same machine representation after compilation as does the first, but stands on its own as self-descriptive.

3.3.20 SIMPLICITY

Software implementation is simple when it is straightforward, clear-cut, and unconfused. Software in this category is usually well thought out in advance and is sometimes programmed several times to find the simplest implementation. The opposite of simple code is sometimes referred to as ''spaghetti code'' because its strands are so interwoven that it resembles the food.

The following are some suggestions for achieving required levels of simplicity during software development:

- Minimize the use of common data blocks.
- Avoid singly used data items in common blocks.
- Use data items only in accordance with their descriptions.
- Make units independent of their input sources and output destinations.
- Avoid encoding knowledge of prior processing in unit sources.
- Provide single entrances to and single exits from units (except for error-related exits).
- Avoid erratic flow of control.
- Avoid GO TOs.
- Avoid the use of conditional branch statements.
- Avoid negative and compound Boolean statements.
- Avoid unnatural exits from loops.
- Avoid nesting beyond three to five levels.
- Avoid multiple statements on one line of code.
- Avoid continuation lines of code.
- Avoid repeated or redundant code (e.g., use macros).
- Do not alter loop variables within a loop.

- Avoid self-modifying code.
- Use the Halstead metric to identify and simplify difficult areas.
- Separate I/O from computation.
- Aggregate similar functions into single packages.
- Avoid initializing global data in one unit and using the data in another unit.
- Minimize fan-out (the number of units invoked by a given unit).

Figure 3–21 shows two designs, the first without any consideration of simplicity and the second with simplicity designed in. The use of negative and compound Boolean decisions has made the first design very difficult to follow and understand. The second decision design results in the same flow as the first, but is simpler and easier to follow and understand.

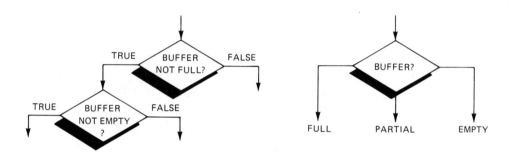

Figure 3-21 Adding simplicity to a software design.

3.3.21 SUPPORT

Software is supportive if it includes tools, data bases, and procedures that ease the management of change after the software is delivered. Although these attributes refer to support software as opposed to operational software, they are important to the latter's fitness for use.

The following are some suggestions for achieving required levels of support during software development:

- Close all program trouble reports before delivery.
- Provide services to support correction and upgrade of software.
- Provide services for on-call consultation.
- Document change management procedures.
- Provide tools to support control over site adaptation of different versions of software.
- Provide tools for change management.

- Provide tools for updates of documentation.
- Provide a data base for testing software and procedures.
- Automate software testing.
- Provide a complete software development environment.
- Provide a library of reusable software components.

Figure 3–22 shows two designs, the first without any consideration of support and the second with support designed in. The first diskette, used to deliver software purchased for programs A and B, contains only programs A and B. If something goes wrong with the programs, or if the user is unable to install it, the user is out of luck because there is no support software or information to help him or her. By contrast, the second diskette contains debugging software, source code, source editing functions, installation instructions, and a help telephone number for consultation.

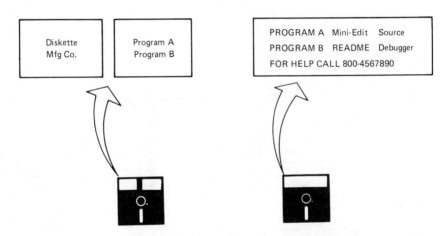

Figure 3-22   Adding support to a software product.

3.3.22   SYSTEM ACCESSIBILITY

The software (including any data bases it interacts with) has good system accessibility if it has complete control over who accesses it and when and how it is accessed. In a word, system accessibility means security, including responding to access violations such as improper access logging and alerts by automatic disconnection.

The following are some suggestions for achieving required levels of system accessibility during software development:

- Limit user access by user identification and passwords.
- Control data access by authorization tables.
- Control the scope of task operations during execution.

- Control network access by authorization tables.
- Keep logs of all system accesses.
- Output alerts in case of access violations.
- Allow only valid data-base operations.
- Monitor data bases to ensure that they are valid.
- Design in the ability to disconnect any interfacing system.
- Password-protect files from unauthorized access.
- Disallow unauthorized modifications to software.
- Protect against loss of services by inadvertent actions.
- Disallow bypass of security features.

Figure 3–23 shows two designs, the first without any consideration of system accessibility and the second with system accessibility designed in. In the first case, the user has mistakenly requested that the main storage disk be wiped clean (''format c:''). The poor design of the software has made the main storage disk easily accessible and allowed it to be thus erased. By contrast, the second software design has made the main disk inaccessible to such disastrous requests.

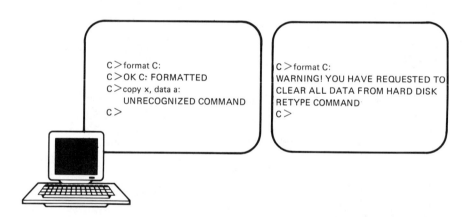

Figure 3-23   Adding system accessibility constraints to a software design.

3.3.23   SYSTEM COMPATIBILITY

Software has good system compatibility when it results in harmonious intersystemic operations, that is, when the hardware, software, and communication functions work together as an interoperating whole. System compatibility is achieved primarily by designing the software around the constraints imposed by the interoperating system.

The following are some suggestions for achieving required levels of system compatibility during software development. (Note that ''compatible'' in this context means compatible with an interoperating system.)

- Use compatible I/O rates.
- Use compatible communication protocols.
- Use common interpretation of intersystemic messages.
- Use common structures and sequences in the contents of messages.
- Use compatible data types, representations, and units.
- Use compatible data-base structures.
- Use compatible data-base access techniques.
- Use compatible word lengths.
- Use compatible interrupt structures.
- Use compatible instruction sets.
- Use compatible source code languages.
- Use compatible operating systems.
- Use common support software.

Figure 3–24 shows two designs, the first without any consideration of system compatibility and the second with system compatibility designed in. In the first, a new system, B, has been designed using a different programming language (and, hence, support environment) from that of the existing system A. Interoperability of these two coexisting systems will very likely not be harmonious because of different data representations, message formats, data structures, and maintenance needs. By contrast, in the second design, system B uses the same language and compiler version as the existing system, thus avoiding the interoperability problems of the first design.

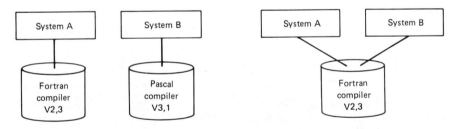

Figure 3-24 Adding system compatability to a software design.

3.3.24 *TRACEABILITY*

Software is traceable when it is easy to find all the code that implements a particular requirement and, conversely, when it is easy to find all the requirements that are implemented by a particular portion of code. Traceability is important in verifying correctness and during perfective maintenance. It is achieved through careful and complete allocation of requirements downward to software components during the design process, and through documentation of the traceability and allocation results.

The following are some suggestions for achieving required levels of traceability during software development:

- Document the origin of each requirement of each software component.
- Document each component to which each requirement is allocated.
- Graphically portray the decomposition of components.
- Implement software in conformity with design specifications.
- Document allocated requirements in unit prologues.

Figure 3–25 shows two designs, the first without any consideration of traceability and the second with traceability designed in. The code in the first design is an untraceable implementation of the specification shown in the center. In terms of traceability it would be difficult for someone looking at the code for the first time to find where function X had been implemented in it, and it would also be difficult to justify the existence of the new functions Y and Z. By contrast, the second design is directly traceable from the specification because it is a straightforward implementation of the requirements.

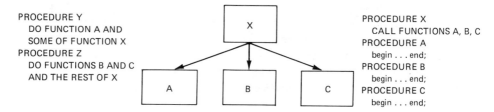

Figure 3-25 Adding traceability to a software design.

3.3.25   *TRAINING*

Software is capable of training users when it includes provisions to help them learn how to use the software to perform their jobs. These provisions include training classes, on-line help capability, and adjustable levels of sophistication in the user interface.

The following are some suggestions for achieving required levels of training during software development:

- Include lesson plans and training materials with software.
- Provide realistic simulation exercises.
- Build in a help system as an integral part of the software.
- Key diagnostic messages toward learning.
- Provide selectable levels of aid and guidance.

Figure 3–26 shows two designs, the first without any consideration of training and the second with training designed in. Judging from the menu, the first design assumes

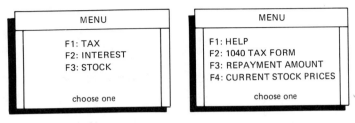

Figure 3-26 Adding training to a software design.

that the user of the program is an expert. By contrast, the second design provides for learning: a help function and more definitive labels for menu choices ease the progression from novice to expert.

3.3.26 VIRTUALITY

Software has the attribute of virtuality if it represents different physical components by the same logical or *virtual* component. The representation can occur across any interface: user interacting with software, units calling other units, or software interfacing with devices. The importance of the representation is to be able to replace devices or functions without disrupting or changing the interface.

The following are some suggestions for achieving required levels of virtuality during software development:

- Present a logical (not physical) view of the system to the user.
- Isolate I/O interfaces to single units.
- Use logical record interfaces.
- Avoid encoding knowledge of the physical properties of the system.

Figure 3–27 shows two designs, the first without any consideration of virtuality and the second with virtuality designed in. From the viewpoint of the function "GET USER'S CHOICE" in the first design, screen coordinates are input from a specific pointing device with specific characteristics and specific interface commands. There is no representation here. By contrast, the same function in the second design sees a logical pointing device. This virtual interface requires no knowledge of type, model number, or command language.

3.3.27 VISIBILITY

Software is visible if there is insight into its progress as regards coding and testing. Insight is gained through objective evidence of the correct functioning of the software during execution, primarily through the thoroughness of testing and the success of the

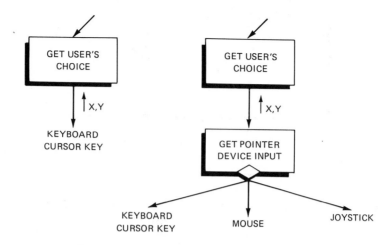

Figure 3-27 Adding virtuality to a software design.

test results. Visibility is equally applicable to both initial development and maintenance changes. It is added to the software by embedding self-testing in the code and through completeness of software testing procedures.

The following are some suggestions for achieving required levels of visibility during software development:

- Provide tests for all software performance requirements.
- Design test scenarios to maximize the number of units tested.
- Document inputs and outputs for performance test cases.
- Provide tests for all unit-to-unit interfaces.
- Provide tests for all parameters in each unit interface.
- Provide tests for all execution paths in each unit.
- Add monitors to detect intermittent errors and marginal performance.
- Add built-in test software to isolate defective components.

Figure 3–28 shows two designs, the first without any consideration of visibility

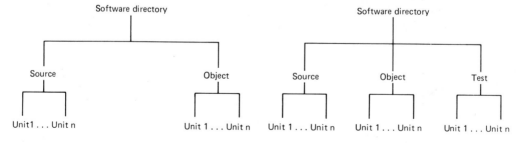

Figure 3-28 Adding visibility to a software design.

and the second with visibility designed in. In the first design, the software directory contains only source and object code. This design did not consider the need for test software to reverify changed code during maintenance. By contrast, the second directory contains test software in addition to the source and object code. This design will result in better visibility because of the ability to verify the condition of the software during maintenance.

3.4
Mapping User Needs to Engineerable Criteria

The 15 software quality factors described in Section 3.2 are the objective of software quality engineering. However, software engineers have a problem relating these fitness-for-use requirements to daily decision making during design and implementation. For example, how should a structured design be changed to meet a reliability requirement of 200 hours mean time between failures?

In a similar manner, users have a problem relating the 27 engineering quality criteria just described to fitness-for-use requirements. For example, how much reliability is added to the software by making the code more simple?

Table 3–2 is a mapping between user needs for quality and the criteria that can be designed in during development. Based on this mapping, we are able to specify what levels of quality should be implemented during design to meet certain levels of fitness-for-use requirements. (See Chapter 4.)

Figure 3–29, which summarizes the quality factors, engineering criteria, and their interrelationships, may be used as a quick reference guide to the information presented in this chapter.

TABLE 3-3

Fitness-for-Use Factors	Correctness	Efficiency	Expandability	Flexibility	Integrity	Interoperability	Maintainability	Manageability	Portability	Reliability	Reusability	Safety	Survivability	Usability	Verifiability
Engineering Attributes															
Accuracy										*			*		
Anomaly Management										*			*	*	
Augmentability			*												
Autonomy													*		
Commonality						*									
Completeness	*						*								
Consistency	*						*								
Distributivity													*	*	
Quality of Documentation								*			*				
Efficiency of Communication		*													
Efficiency of Processing		*													
Efficiency of Storage		*													
Functional Scope						*					*				
Generality			*	*							*				
Independence						*			*		*				
Modularity			*	*		*	*		*		*				*
Operability														*	
Safety Management													*		
Self-descriptiveness			*	*			*		*		*				*
Simplicity			*	*			*			*	*				*
Support								*	*		*				*
System Accessibility					*										
System Compatibility						*									
Traceability	*						*								*
Training														*	
Virtuality			*												
Visibility							*								*

SOFTWARE QUALITY FACTORS

Correctness	What was produced is what was specified, and vice versa
Efficiency	The number of resources required is affordable
Expandability	It is easy to change the software to add new capabilities
Flexibility	The software is adaptable to a wide range of different environments
Integrity	The user is reasonably certain that the software and data are not being tampered with or stolen
Interoperability	The software produces or uses results that comply with industry standards
Maintainability	The software is productive during the maintenance life cycle, from error detection to new release
Manageability	The support environment is complete and easy to use
Portability	The software may be used on a wide range of operating systems and computers
Reliability	There is an acceptably long time between failures
Reusability	There is a large library of software building blocks
Safety	The software can be trusted
Survivability	Essential functions are still available even though some part of the system is down
Usability	It is easier to use the software than not to use it
Verifiability	The software is productive during certification

SOFTWARE QUALITY CRITERIA

Accuracy	Achieving required precision in calculations and outputs
Anomaly management	Nondisruptive failure recovery
Augmentability	Ease of expansion in functionality and data
Autonomy	Degree of decoupling from execution environment
Commonality	Use of standards to achieve interoperability
Completeness	All software is necessary and sufficient
Consistency	Use of standards to achieve uniformity
Distributivity	Geographical separation of functions and data
Document quality	Access to complete understandable information
Efficiency of communication	Economic use of communication resources
Efficiency of processing	Economic use of processing resources
Efficiency of storage	Economic use of storage resources
Functional scope	Range of applicability of a function
Generality	Range of applicability of a unit
Independence	Degree of decoupling from support environment
Modularity	Orderliness of design and implementation
Operability	Ease of operating the software
Safety management	Software design to avoid hazards
Self-descriptiveness	Understandability of design and source code
Simplicity	Straightforward implementation of functions
Support	Functionality supporting the management of changes
System accessibility	Controlled access to software and data
System compatibility	Ability of two or more systems to work in harmony
Traceability	Ease of relating code to requirements and vice versa
Training	Provisions to learn how to use the software
Virtuality	Logical implementation to represent physical components
Visibility	Insight into validity and progress of development

Figure 3-29 Software quality factors and engineering criteria.

Specifying Software Quality Requirements

What do you look for in terms of quality when you are shopping for an automobile? Is a touch-sensitive command console important to you? Leather seat covers? Top speed of 150 miles per hour? Large trunk space? Low maintenance costs? Resale value? Safety?

It all depends on how you intend to use the automobile, who will be driving it, what area of the country you live in, how much you are willing to spend, and so forth. If you only want a reliable car for traveling back and forth to work, then your needs are different from those of someone who wants to chauffeur dignitaries to corporate headquarters.

The analogy is true for software quality as well. Depending on intended use, cost, environment, and many other factors, levels and types of quality needs will differ. Thus, in keeping with the phrase "you can't achieve quality unless you specify it," a specification process must be followed to tailor the many possible software quality attributes to a subset uniquely applicable to a particular software development project.

This chapter is organized around the model shown in Figure 4-1, which shows the steps that are followed to analyze a unique need for quality, and based on that need,

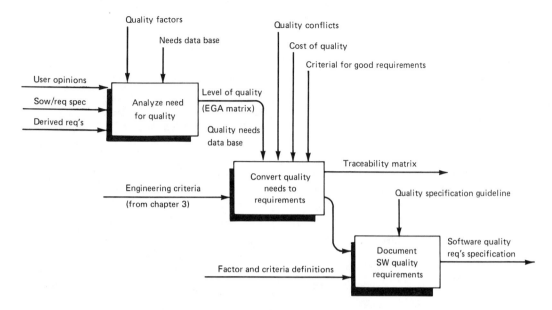

Figure 4-1 Overview of software quality specification process.

tailor general quality attributes to specific requirements. Given the quality requirements, designers can proceed to engineer in quality. Each model activity is briefly described in the following paragraphs.

Analyzing the need for quality results in an understanding of the unique quality requirements of a given software project, documented in the form of a quality needs data base and a level-of-quality matrix. Quality needs are based on the statement of work, system requirements specification, system design specification, and any other sources that afford a clue as to what the end user needs. The level-of-quality matrix, which is based on the user's viewpoint, gives the level of quality needed for each software component for each quality factor. Controls on this activity are a suggested format for a needs data base and the 15 quality factors described in Chapter 3. Subactivities of the quality needs analysis are:

- Collecting and organizing quality needs
- Determining the level of quality required

Converting quality needs to requirements results in a precise specification of the quality required in a piece of software. The quality needs from the analysis activity and the 247 engineering criteria from Chapter 3 (the list of suggestions under each of the 27 criteria) are used as the basis for the quality specification. This activity is controlled by the level-of-quality matrix from the analysis activity, interfactorial quality conflicts, the cost of quality, and the criteria for good requirements given in Section 4.2. Subactivities of the quality needs conversion are:

- Deriving requirements based on needs
- Conversion to testable, objective statements
- Meeting good requirement criteria
- Allocating quality requirements to software components

Documenting software quality requirements results in a software quality specification that is used for negotiation between the developer and user and as an input to the design process. The specification is based on the quality requirements from the quality needs conversion, the definition of each quality factor and engineering criterion from Chapter 3, and the factor/criterion interrelationship chart of Chapter 3. A quality specification style guide is a control on this activity.

Appendix 1 contains a sample software specification developed in accordance with DOD-STD-2167's data item description for Software Requirements Specifications (DI-MCCR-80025). It may be useful to refer to this appendix while reading through the rest of this chapter.

The word "component," as used in this chapter, is meant to be generic. It refers to a manageable subpart of the whole software program, or, more precisely, a subpart that could have an entire software requirements specification written for it. On a U.S. government contract under DOD-STD-2167, "component" would be replaced by "computer software configuration item" (CSCI).

Software quality specification is necessary to all software development efforts. However, the degree of formalism and amount of effort it involves may vary depending on the size of the project. For example, quality needs may be simply handwritten notes for the development of a personal computer program for calculating baseball statistics. On the other hand, there may be several person-years of effort and formal customer deliverables involved in specifying software quality for an air traffic control system.

This chapter is written to satisfy the needs of the latter, large-system development effort. Tailoring downward to a smaller software development effort is done by reducing the amount of effort performed in each activity. At a minimum, you simply select, from the list of engineering criteria in Chapter 3, those quality attributes that you want to achieve, mark them in this book, and let the marked-up book be your "specification."

4.1
Analyzing the Need for Quality

As mentioned previously, the goal of the quality needs analysis is to understand the unique needs for quality that a given software project has. This understanding is documented in two products:

- The quality needs data base
- The level-of-quality matrix

(*Note:* We use the word "need" to talk about software quality desires before they have been analyzed, sorted, and converted into testable specifications. Needs can come from any source and may or may not be in testable, objective form when discovered.)

Table 4–1 shows some sample quality needs. (The sources are fictitious.)

The quality needs data base should contain the following information for each unique need identified:

NEED	Textual description of the quality need
SOURCE	Precise description of the source of the need
IMPORTANCE	Importance of the need
REQUIREMENT	Keyword for each requirement imposed by the need
SUBJECT	Keyword for the subject of the need

The NEED field is a terse, but complete specification of the quality need. It is one sentence using one subject and one requirement on that subject. Thus, wordy specifications will need to be decomposed into single, complete subparts to become records in the needs data base. The key idea is one need per record.

The SOURCE field documents the traceability of the need. If the source is a document, the user should identify the document and include either the physical position (page, paragraph, and line number) or the logical position (section and sentence number) of the need within the document. If the source is an interview, the user should include the name of the person interviewed and the date of the interview.

TABLE 4–1

Need	Source	Importance	Requirement	Subject
The objective is to obtain new software that uses modern software engineering techniques	SSS/250(a) pg 263, p 2, s 4	9	modern	design
The precision and accuracy of inputs shall be preserved in all calculations	SSS/250(a) pg 346, p 6, s 2	5	precise	arithmetic
Design emphasis will be placed on fault tolerance	STD-1213 pg 45, p 6, s 8	5	fault tolerant	design
Code shall be regeneratable using delivered software	SOW-250(b) pg 23, p 5, s 2	3	complete	support software
Software should adapt to individual user needs and personal convenience	P. Smith 9/23/84	8	adaptable	MMI

The IMPORTANCE field records any information the user finds that emphasizes the priority of the need relative to other needs. For example, a scale of 1 to 10 might be used, where 10 means that satisfaction of the need is mandatory and 1 means that satisfaction of the need is almost unnecessary.

The REQUIREMENT field is an optional one- or two-word abstract (an adjective) of the requirement imposed by the need. If included, it can be used to sort needs based on their requirements. This is especially useful in working with large data bases.

The SUBJECT field is an optional one- or two-word abstract (a noun) of the subject of the need, used in conjunction with the REQUIREMENT field.

4.1.1 COLLECTING AND ORGANIZING QUALITY NEEDS

SCAN EXISTING DOCUMENTATION. The following documents, if they exist, are potential sources of determining software quality needs:

- Request for proposal
- Statement of work
- System or segment requirements specification
- Proposals used for acquiring the contract
- System design documents
- Previous studies about the current system
- Planning documents that describe future needs
- Required software development standards
- Software quality assurance requirements

Given the current state of understanding of software quality, you will probably not find much in the way of software quality requirements in these documents. And even when a requirement is found, it is likely to be subjective and difficult to understand. However, any such requirements in the document are important to capture because (1) they are attempts to specify what is required, (2) they give us a clue as to what is important to the user, and (3) they are a source from which you can derive testable requirements later on.

Hints:

Be Sherlock Holmes in search of quality needs.

Be thorough!

Set an example of quality work.

SURVEY USERS AND EXPERTS. The following people are rich sources of real insight into what kinds of quality should be built into the new system:

- Current or past users of the current system or software
- Planners of the new system
- Senior technical leaders of the development effort

It is sometimes difficult to capture a user's real need in a formal, legalistic document used for contract negotiation. For example, although "easy to use" may be the best way to describe the need, such a phrase is too vague to test and too difficult to price the effort required to achieve it. However, with just a few minutes' time, an interview or survey can zero in on what "easy to use" means and lead to a real understanding of quality needs.

In addition to users, people considered to be experts in similar software can be a rich source of what "high quality" means.

Hints:

Users understand fitness for use better than purchasers do.

Structure the survey around the fitness-for-use factors.

Try the old system yourself . . . what would you want?

ANALYZE NEEDS. If there is enough time and it hasn't been done yet, a needs analysis study is certain to identify a rich source of quality needs. A popular form of needs analysis today is the *quality circle* used by industrial employees to help solve problems in productivity and quality. A needs analysis study consists of the following activities:

- Gathering observations of the existing system.
- Determining problems based on observations.
- Identifying needs based on problems.

Gathering observations leads to knowledge and assertions about the existing system. These may be productivity and defect rates, trouble spots, ease-of-use indicators, personal opinions, technology assessments, assessments of the availability and reliability of resources, and the like.

Based on the observed facts, a cause-and-effect graph is developed that systematically relates causes to the observations, and then causes to causes, etc., until root causes are discovered. The root causes resulting from cause-and-effect graphing are the basis for determining needs. Basically, a need is stated as a requirement for a solution or solutions to the root cause of a problem. Deriving needs is a design technique; that is, it involves creating a solution that eradicates the problem. The following section gives some ideas for solutions.

USING CHAPTER 3 AS A GUIDE. The 247 suggestions regarding quality criteria in Chapter 3 can be used as a checklist to determine what is needed. Each suggestion is a specific solution to some quality problem. As such, for each one, you can ask whether or not the planned software needs such a solution; that is, does there exist a problem that requires this solution? When such a problem is uncovered, you have identified a need. (*Hint:* There may be problems without a solution in the suggestions.)

ORGANIZE COLLECTED NEEDS.   On a large project, you may find as many as 500 or even more needs. You can expect that some of these will be redundant and have to be eliminated. However, they may be stated differently enough to make it difficult to determine just which ones are in fact redundant. Then the potentially enormous task of comparison (500 needs require 125,250 comparisons!) plus the required manipulation of these needs in the next phase of organization are manageable only by using organization skills and a computer data-base management system.

To perform the task, record each need in a data-base record formatted as previously suggested—that is, source of need, importance of need, requirement key, and subject key. While recording each need, it is helpful to write down the requirement and subject keys on paper as the rows and columns of a matrix whose elements are the number of requirements with those attributes. This minimizes the number of unique keys and helps you decide on a key based on those keys that have already been defined.

When the data base is built, sort by requirement key. If any redundant requirements exist, they will be grouped after this sort (depending, of course, on how consistent you were in assigning keys). Next, sort by subject key to eliminate any subject redundancies. This will eliminate many, but not all, redundancies. Just as important, you will begin to become intimately familiar with your quality needs. (In the end, you must be an expert.)

An illustration of the relationship between the requirement key and the subject key is shown in Figure 4–2. The numbers in the matrix are the numbers of needs that have the same requirement key and subject key in common.

4.1.2 DETERMINING THE LEVEL OF QUALITY REQUIRED

Unconstrained, the process of software quality specification could end up with a Cadillac when only a bicycle is needed. Thus far, we have not constrained the process. Indeed, the process should not have been constrained because we need to make sure that all possible needs have been identified before we can intelligently trim them back based on what we can afford.

However, at this point we can begin worrying about what is possible or practical within the constraints of the software project. The two major steps in this regard are:

- Determine the level of quality needed.
- Tradeoff levels, conflicts, costs, and the schedule.

DETERMINE THE LEVEL OF QUALITY NEEDED.   If we were trying to determine the optimum type of transportation for a group of people, we might design a questionnaire that asked questions like the following:

At what times do you use transportation most?   AM ___ PM ___

SUBJECT (columns) vs. **REQUIREMENT** (rows)

REQUIREMENT	Algorithm	Code	CSC	CSCT	CSCTIO	Data	Data representation	Documentation	Fault tolerance	Global data	Interunit protocol	Language/compiler	MM	Network protocol	Performance	Resource management	SW architecture	System control	Unit	Usage procedures
Accessible								3										5		
Adaptable	1				1															
Allocate downward			1												1					
Alternate routing																		2		
Autonomous				2																
Average size LE 100																			1	
Centralized									1									6		
Centralized control				3																
Comment standard		8	1	1	7				1										3	
Common language												1								
Complete								3						4						
Data integrity									1											
Diagrammed																	4			
Documented																				5
Dynamic allocation																5				
Efficient		4	1		5										1	1			3	
For all errors									6											
Help capability												2								
Interoperable			9	4														1		
Keep record of												1						1		
Limit local data																			2	
Limit services used																			1	
Limited retries																			1	
Logical E of												1								
Maximize cohesion			2		1														6	
Maximize defaults												1								
Maximize fan-in																			1	
Maximize spare																5				
Minimize coupling			1	1															5	
Minimize fan-out																			1	
Minimize formats														3						
Minimize keystrokes													1							
Minimize non-hol		2																		
Minimize control data											2									
MSG completeness														2						
Naming standard					3															
Network integrity									1											
No mixed data types		2																		
No overlay																1				
No self-modification		2																		
No time constraint															2					
No unit access									1											
None unused					1						1									
Only computed/global					1															
Only parms/global											4									
Periodic check							2													
Precise																2				
Redundant									1									2		
Report to operator								1										3		
Restricted set/use									1											
Return to caller											1									
Reusable		6		2	1						1								4	
Simple/consistent																				
Standardized		5		4	5	3	4					2		6			2			
Standardized subset		1									1									
Structured		14											1				2			
Synchronization limit															1					
Test data available	1																			
Thoroughly tested		1									1					1			2	
Understandable							1						3							
Unique name			1	1																
Usage standard				1	1			3												
User modifiable																	2		1	
User options																5				
Validate				8	2															
Variable initialization					1															
Verify	1																			
Version consistency				2																
Virtual																	1	2		

Figure 4-2 Sample subject key vs. requirement key cross-reference table.

| | Are you willing to pay extra for luxury items? | YES __ NO __ |
| | How much space do you require? | ____ sq feet |

In this transportation questionnaire, we are trying to zoom in on requirements that are uniquely adapted to a specific user or set of users so that we neither overspecify nor underspecify what is needed. After all, in one case luxury may be most important and in another space may be. The subject of each question (time, luxury, space) is the requirement criterion.

Time, luxury, and space in these questions are analogous to the 15 fitness-for-use concerns (maintainability, efficiency, etc.) regarding software quality. In one case portability may be most important, and in another survivability may be most important. We need to uniquely adapt the fitness-for-use concerns to each software component that we are developing. In effect, our goal is to fill in the matrix shown in Figure 4–3 with indicators of level of importance. In doing so, we can choose the easiest metric to relate a software component to the 15 software quality factors by importance level (for example, 1 to 10 with 10 high). The following is one possible metric scheme:

E . . . Excellent quality is required for this factor. Use all quality criteria in Chapter 3 that are applicable. Exceptional techniques should be used for design, reviewing, and testing.

G . . . Good quality is required for this factor. Use most quality criteria in Chapter 3 that are applicable. Better than average techniques should be used for design, reviewing, and testing.

A . . . Average quality is required for this factor. Use some quality criteria in Chapter 3 that are applicable. Normal corporate practices should be used for design, reviewing, and testing.

Software component

Correctness																	
Efficiency																	
Expandability																	
Flexibility																	
Integrity																	
Interoperability																	
Maintainability																	
Manageability																	
Portability																	
Reliability																	
Reusability																	
Safety																	
Survivability																	
Usability																	
Verifiability																	

Figure 4-3 Software ranking matrix.

NI . . . Quality is not an issue for this factor. No special quality requirements or techniques are needed.

The use of "all," "most," and "some" in the preceding can be replaced with percentage thresholds once we have established a corporate data base of quality requirements based on the quality criteria of Chapter 3. Or better yet, three data bases could be established corresponding to the excellent, good, and average levels.

How do we select the quality level desired for each software component? One way is to use the previous suggestions for collecting needs. For example, the level-of-importance values in the needs data base could be used. Normally, however, there is not enough information to determine these values from source documents. Instead, a formal needs analysis might be required that would result in levels of priority which could be used for the matrix.

If users of the current software are available, the best source for determining level of quality is a survey of these users. A sample survey package is shown in Figure 4–4 with a blank quality matrix like the one in Figure 4–3 filled in with software component names, definitions of the quality factors, and a description of each software component.

Some useful hints for designing the survey are as follows:

- A personal touch helps the quantity and quality of results.
- Rules are needed regarding when a consensus exists among respondents.
- It takes about 10–20 minutes per column to fill out the matrix.

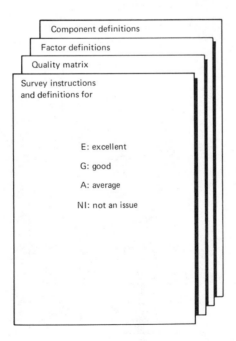

Figure 4-4 Sample survey package.

TRADE OFF LEVELS, CONFLICTS, COST, AND THE SCHEDULE.   While necessary for determining quality, the level-of-quality matrix is not enough. First, there are some conflicting relationships between quality factors that may make it impossible to generate a consistent resultant matrix. And second, the matrix may be a wish list, some of whose elements may not be affordable.

Figure 4–5 shows a matrix with conflicting and complementary relationships among the software quality factors. (The interested reader will find more on the basis for these conflicts in G. M. Weinberg's *The Psychology of Computer Programming*, Van Nostrand, New York, 1972.) The way to read the matrix is as follows. When the level of quality specified is raised for a factor in one of the left-hand rows, the effect on the factors in the columns is either complementary ($+$), conflicting ($-$), or nonexistent (blank). A complementary relationship comes about when, by raising the specified quality of a given factor, the level of quality of another factor is raised as a by-product. A conflicting relationship comes about when, by raising the specified quality of a given factor, the level of quality of another factor is lowered as a by-product. Thus, specifying a higher level of reliability lowers the efficiency of the software but raises its usability.

Given this matrix of relationships, we can go back to the level-of-importance matrix and adjust it by using the following procedure:

1. For the first software component (first column),

2. For the first conflicting relationship ($-$) between factor A and factor B,

3. Adjust the two levels of quality as shown in Table 4–2. (This table is for guidance only; the matrix will need to be adjusted depending on the specific environment involved.)

4. Repeat step 3 for the second conflicting relationship, and then the third, etc.,

Raising the level of quality for the factors in the rows results in:

Raising ($+$)

Lowering ($-$)

No change to the factors in the columns (   )

	Correctness	Efficiency	Expandability	Flexibility	Integrity	Interoperability	Maintainability	Manageability	Portability	Reliability	Reusability	Safety	Survivability	Usability	Verifiability
Correctness			+	+			+				+				+
Efficiency							−		−						−
Expandability	−			−	+					−				−	
Flexibility	−		−		+					−				−	
Integrity	−														
Interoperability	−				−										
Maintainability	−		+	+							+				+
Manageability									+		+				+
Portability	−														
Reliability	−													+	
Reusability	−			−	+	+		+	−					−	
Safety	−			+						+			+	+	
Survivability	−	−	−	−		+			−					−	
Usability	−					+									+
Verifiability	−														

Figure 4-5   Factor conflicts.

TABLE 4-2

If specified for factor A	Then at most for factor B
E	NI
G	A
A	G
NI	E

until there are no more conflicts. Then revisit previously adjusted relationships to make sure that they haven't been changed.

5. Repeat step 2, one column at a time, for each additional software component (row).

In step 3, the levels of quality are being tampered with, which means that we will almost certainly end up with a software product that doesn't meet the user's needs. However, such tampering is necessary to generate a consistent level-of-quality matrix. But the trade-offs will need to be coordinated and explained to the user, and some studies may be required to be able to decide what trade-offs are necessary. For example, one might have to ask how many resources are available to lower or raise the level of efficiency.

Some useful hints for trading off among elements in the quality matrix are as follows:

- There is no need to adjust complementary relationships.
- There's no better rule than common sense.
- The goal is to achieve no more and no less than what is needed.

The level of importance matrix resulting from this procedure may contain levels of quality that are unachievable within the budget and time available. So development costs and scheduling conflicts must be resolved. We start by assuming that a budget and schedule for normal software development have been determined. (Chapter 14 discusses the cost and schedule expansion factors based on the level-of-quality matrix.)

At this point in time, the state of the technology is insufficient to specify an algorithm for trading off level-of-quality and cost factors. There are simply too many variables required to determine cost expansion factors based on software type, analyst experience, etc. However, on a macroscopic level, the matrix may be adjusted by replacing each E, G, A, and NI in it with an expansion factor in the range of values (both cost and schedule) given in Chapter 14 and then computing the average for each software component. This yields the average software cost and schedule expansion for the development of each software component based on the perceived level of quality. Beware! This is a rough order of magnitude estimate.

Figure 4-6 shows an example in which the midpoint of the ranges from Tables 14-3 and 14-5 were taken for cost and schedule. The average values indicate a 17 percent increase in cost and a 5 percent increase in time scheduled to implement this

	Level of quality	Relative cost	Relative schedule
Correctness	E	1.85	1.23
Efficiency	A	1.05	1.02
Expandability	A	1.05	1.02
Flexibility	A	1.05	1.02
Integrity	NI	0.04	0.04
Interoperability	A	1.05	1.02
Maintainability	G	1.20	1.07
Manageability	E	1.05	1.29
Portability	NI	0.04	0.94
Reliability	G	1.29	1.07
Reusability	A	1.05	1.02
Safety	NI	0.04	0.94
Survivability	G	1.29	1.07
Usability	G	1.29	1.07
Verifiability	G	1.29	1.07
Average		1.17	1.05

Figure 4-6 Calculation of cost and schedule expansion for sample level of quality.

level of quality. (Note, for this example the range is 2 percent to 32 percent expansion for cost and 0 percent to 9 percent expansion for schedule.) If these expansions in cost and schedule are unacceptable, then the level-of quality matrix must be adjusted to reflect lower values of quality (e.g., are the E's really necessary, or could they be replaced with G's?).

In sum, we have collected all perceived needs for quality, recorded them in an organized data base, removed redundant needs, established a level-of-quality matrix, and traded off quality levels with conflicts, costs, and the schedule. The two major results are the needs data base and the level-of-quality matrix. The former will be used as a source for determining software quality requirements, the latter to control the quality specification process.

4.2
Converting Quality Needs to Requirements

The needs data base is filled with a variety of quality statements. Some are from interviews (e.g., "I'd like to have . . ."), some are from formal requirements specifications (e.g., "The software shall . . ."), and some are from planning documents (e.g., "Modernness is the goal."). None, however, are genuine requirements.

For a software quality requirement to be good means that we can use it to design software that has the required quality attribute and that an independent observer can objectively verify that the implemented software exhibits the specified attribute. Oftentimes, however, a software designer does not know how to design software to meet a user-oriented quality need, as, for example, mean time between failure (MIBF). Similarly, a need such as "modern software" is neither objective nor testable. Thus, such needs must undergo a transformation before they can be classified as genuine software quality requirements.

To help in the transformation process a data base of quality requirements that has the following content is needed:

REQUIREMENT	Text of actual requirement
SOURCE	Source of requirement
CRITERION	One of 27 criteria that requirement belongs to
DESIGN	"x" if requirement is verifiable in design phase
CODE	"x" if requirement is verifiable in code phase
TEST	"x" if requirement is verifiable in testing phase
DOCSORT	Sort order of final requirements document

The SOURCE field is necessary for traceability and should also contain an indicator as to whether the requirement was derived on the basis of an original need. The DESIGN, CODE, and TEST fields are useful for sorting the requirements for quality goals to be designed in and for internal review checklists. It may also be desirable to add requirement and subject keys as with the needs data base, to help in eliminating redundancies and inconsistencies.

If there are many software components, it is advisable to build one requirements data base to act as a superset for all the components. If this approach is used, the requirements data base should be designed to meet the most stringent quality requirements ("E" in the level-of-quality matrix). The last step in the process will then be to allocate requirements to each software component and adjust them on the basis of the level of quality needed.

The general approach to generating good software quality requirements can be summarized as follows:

- Derive requirements based on needs.
- Convert stated needs to testable, objective statements.
- Meet good requirement criteria.
- Allocate quality requirements to software components.

DERIVE REQUIREMENTS BASED ON NEEDS. Each need in the needs data base will become one or more requirements in the requirements data base. The first transformation is to convert each need to a potential requirement. In this regard, there are two kinds of needs: a need that can be restated as one requirement (i.e., one required quality attribute), and a need that results in many derived requirements (i.e., many quality attributes). A sample of each type is shown in Table 4–3.

We can distinguish between the two types by asking whether there is one test that could be performed to validate that the requirement has been implemented. For example, in the case of the first need, one test, viz., testing whether all decision points are accompanied by comments, can indeed be used to validate that the source code is liberally commented. But there is no single test that could validate the second need, that the software be fault tolerant, because many functions are required to implement fault tolerance.

TABLE 4-3

Need	Requirement(s)
Code shall be liberally interspersed with comments.	Code shall be liberally interspersed with comments.
The software shall be fault tolerant.	Validate all external inputs. Recover from invalid inputs. Report all discovered faults.

The first step, then, is to go through the needs data base one need at a time, developing the requirements data base. For needs that are single, software-designable requirements, a simple copy operation is all that is needed (in addition to filling in the other associated data fields). For needs that are implemented by more than one requirement, on the other hand, some extra work is involved. A necessary set of requirements must be defined that satisfies the need. Where do these ''extra'' requirements come from?

As a shortcut, one may pick and choose the requirements that satisfy the need based on the 247 engineering criteria of Chapter 3. For example, one may pick and choose requirements from the anomaly management and distributivity criteria to fulfill the need for fault tolerance.

CONVERT TO TESTABLE, OBJECTIVE STATEMENTS.   Two important attributes of a requirement are that it be objective and that it be testable. A requirement is objective if it is not dependent on personal opinion (i.e, not subjective); a requirement is testable if there is some finite, cost-effective process that can be used to validate that the requirement has been implemented.

Unfortunately, software quality requirements are oftentimes subjective and untestable. Consider the first requirement from Table 4-3, ''Code shall be liberally interspersed with comments.'' Does this mean that comments are to be written by a left-wing liberal from San Francisco? Should every statement have a comment, or every other statement? Is it sufficient to have 25 percent of the total code be comments, or are there certain statements that need comments while others do not? Do prologues count as comments? Do descriptive names count as comments? How about comments on the same line as a statement? Embedded within the statement?

Obviously, the requirement, as stated, is not objective. If we change it to ''All decision points in the code shall be accompanied by comments,'' then it is more objective and close to testable. In that case, which statements in the language are ''decision points'' is the only item where there is room left for interpretation. (We are not now considering how good the comment is, only whether there is or is not a comment.) Once that has been decided and documented, a program could be written to validate the requirement by automatically scanning all the source code for decision points and associated comments. The most objective and testable version of this example would list all programming language statements that require comments, for example:

There shall be an explanatory comment associated with each of the following programming statements: IF-THEN-ELSE, CASE, GOTO, EXIT, RAISE.

Certain quality attributes may be impossible to state in an objective, testable manner. A good example of this is cohesion. Cohesion is the attribute of a software design that relates the internal parts of a component together. If there is no meaningful relationship among the parts of a component (i.e., they just happen to be together for convenience), then that component has a low cohesion value. If, instead, all the elements within the component are purposefully related to the performance of a single function (i.e., the binding is *functional* rather than just coincidental), then that component has a cohesion value. There are several levels of cohesion. It is neither possible nor even desirable to achieve 100 percent functional binding in a design. Furthermore, since deciding on what type of cohesion any particular software component has is open for interpretation, the best we can require in the general case is to maximize cohesion, and even this is not strictly testable. In such cases, there is a range of acceptable results and the requirement should be stated in that manner.

There are no cookbook techniques for making each requirement in the requirements data base objective and testable. Doing so requires invention on the part of the designer and review by others for objectivity. For the latter, a test engineer, if available, is the best reviewer. One good approach is to try to get designers involved in the objectivity review. They are good judges of objectivity, and you will be training them in the software quality requirements at the same time.

MEET GOOD REQUIREMENTS CRITERIA. Software quality requirements should be quality software requirements. Accordingly, the next step in quality engineering is to review and revise the requirements for quality to meet the criteria for good software requirements.

The following attributes of good software requirements are related to goals as shown in Figure 4–7:

1. *Compliant With Contract.* A requirement is compliant with the contract if it meets the specifications given in

   • The system-level specification (SLS).

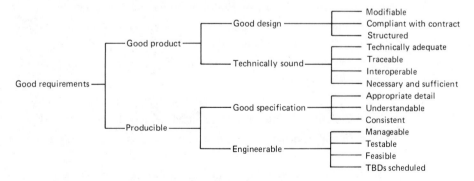

Figure 4-7 The attributes of good requirements.

- The statement of work (SOW).
- The system/segment specifications (SSS).
- Other specifications referenced by the preceding three.

2. *Consistent.* A requirement is consistent if it does not conflict with any other requirement in any of the following ways:
   - The same object is referred to by more than one term.
   - The same object is defined by more than one set of characteristics that conflict.
   - There is a logical or temporal conflict between two specific actions.

3. *Feasible.* A requirement is feasible if it can be implemented within the constraints of
   - The technological state of the art.
   - All schedules and budgets.
   - Available tools and techniques.
   - The performance goals.

4. *Interoperable.* A requirement is interoperable if it is complete with respect to requirements that address interoperating systems (an existing system into or with which the software in question will be integrated).

5. *Appropriate Level of Detail.* A requirement has the appropriate level of detail if it contains enough but no more than the information needed to meet its intended use. The primary uses of quality requirements are as
   - Specifications of quality that the buyer can use to assess the adequacy of the quality of the software before development begins.
   - Specifications of quality that software engineers can use to design in quality during development.

6. *Manageable.* Requirements are manageable if they can be organized around assignable development activities or organizations (i.e., if they can partition the requirements into administrative organizations or phase-related activities).

7. *Modifiable.* Requirements are modifiable if their structure and style are such that any necessary changes to the requirements can be made easily, completely, and consistently. To be modifiable, requirements generally:
   - Must have a coherent and easy-to-use organization with a table of contents, an index, an explicit cross-referencing.
   - Are not redundant, i.e., the same requirement does not appear in more than one place.

8. *Necessary and Sufficient.* Requirements are necessary and sufficient if they
   - Contain all of the quality required to meet the system-level requirements.
   - Contain no more than what is required to meet the system-level requirements.

9. *TBDs Are Scheduled.* A requirement has this attribute if, for each item TBD

(to be determined; also known as to be specified), there is an action with a scheduled completion date and responsible person assigned.

10. *Technically Adequate.* A requirement is technically adequate if

   - Its overall approach is sound.

   - No known facts or principles are violated.

   - The approach is consistent with approaches known to be successful on other projects.

   - It is well researched or based on proven prototypes.

   - It is well thought out and not thrown together.

   - Its approach makes sense both technically and practically.

11. *Traceable.* A requirement is traceable if it satisfies all of the following:

   - It fully implements the applicable stipulations in the SLS and/or SSS.

   - It has its basis in the SLS and/or SSS (i.e., no untraceable material has been introduced).

   - It does not contradict the SLS and/or SSS.

12. *Structured.* Requirements are structured if they are cohesive, independent, not coupled to other requirements, and based on a hierarchical architecture derived from system-level requirements.

13. *Testable.* A requirement is testable if there exists some finite cost-effective process by means of which a person or machine can check that the software product meets the requirement.

14. *Understandable.* A requirement is understandable if it is clear, unambiguous, meaningful, and simple.

ALLOCATE QUALITY REQUIREMENTS TO SOFTWARE COMPONENTS. Once a superset of requirements has been developed to cover all software components, it is time to allocate each requirement to each component. The level-of-quality matrix developed earlier is used to select applicable requirements and, if necessary, to adjust the level of quality required.

First, the data base of requirements is duplicated for each software component. Then, for each requirement in each resulting data base, the following is done:

   - If the requirement is not applicable to the software component, delete it. (*Note*: If the requirement is applicable to any software subpart anyplace in the software component, then it must not be deleted. During the design phase, the requirements will be allocated downward only to those software subparts to which each requirement is applicable.)

   - For requirements that were not deleted, tailor the requirement in accordance with the level-of-quality matrix as follows:

   (a) Using the criteria-factor relationship matrix from Chapter 3, determine the fitness-for-use factor that the requirement belongs to. (The criteria come from the requirements data base record.)

(b) Using the level-of-quality matrix for the software component in question, determine the level of quality needed (E, G, A, or NI) for the factor in question.

(c) Tailor the wording of the requirement to match the level of quality.

Following are some suggested word-tailoring approaches:

1. If the level of quality is not an issue (NI), delete the requirement.

2. If the requirement is written to apply to all items of a given class (e.g., "All external inputs shall be checked for reasonableness"), then rewrite the requirement to list the things to which it will apply, and then choose a subset of that class (e.g., "The following external inputs will be checked for reasonableness . . .")

3. Use the word "shall" to specify a binding requirement that must be validated by some type of test. Use the word "will" to specify a nonbinding goal of the design.

4. Use "minimize" and "maximize" as replacements for specific, testable requirements (e.g., replace "No unit shall use machine-dependent code" by "Minimize the number of units using machine-dependent code").[1]

5. The word "critical" is used in many requirements to specify special processing for important software or data. For less important components, redefine the word "critical" to reduce the scope of software to which these requirements apply.

In general, since the allocation of quality requirements to software components depends on expert knowledge of those components, it is best to get the person who is responsible for specifying functional requirements to be involved in or to perform the said allocation.

4.3
Documenting Software Quality Requirements

DOCUMENTING SOFTWARE QUALITY REQUIREMENTS UNDER DOD-STD-2167. On U.S. government contracts, formal documentation is a large part of the contract effort. Indeed, in the slimmed-down version of the new software standard, DOD-STD-2167, there are 286 pages of data item descriptions (DIDs) needed to describe the required content of 26 types of software document to be delivered on a full-scale development contract. On a recent 1,000,000-lines-of-code contract under this standard, the software requirements specification (just one of the 26 types of document) printed on both sides of the paper was four feet thick. This was just one of approximately 100 copies and only

---

[1] Neither of the last two methods are recommended if there are alternative approaches: use of the words "will," "maximize," and "minimize" reduces the testability of the requirement and, therefore, reduces the chance of negotiating a common agreement as to what "high quality"means.

one of approximately five versions (a total of approximately 12,000,000 printed pages of information for each type of document!).

DOD-STD-2167 is organized around the fitness-for-use factors discussed in Chapter 3 of this book. Figure 4–8 illustrates the format involved, and Appendix 1 presents a completed software quality requirements specification under this format.

The software quality fitness-for-use factors of DOD-STD-2167 are those of Section 3.2.1 of this text, viz., correctness, efficiency, etc. As we have interpreted the DOD standard, each factor is to be defined and followed by a listing of its static quality requirements and dynamic quality requirements. In defining the fitness-for-use factors the wording of the definitions should be carefully negotiated to avoid misunderstanding and to avoid committing to something beyond what can be achieved by implementing the requirements data base.

As discussed in Chapter 1 there are two types of quality attributes: static and dynamic. They are distinguished at this level of the quality specification. Dynamic quality attributes are those that are exhibited after the software is developed and/or is executing. Example metrics are:

- Mean time between failures (MTBF)
- Mean time to repair (or restart) (MTTR)
- Mean labor to repair an error

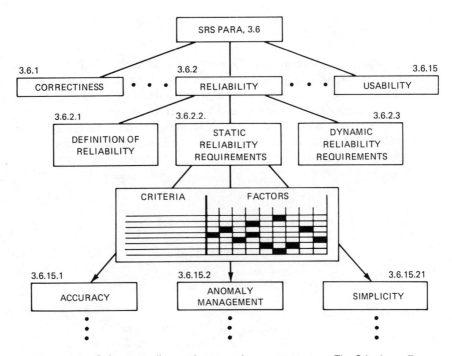

Figure 4-8 Software quality requirements document structure. The Criteria vs. Factor Table maps user requirements (factors) into engineering requirements (criteria).

- Software resource utilization
- Algorithm accuracy
- Effort to learn how to use a function
- Effort to port software to another machine
- Effort to release a new version of the software

Although a part of the DOD standard, dynamic quality requirements will not be discussed any further in this book. Certainly they are important metrics, because they are after-the-fact measures of how well static quality requirements have been designed into the software, reviewed, and tested. However, software quality technology is not mature enough to be able to credibly correlate dynamic quality attributes with successful achievement of static quality attributes (or vice versa). Nor is the technology surrounding the dynamic attributes able to provide measurements during development that can be used as an in-process gauge of success in achieving software quality. (See Tom Gilb, *Software Engineering Templates*)—(a companion handbook for the Design by Objectives method) and IEEE Draft Standard P982, *Measures to Produce Reliable Software*).

Static quality requirements are exhibited in designs and source code. All the requirements discussed in this chapter are static requirements. The static quality requirement for each factor defined in the DOD standard is to implement the quality criteria that are called out in Table 3–2 and specified in the appropriate subsections of this text. For example, the static requirement for reliability would be that

> This software component will meet the quality criteria identified in Table 3–2 and specified in subsection 3.6.15.

DOCUMENTING SOFTWARE QUALITY REQUIREMENTS FOR ENGINEERING USE. The electronic data base of quality needs should be invoked as the baseline for negotiation with the end user to reach an agreed-upon definition of what ''high quality'' is. A minimal documentation set should be captured for reference and should include one printed copy of the data base and a summary of how the data base was tailored to fit the actual requirements of each software component. An extract from a sample of such a summary is shown in Figure 4–9.

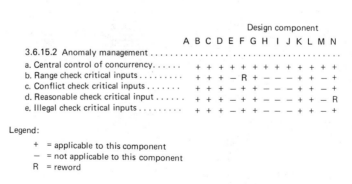

Figure **4-9** Summary of SRS paragraph 3.6.15.2 tailoring.

Achieving Software Quality
Specifications

Contrary to what many may imagine, modern programming practices are not the only way to achieve quality during design. There are many software quality engineering techniques, some of which include the structured design techniques and others of which involve good old-fashioned common sense. In this chapter we shall consider the following major categories of techniques:

- Using design and coding standards
- Allocating quality requirements to design components
- Straightforward implementation of requirements
- Design iteration
- Modern design and coding techniques
- Automated tools that help achieve quality
- External decisions that can help or hinder
- Special quality engineering techniques

TABLE 5-1 POTENTIAL OF ENGINEERING TECHNIQUE TO ACHIEVE QUALITY REQUIREMENTS

Legend:
- ■ Significant support
- ▨ Support
- □ Insignificant support

Quality criteria

Engineering technique	Accuracy	Anomaly management	Augmentability	Autonomy	Commonality	Completeness	Consistency	Distributivity	Quality of documentation	Communication efficiency	Processor efficiency	Storage efficiency	Functional scope	Generality	Independence	Modularity	Operability	Safety management	Self-descriptiveness	Simplicity	Support	System accessibility	System compatibility	Traceability	Training	Virtuality	Visibility
Standards	□	□	▨	□	■	■	▨	□	□	□	□	□	□	▨	□	▨	□	□	■	▨	□	□	□	▨	□	□	□
Allocation	▨	▨	▨	□	■	▨	□	▨	□	□	□	□	□	▨	▨	▨	□	▨	□	▨	▨	▨	▨	▨	□	▨	□
Straightforward	▨	▨	▨	▨	□	▨	▨	□	□	□	□	□	□	▨	▨	▨	▨	▨	▨	▨	□	□	□	▨	□	□	▨
Design iteration	▨	▨	▨	□	□	□	□	□	□	□	□	□	□	▨	▨	▨	□	▨	□	▨	□	□	□	□	□	□	□
Modern techniques	□	□	▨	□	■	■	▨	□	▨	□	□	□	▨	■	■	■	□	▨	▨	■	□	□	□	□	□	▨	□
Automated tools	□	□	□	□	□	■	□	□	▨	□	□	□	□	□	□	□	▨	□	▨	▨	□	□	□	□	□	□	□
External decisions	■	▨	▨	▨	□	▨	□	□	■	□	□	□	□	□	□	□	■	□	□	□	□	□	□	□	□	▨	□
Special techniques	■	□	□	□	▨	□	▨	□	□	□	□	□	□	□	□	□	□	■	□	□	□	□	□	□	□	□	□

Table 5-1 illustrates the potential of these various engineering techniques to achieve quality requirements. Each quality criterion defined in Chapter 3 is considered as a whole, complete unit. An engineering technique is shown as a dark square in relation to a criterion if the technique is a significant contributor to the achievement of the requirements in that criterion. If the technique provides some, but not crucial, support toward achievement of the requirements in that criterion, then a slashed square is shown. If the technique does not provide any significant support, then a blank square is shown. The table can be used to choose the type of technique and amount of emphasis to be applied for any unique set of software quality requirements.

We will not cover all techniques of quality engineering here—just those dealing with the technical aspects of design. Techniques discussed in other chapters include reviewing for defects (Chapters 6 through 10), testing for errors (Chapters 12 through 14), the software technical assurance role (Chapter 16), and the use of team techniques (Chapter 17).

5.1
Using Design and Coding Standards

A glance at Chapter 3's 247 suggested software quality attributes reveals many requirements for standardization. Standards are especially important to the fitness-for-use factors of correctness, maintainability, interoperability, and reusability.

To better appreciate why the use of standards is such an important ingredient during design, Figure 5-1 illustrates the effect of their use. Design products and code are subjected to review techniques to determine whether they meet the specified quality

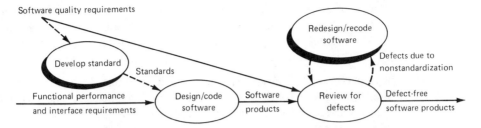

Figure 5-1 Standards are an important part of engineering-in quality

requirements, including standardization. Thus, if standards are specified beforehand and used as criteria during design and coding, products will not need to undergo rework as a result of finding defects due to nonstandardization during review.

The following activities are required to implement standards as part of the software engineering process (preparation cannot be overemphasized; the standards must be in place and training must be completed before design begins.):

- Developing the standard (use the list that follows as a checklist)
- Training the engineers in the meaning and application of the standard
- Disseminating the standard to all users
- Making sure that the standard is being used (spot-checking) during design
- Including the standard in a checklist of review activities

Following is a list of standards that should be considered:

Naming Conventions Guidelines for the names assigned to units of data or functions. May include special designators or acronyms, length limits, required prefixes or suffixes, and the use of numbering.

Documentation Standards Style guides for the content and format of documents developed to describe the software or in support of the use of the software. May include paragraph outlines and the required content thereof, formatting of tables and figures, and required appendices.

Interunit Protocol Standardization of the interface between two units which pass data. May include how the data get passed (by value or reference), the use of standard error indicators, and the order of values (e.g., input before output).

External Message Protocol Standardization of the interface between two functions which may reside on different devices. An example is the IEEE 802.3 standard for Ethernet communication at the lowest level of the Open System Interconnect (OSI) seven-layer model.

External Message Format Guidelines for the formatting and content of messages communicated across external interfaces. May include header and footer standards, required fields and field uses, and content descriptors.

Data Representation Formatting standards for representing the alphabet, numbers, and special characters on a computer. Examples are the American Standard Code for Information Interchange (ASCII), Binary Coded Decimal (BCD), and Extended Binary Coded Decimal Interchange Code (EBCDIC).

Design Representation Formatting and content of design drawings and descriptions (not to be confused with document standards). May include syntax, semantics, and graphic standards for design symbols; page size limitations; and off-page connection references.

Global Data Usage Establishing and enforcing the restricted definition and use of data shared by more than one function. The goal is to ensure that a global data item is used consistently and only for its intended purpose.

Error Handling Guidelines for the consistent handling of error conditions. May include error identification, error communication, error-handling responsibility, and global error recovery and reporting functions.

External System Vocabulary Establishing and enforcing the restricted definition and use of data shared by more than one interfacing system or subsystem.

Coding Standards Guidelines for the consistent and self-descriptive use of a specific programming language. The following are suggested coding standards (some of the quality requirements of Chapter 3 should also find their way into these standards):

- Use of a common higher order language
- Delineation of allowable programming language constructs
- Delineation of a programming language subset for critical units
- Unit and data structuring
- Blocking and indenting guidelines
- Prologue format and content
- Code commenting
- Global data commenting

5.2
Allocating Quality Requirements
to Design Components

If you have specified quality requirements before beginning design (as this book suggests), at this point you have quality requirements for a major software component (e.g., a computer software configuration item, or CSCI). This major software component will be systematically decomposed into smaller and smaller components until many programmable units are specified.

Do all specified quality requirements apply to all units?

Fortunately, no. If you used the 247 suggested quality considerations given in Chapter 3 as a basis for your requirements, you will notice that they relate to many different kinds of software products—for example, code, data, documents, and design. There are even some requirements that relate to the design process rather than a product of the design process. Therefore, not all 247 requirements will be applicable to all programmable units. Table 5–2 illustrates this fact by showing some of the quality criteria of Chapter 3 in relation to sample categories of software. (A check means applicable, a blank means not applicable.)

TABLE 5-2 SOFTWARE QUALITY REQUIREMENTS APPLY TO DIFFERENT SOFTWARE PRODUCT CATEGORIES

Sample quality requirement		Critical	Support	I/O	Data	Computational	Environment	MMI	Documentation	Design
Replicate critical components	(Distributivity	√								
Library of tests for all units	(Visibility		√				√			
Standardize I/O protocol	(Consistency				√		√			
Separate adaptation and fixed data	(Independence				√	√	√			
Avoid unreachable code	(Completeness	√	√	√	√	√				
Avoid memory overlays	(Efficiency of processing	√					√			
Limit user access	(System accessibility						√	√		
Standardized design representation	(Consistency								√	
Use Structured design technique	(Modularity									√

The software design process results in levels of design. For example, functional requirements may be first partitioned and then synthesized into a task (concurrent process) communication architecture. Then each task may be partitioned into an interunit invocation control architecture (e.g., a structure chart). Then each unit may be partitioned into an internal unit architecture (e.g., a program design language (PDL) description). There may be other intermediate levels of functional design and other levels associated with data and interface design.

Allocation of quality requirements is done at each level of design. One or more of the requirements applicable at the next higher level (level 0 is the quality requirements specification itself) are allocated to each design component at the next lower level of design. At the bottommost level, there may only be a fraction of the original 247 requirements applicable to any single program unit.

Applicability is the only criterion for decision making regarding allocation. For any given design component, we ask, "Is this requirement applicable to this component," for each quality requirement from the next higher level allocation. If it is applicable, it becomes part of the requirements set for the given level of design. Some requirements (e.g., design architecture requirements) may be applicable only to an intermediate level of design and, therefore, will not be allocated down to the lowest level.

Allocation needs to be done continually throughout the design process. The result is used as requirements to be met by the software designer who is trying to engineer in quality.

The results of the allocation process should be captured in a table which can then be used as a checklist to support the design and coding review process. For each design component, all quality requirements that are applicable to it are listed. If software development files (also known as software development folders or unit development folders) are being used, they are a good place to record the allocation results. An example format for the allocation report is given in Fig. 5-2.

```
                                              Design component

                                       A B C D E F G H I J K L M
3.6.15.2 Anomaly management . . . . . . . . . . . . . . . . . . . . . . . . . . . . . . . . . . . . . .
a. Central control of concurrency . . . . . .   + + + +  + + + + + + + + +
b. Range check critical inputs . . . . . . . . .  + + + −  + + − − − + + − +
c. Conflict check critical inputs . . . . . . . .  + + + −  + + − − − + + − +
d. Reasonable check critical input . . . . . .   + + + −  + + − − − + + − +
e. Illegal check critical inputs . . . . . . . . .  + + + −  + + − − − + + − +
```

Legend:
+ = applicable to this component
− = not applicable to this component

Figure 5-2 Quality requirements allocation summary

The following categories may be useful for deciding on the applicability of a quality requirement to a software component. They were derived from the quality criteria of Chapter 3 and are not mutually exclusive.

1. *Critical or noncritical?* Certain requirements are only applicable to critical software; that is, there is extra quality required for this type of software. Depending on the application, "critical" may be defined as pertaining to safety, efficiency, reliability, or software on the critical path of a schedule. You need to define what critical means to your application and, based on this definition, decide what critical requirements apply.

2. *Operational or support?* Some of the quality requirements deal with the on-line functionality of the software, while others deal with off-line maintenance support software.

3. *I/O, data, MMI, or computational?* The quality requirements pertain to either I/O software, data design and coding, man-machine interface (MMI) design, or normal computational design and programming.

4. *Process or product?* Some of the quality requirements may specify how to perform design rather than the attributes of the product resulting from design.

5. *Run-time environment or application software?* Some of the requirements deal with the run-time environment and have nothing to do with the application software. For example, operating system, data base management, process scheduling, and memory management requirements are all requirements of the run-time enivronment.

6. *Documentation/design representation or software?* Some of the quality requirements will deal with code-related products, while others will deal with the documentation of the code-related products.

5.3
Straightforward Implementation of Requirements

This section deals with implementation techniques that do not have a label like ''structured design.'' They are bundled together under the name ''straightforward'' for lack of a prestigious label. However, they are no less important to quality engineering than their better known counterparts.

Figure 5-3 is the example used in Chapter 3 (p. 52) to illustrate the anomaly management criterion. Let us examine what the real difference is between the lower quality design on the left and the higher quality design on the right.

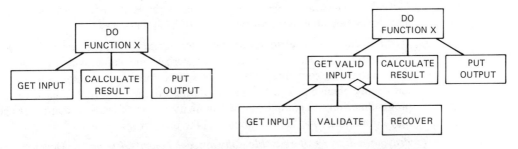

Figure 5-3 Straightforward implementation of anomaly management requirements

Both designs accomplish the same function. However, the design on the right is more reliable than the one on the left because it recovers in the case of an invalid input; the design on the left will continue processing with unpredictable results. This is the difference in quality between the two designs, but what difference is there in the techniques used by the two different designers to design in that quality?

Both designers used structured design to design in the basic functionality. However, there were two additional factors present to the quality-minded designer:

- Prior to design, there were anomaly management requirements in addition to functional requirements.

- Additional functionality was added to the same basic design to meet those requirements.

We can't call this structured design; it's just good quality engineering practice.

There are many such "straightforward" quality engineering techniques used to implement quality requirements. They are straightforward because they are based not on a formal design methodology, but instead, on commonsensical extensions to existing designs or implementation of the requirements. Some further examples from Chapter 3 may help to solidify the concept in the reader's mind:

1. *Develop a user's manual as part of the design process (commonality).* This requirement helps to clarify the man-machine interface before design of it begins. To implement the requirement means no more and no less than creating a separate activity to develop the manual.

2. *Avoid unused parameters in a procedure argument list (completeness).* During design and coding, review all unit interface statements to ensure that there are no unused arguments.

3. *Use data compression for communication messages (efficiency of communication).* Add compression/decompression functions to existing communication software.

4. *Use an optimizing compiler or assembly language if necessary (efficiency of processing).* Decide which cases an optimizing compiler or assembly language is necessary for and use the technique for those cases.

5. *Make error messages clear to the user (operability).* Prototype error messages and survey potential users for the clarity of such messages.

6. *Use the Halstead metric to identify and simplify difficult areas of code (simplicity).* The Halstead metric characterizes the complexity of code by counting certain constructs in the code and performing calculations based on the counts obtained. Use the metric during coding to give feedback to the programmer on the complexity or simplicity of the product so that he or she may correct the code before submitting the product for review.

7. *Provide a library of reusable software components (support).* Develop and deliver, along with the operational software, a library containing all the primitive components resulting from the development effort.

5.4
Design Iteration

In software development, we rarely succeed at first. Indeed, frequently we don't succeed the second time, and in some cases we never succeed! So why do most software development plans show milestones like "design complete" or "coding complete" when there's rarely time or planned activity to rework a design before it is "completed"? As a matter of fact, they shouldn't; or at least, if they do, they should plan for such milestones and completions in the context of *iteration*.

Iteration is a fundamental software quality engineering technique. We single it out as a technique because it is such an important ingredient in quality and because some software design methodologies either underemphasize it or don't include it at all.

The flowchart shown in Figure 5-4 illustrates the role of iteration in software design. It is extracted from a procedure describing a framework for the design of large real-time systems. This particular part of the procedure deals with the partitioning process during the sequential phase of design (for example, the design of the intervals of a

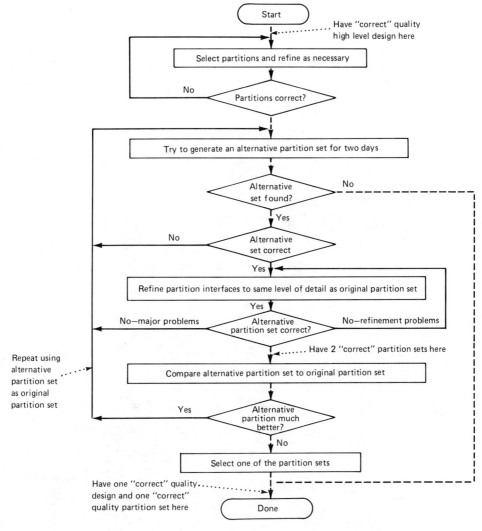

Figure 5-4 Partition process for the high/medium phases

concurrent process). "Partitioning" refers to the breaking up of a component into parts that have specifiable interfaces.

Notice the solid lines in the flowchart; they emphasize iteration paths. For example, based on the decision "partitions correct?" in the first diamond of the flowchart, there is iteration until a correct partition is designed. Indeed, there are usually several iterations before a correct partition is discovered, each taking time—time to brainstorm, record thoughts, and review for correctness. Properly done, iteration will not stop until a correct partition results (as opposed to a scheduled milestone coming due). Let us call this partition A.

The next iteration to notice is the outside loop based on the decision "alternative partition much better?" (the bottommost diamond). An alternative partition, say, partition B, is designed and then compared with the previous partition A. Iteration continues based on the relative difference between the two partitions. Big differences imply continued iteration is needed; small deviations indicate a zeroing in on a solution. (Notice that this iteration is controlled by a two-day maximum for redesign).

As illustrated by this example, design iteration is a technique in and of itself, independent of the particular design methodology used. Furthermore, design iteration based on a comparison of two competing solutions leads to a better quality design than one in which we accept the first correct solution. Three fundamentals illustrated by the example are:

- Iterate until the design is correct.
- Develop and compare at least two alternative designs.
- Iterate until design closure (differences converge).

If we abstract these fundamentals out of the example, we end up with the design iteration process illustrated in Figure 5–5. First a correct design is developed. Then an

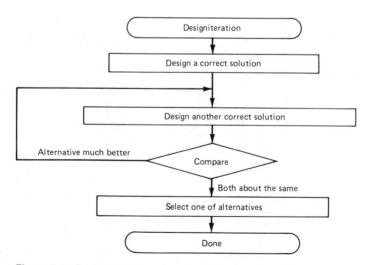

Figure 5-5 Design iterations: Iterate until design alternatives converge

alternative correct design is developed. Then the two designs are compared, and, if the alternative is much better, another alternative is designed. The process continues until design closure, when one of the alternatives is chosen as the final correct design.

Recall from Chapter 3 that ''correct'' means conformance to requirements. These requirements include quality attributes. Therefore, a correct design is one that implements all functional requirements and is high quality by definition. Why, then, is it necessary to iterate a design? How can it get better?

First, by taking a different approach to the solution of a problem, the structure of the solution is often much different. Many times this leads to better insight into the problem and a solution structure that matches the structure of the problem more closely. Given two designs that are correct, the one whose structure more closely matches the problem is better.

Second, some quality requirements have a range of correct implementations from minimally acceptable upward (e.g., efficiency of processing, coupling, and cohesion). A correct design may be made better by achieving higher levels of quality for these quality requirements that have a range of correct solutions.

A conflict may be obvious to some at this point, viz., the conflict between schedule and quality. This conflict was discussed in Chapter 1, where it ended with the question, ''Is there a compromise'' (between management and engineering)? Typically, plans fail to take design iteration into account and result in a premature termination of the iteration process. Indeed, to develop just two competing designs is heresy to some crisis management planners. Two criteria can be defined and used to negotiate a compromise: limit the time spent in designing an alternative, and allow for greater differences in comparison of designs.

A final note on design iteration: it is generally accepted that five to seven iterations each of brainstorming, solution outline, and review are needed to develop a good solution to difficult problems. Fewer than this means either that you are refining an existing solution or that quality is being sacrificed for something else.

5.5
Modern Design and Coding Techniques

Techniques for designing and coding software have evolved over the last two decades. To a large extent, the evolution has come about because of increased understanding of software quality. Modern techniques take advantage of this, as well as of the increased availability of resources (decreasing time and memory constraints), modern higher order languages, and the lessons learned from methodology pioneers. Because of all these, proper use of a modern design or coding technique will automatically result in achieving some subset of the required quality attributes.

In what follows, we deal primarily with the principles employed by design and coding techniques rather than the specific techniques themselves. No specific technique is recommended, because the intent is to arm the reader with enough information to be able to make a rational decision depending on the level of quality required versus the ability of any specific technique to achieve those requirements.

5.5.1 PRINCIPLES OF DESIGN AND CODING TECHNIQUES

The following terms embody principles of modern design and coding techniques that may be used as a decision-making rationale for choosing a design method:

Abstraction The extraction of essential properties while omitting inessential details. Model of the solution that hides the details of implementation.

Modularity Purposeful structuring of the solution. Divides programs into subprograms that interrelate, achieving strong cohesion within a component and loose coupling between components. A single-entrance, single-exit design.

Uniformity The lack of inconsistencies and unnecessary differences in design or code representations.

Information Hiding Making unnecessary details inaccessible to the user. Postpones binding decisions to the lowest level of implementation, and defines and enforces access constraints.

Completeness The quality of being able to assess the correctness, the extent of satisfaction of the requirements, of a solution at each level of design.

Divide and Conquer Approach to managing complexity. Breaking apart large, unsolvable problems into smaller, solvable problems. Also called partitioning and hierarchical decomposition.

Problem Oriented Matching the design structure to the problem structure. Facilitates discovery of the underlying structure of the problem and is a natural representation of the object to be built.

Verifiable Quality Quality discerned by objective rules for deciding the better of two alternatives. Use of the five structured programming constructs: sequence, IF-THEN-ELSE, DO-WHILE, DO-UNTIL, and CASE.

Disciplined Taking a structured approach to problem solving. Avoiding code until design is complete.

Unambiguous Having one and only one meaning. Said of design or code representation.

5.5.2 PRINCIPLES VERSUS QUALITY REQUIREMENTS

The principles of good design and coding techniques can be related to software quality requirements. Table 5–3 shows how the 27 quality criteria defined in Chapter 3 are related to the 10 principles just described.

The requirements for each criterion are considered as a whole in their relation to the 10 principles. If applying a principle results in achieving a significant portion of the

TABLE 5-3 POTENTIAL OF SOFTWARE DESIGN PRINCIPLE TO ACHIEVE QUALITY REQUIREMENTS

Legend:
- ■ Strong relationship
- ▨ Weak relationship
- □ No relationship

Design and code principles	Accuracy	Anomaly management	Augmentability	Autonomy	Commonality	Completeness	Consistency	Distributivity	Quality of documentation	Efficiency of communication	Efficiency of processings	Efficiency of storage	Functional scope	Generality	Independence	Modularity	Operability	Safety management	Self-descriptiveness	Simplicity	Support	System accessibility	System compatibility	Traceability	Training	Virtuality	Visibility
Abstraction													W	S													
Modularity			W				W									S											
Uniformity					S														W								
Information hiding				W											W	W											
Completeness			W			S																		W			
Divide and conquer								W											W								
Problem oriented																											
Verifiable quality																											
Disciplined																											
Unambiguous								W										W	W	W							

requirements within a criterion, a strong relationship (dark box) is shown. If applying a principle results in only some requirements being achieved a weak relationship (hashed box) is shown. Otherwise, no relation (a blank box) is shown.

Where strong or weak relationships are shown, design or coding methods that employ the principles in question lead to quality attributes that are required for the criterion in question.

The matrix is noticeably sparse. One may conclude from this that "modern methods" are not all that is needed for software quality. One may also conclude that "modern methods" have evolved for other than achieving software quality attributes—for example, for management of complexity, organizational control of large-scale projects, design iteration, and achieving flexibility in problem orientation.

5.5.3 CHOOSING DESIGN AND CODING TECHNIQUES

Unfortunately, there are so many variables involved in choosing a design or coding technique that no definitive answer can be given here as to which types of design or code technique to select. Some of the variables that make each situation unique are the following:

- *Type of problem.* The type of problem being solved can be data-flow (e.g., payroll) or control-flow (e.g., nuclear power station) oriented. The design and coding techniques chosen should match the problem orientation.

- *Level of design.* Design occurs at a high level (e.g., task architecture), at a medium level (e.g., program architecture), and at a low level (e.g., unit architecture). The design and coding techniques chosen should match the level of design.

- *Size of problem.* Software projects can range from 1,000,000 lines of code with a staff size of 400 people to 1,000 lines of code produced by one person. The design and coding techniques should be chosen to accommodate the difference between large- vs. small-scale programming.

- *Environment.* The software engineering environment consists of certain people with a certain amount of experience and training, certain tools, and certain facilities. The design and coding technique should be chosen to fit into this environment.

Following are 12 references from which design and coding techniques may be chosen. The list is far from complete, and no technique is recommended per se because of the large number of variables involved. Rather, each unique situation requires a unique technique. The reader is encouraged to evaluate whether a technique of his or her own choice satisfies the aforementioned principles and, as a consequence, his or her software quality requirements. The references mentioned are meant not as endorsements, but as samples only.

Sample Design and Coding Techniques

- G. Booch, "Object Oriented Design" in *Software Engineering with Ada* (New York: Benjamin/Cummings, 1983).

- E. Yourdon and L. Constantine, *Structured Design* (Englewood Cliffs, N.J.: Prentice-Hall, 1979).

- P. Ward and S. Mellor, *Structured Development for Real-Time Systems* (New York, N.Y.: Yourdon Press, 1985).

- R. J. A. Buhr, *System Design with Ada* (Englewood Cliffs, N.J.: Prentice-Hall, 1984).

- M. Jackson, "Jackson Design Methodology" in *Tutorial on Software Design Techniques*, IEEE Computer Society, Long Beach, Ca., 1977.

- M. Alford, "Software Requirements Engineering Methodology," in Proceedings of International Computer Software and Application Conference (COMPSAC), Chicago, Ill., 1980.

- G. Cherry, *Process Abstraction Method for Embedded Large Applications* (Reston, Va.: Thought Tools, Inc., 1985).

- M. Carrio, "Technology for the Automated Generation of Systems," in *Computer*, vol. 18, No. 4, 1984.

- C. A. Hoare, *Communicating Sequential Processes* (Englewood Cliffs, N.J.: Prentice-Hall International, 1985).

- T. Clark, *Digital System Development Methodology* (Pittsburgh, Pa.: Computer Sciences Corporation, 1985).

- F. T. Baker, "Structured Programming," in *IEEE Transactions on Software Engineering*, June, 1975.

- H. Gomma, "A Software Design Method for Real-Time Systems," in *Communications of the Association for Computing Machinery*, vol. 27, no. 9, 1984.

5.6
Automated Tools That Help Achieve Quality

An automated tool is a software program that performs repetitious design or coding tasks. That is, it involves the use of a computer to replace some manual aspect of the design or coding activity. A compiler is a good example; it replaces the manual translation of human-readable language statements into machine-language statements. Today, there are many sophisticated tools that replace design and coding activities such as drawing, design and code management, review, and testing. Automated tools are primarily software productivity implements.

Automated tools can also be software quality implements. Those aspects of tools that support quality engineering are (1) standards enforcement, (2) design rule enforcement, and (3) documentation quality. Some of the standards mentioned at the beginning of this chapter have been encoded in tools to assure that a design or program adheres to the standard. For example, there exist code auditor tools that ensure adherence to programming standards and design-drawing tools that ensure adherence to design representation standards. The use of such tools will automatically achieve the quality attributes associated with standardization.

Some of the required quality attributes are associated with design rules such as "define all options for decision points," "avoid unreachable code," and "partition software to be logically complete and self-contained." Modern tools are beginning to encode such design rules into the logic of the tool. The use of such tools will not guarantee achievement of the quality requirements for design rules, but will support design iteration by providing feedback during the design process.

An example of such a capability is illustrated in Figure 5–6. The structure chart on the left looks cluttered because of the fan-in to the two units, A and B. On the right, as a result of defining the two units as reusable library units (and meeting certain required constraints), the tool has replicated the units and used spatial significance to portray a higher quality design.

Finally, the use of tools coupled with modern computer equipment can result in automatically achieving some of the requirements in the documentation quality criteria. For example, the use of such tools can ensure correct spelling, tables of contents, and subject indexes, and readability gained from high-quality document formatters and laser printers.

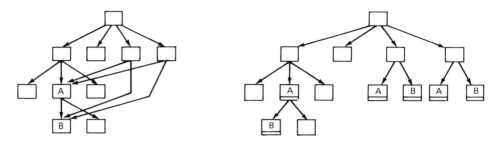

Figure 5-6 Automatic visual feedback on design quality (Source: R. R. Willis, "AIDES Computer-Aided Design of Software Systems—II," *Software Engineering Environments*. Amsterdam: North Holland, 1981)

5.7
External Decisions That Can Help or Hinder

The environment in which the software will reside can affect the extent to which software quality requirements can be achieved. For example, the number of devices and their configuration will limit the ability to achieve requirements in the distributivity criterion. Therefore, either making or influencing decisions about the environment is a method of achieving quality.

Following is a listing of environmental features and sample decisions that can affect software quality:

System Architecture   The arrangement and connection of computer devices, including centralized versus distributed devices, the fault tolerance of each device, device redundancy, and the performance of the devices.

Security   The accessibility of the computer system, including the system's physical and operational controls, housing the computer center, the distributivity of the system, and whether or not the system resides on a network.

Resource Capacity   The total number of instructions processed per second, memory storage bytes, and bytes communicated per second under control of the software.

Physical MMI   The design of the physical man-machine interface including the use of a keyboard, mouse, or pointing devices for input, monochrome vs. color screen capability, and graphics capability.

Hardware Selection   The making of decisions about the specific manufacturer of the computer, storage, or communication devices, including considerations such as storage expandability, word size, the instruction set of the computer, reliability, data representation, and error detection capability.

OS Selection   The making of decisions about the operating system, including considerations such as scheduling strategy, functionality of fault detection and correction, kinds of support features available, system reliability, and language compatibility.

DBMS Selection The making of decisions about the data-base management system, including considerations such as recovery capability, storage efficiency, data representation and input/output compatibility, and access control.

Language Selection The making of decisions about the programming language, including considerations such as use of structured programming constructs, exception-handling features, information-hiding features, constructs for unit structuring, and data definition and representation features.

Compiler Selection The making of decisions about the system compiler, including considerations such as accuracy, reliability, storage and processing efficiency, compatibility between computer types, effective commenting and data naming, and the extent of error checking.

Table 5–4 illustrates how important these decisions are to software quality. Each of them is shown in relation to the software quality criteria described in Chapter 3. A dark square signifies that the decision can significantly affect, positively or negatively, the ability to achieve the quality requirements of the criterion in question. A hashed square indicates either a contribution toward or constraint on the ability to achieve the given quality requirements.

TABLE 5-4 POTENTIAL OF EXTERNAL DECISION TO ACHIEVE QUALITY REQUIREMENTS

Legend:
- ■ Significant impact
- ▨ Some impact
- □ Insignificant impact

External decision	Accuracy	Anomaly management	Augmentability	Autonomy	Commonality	Completeness	Consistency	Distributivity	Quality of documentation	Effeciency of communication	Efficiency of processing	Efficiency of storage	Functional scope	Generality	Independence	Modularity	Operability	Safety management	Self-descriptiveness	Simplicity	Support	System accessibility	System compatibility	Traceability	Training	Virtuality	Visibility
System architecture		■				■																▨					
Security design																							■				
Resource capacity			▨			▨					■	■															
Physical MMI				▨																				▨		▨	
Hardware	■	▨		▨																							
Operating system		▨	▨	▨						▨	▨	▨										▨	■	▨			▨
Data-base manager			▨								▨	▨			▨	▨							■				
Programming language	▨	▨			▨	▨									▨	▨	▨		▨				■				
Compiler	▨	▨		▨	▨	▨					▨	▨				▨	▨										

5.8
Special Quality Engineering Techniques

The preceding techniques for achieving software quality requirements may not be enough. In some cases, extra emphasis is needed on certain criteria. For example, the high level of reliability required in nuclear power control systems may not be achievable using typical structured design methods. Exotic requirements may sometimes justify exotic approaches where cost is not as much an issue as the required level of quality.

Special quality engineering techniques generally have as their objective either (1) to achieve an exceptional level of quality in certain criteria, or (2) to achieve a higher level of quality during design iteration. In the first category, specific techniques have been developed to achieve specific quality requirements. For example, fault-tolerant design techniques support the anomaly management criterion. In the second category are found techniques that help to verify the correctness of the evolving design. Simulation modeling is such a technique; it provides "proof" that the design is correct from a performance standpoint. These correctness-proving techniques are an integral part of the engineering process.

Following is a sample list of special techniques that aid in achieving exceptional levels of quality for the criteria mentioned:

Algorithm Modeling Prototyping critical algorithms to ensure that they are feasible and that they can achieve accuracy requirements.

Simulation Modeling Prototyping software time and memory utilization and software execution control to ensure that predicted performance is within resource requirements.

Proofs of Correctness Using formal notation and induction to prove that an algorithm is correct.

Fault-Tolerant Design Designing specifically to have tolerable functional capability in the presence of faults so that failures may be more readily avoided.

N-Version Programming From one specification, the development of N versions of software by N software development teams, and the use of these N versions to achieve a consensus when execution results differ. Analogous to triple-modular redundancy ($N = 3$) in hardware. (See Section 10.2).

Software Hazards Analysis and Fault Tree Analysis Tracing system-level hazards (e.g., unsafe conditions) through design or coding structures back to software implementations that could cause the hazards.

Partition Interface Specifications The use of formal interface specifications at each level of design to verify the feasibility and completeness of interfaces between partitions.

Reliability Modeling The use of software reliability models to predict software reliability (e.g., MTBF) based on the rate of occurrence of defects and errors.

5.9
Quality Level Guidelines

Table 5–5 may be used as a summary guideline for achieving quality in software. It shows how the techniques discussed in this chapter relate to the four levels of quality, "not an issue," average, good, and excellent discussed in earlier chapters.

TABLE 5-5 CONFIGURING A SOFTWARE ENGINEERING METHODOLOGY AROUND LEVEL OF REQUIRED QUALITY

	Standards	Design iteration	Modern[1] design techniques	Auto-[2] mated tools	Special techniques	External decision	Other
Not an issue	External MSG protocol External MSG format Data representation	One correct design	Experimental use of some modern development practices (MDPs)	Primitive or basic tool set		Laissez-faire	Requirements allocation Straightforward implementation
Average	Global data usage Naming conventions Coding conventions	One correct design	Experienced use of some MDPs	Interactive tool set		Some influence	
Good	Error handling Design representation Documentation style guide	Two correct designs	Experienced use of most MDPs	Modern tool set	Fault-tolerant design Partition interface specs Algorithm modeling Simulation modeling	Strongly influence	
Excellent	External system vocabulary Interunit protocol	Iterate until design closure	Routine use of all MDPs	Advanced tool set	Correctness proofs *N*-version programming SW hazard analysis Reliability modeling	Make decision to meet requirement	

(1) Based on R. Jensen's Seer software cost estimation model variable "MODP"
(2) Based on R. Jensen's Seer software cost estimation model variable "TOOL"

Part III

Using Verification and Validation to Review Out Defects and Test Out Errors

Introduction to Verification
and Validation

6.1
Scope of Verification and Validation (V & V)

Quality software is produced by engineering in quality, reviewing out defects, and testing out errors. The interplay among elements of this three-tiered quality model is diagrammed in Figure 6–1. The model emphasizes the definition and engineering of quality requirements into the product. The reviewing and testing functions of the model essentially outline the scope of verification and validation. Review activities are provided to identify defects in quality. Corrective action is referred back to the engineering process to rectify any defects discovered. Testing of the product proceeds in a similar manner. Whenever defects in quality are found by the testing process, the corrective action system refers those defects back to the engineering process for correction. From an economic viewpoint, correct engineering is of course preferable to either reviewing out the defects or testing out the errors, but given the limitations of human beings, it is at best an ideal to be striven for. Of the two verification and validation functions, testing is about an

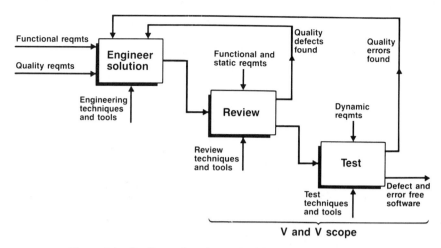

Figure 6-1 Quality engineering and verification and validation

order of magnitude more costly to carry out than reviewing, which in turn is more costly than correct engineering.

For convenience, we have identified verification and validation and diffferentiated it from the engineering process. This is an oversimplification. In reality, a symbiotic relationship exists between the review, testing, and engineering functions that has to do with the specification of quality requirements. Both the review process and the testing process depend upon the up-front definition of the quality requirements. This definition is the basis for identifying and correcting errors. But then, ideally, if we had 100 percent confidence in the engineering solution, we would not need verification and validation. Now, while achieving this degree of confidence may be a noble goal, it can hardly be expected either today or anytime in the foreseeable future. Nonetheless, this ideal does point to the fact that much higher productivity in the software engineering process is possible by gaining more confidence in engineering and hence being able to minimize verification and validation. This is especially important in systems of significant size and complexity, where V&V can actually constitute 50 to 80 percent of the total effort.

All problems require a validation of their solutions. This requirement is particularly exaggerated on software projects, perhaps because of the complexity of the problems that we use software to attempt to solve. Verification and validation should not be viewed as simply an overlay on the development process. Rather, it must be regarded as coproductive with other activities over the development cycle. With the exception of independent verification and validation (IV&V), verification and validation does not constitute its own separate discipline. Instead, it is the responsibility of all elements on the software project to perform it. The system engineering function, software development function, testing function, configuration management function, and quality assurance function all have V&V responsibilities on the software project. IV&V entails using a separate agency to perform analysis and testing in parallel with the developing agency. It is employed when customers want added systematic assurance on the functioning and performance of a system.

6.2
Definitions

The terms "verification" and "validation" fill the literature of the software community and are used with varying expressed or implied definitions. This diversification may be traced to the individual author's need to customize a set of terms that are appropriate and convenient for a specialized area of interest. Often the terms and their definitions are interchangeable; that is, their differences are only apparent and not substantive.

There appears to be a consensus among software engineers that the activities of verification and validation are directed toward determining whether the software performs its intended functions and ensuring the quality of the software. While the specific definitions of the terms are not wholly in agreement, there is enough in common to make a discussion of the concepts worthwhile. The concept of verification concerns the determination whether a candidate baseline of products frozen at a point in the development cycle contains what was intended by its predecessor baseline. Figure 6-2 is illustrative. Alternatively, verification entails a determination whether each product follows logically from the previously established product. There is thus a series of verifications that occur during the life cycle of the project.

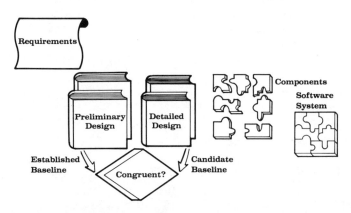

Figure 6-2   Verification: Congruency of baseline

Validation involves a somewhat similar comparison between the products of two life-cycle phases. It establishes an equivalency between a candidate baseline and the objectives of the requirements baseline. (See Figure 6–3.) That is to say, it determines that the intentions of the requirements are established in succeeding baselines. As with verification, there is a series of validations that occurs during the life cycle of a project.

In sum, verification ensures that each step of the development process correctly echoes the intentions of the immediately preceding step, while validation ensures that each product of the development cycle functions and contains the features as prescribed by its requirements specification.

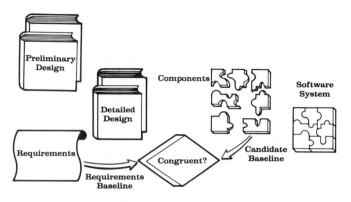

Figure 6-3 Validation: Congruency with requirements baseline

6.3
History of Verification and Validation

Software projects have evolved from small systems involving a few people to much larger systems involving several hundred people. Verification and validation has undergone a commensurate radical adjustment. Originally, V&V was informal and individualized, with a focus primarily on testing. Essentially, it involved the programmer exercising his or her code individually. Unfortunately, as systems became larger and more complex, this self-exercise activity neglected the rigorous definition and execution of test cases and led to unreliable products. By contrast, V&V today is much more formalized. It entails an integrated emphasis involving all organizations in a software project, covering all phases of the life cycle. It may even involve an independent verification and validation agency if added systematic insurance of the progress of development is needed by the sponsoring agency.

The overall technical goal of verification and validation is to assure that the required quality is achieved. Also, it is desired that periodic feedback be provided regarding those goals. The corresponding management goal is to provide continual visibility into the status of the product in order to determine whether the quality goals are being met. Visibility is achieved by feedback, which is the strength of verification and validation technology. Thus, as verification and validation has progressed historically, it has become a very powerful management tool. It provides the information for management to exercise options regarding a candidate baseline of products. If the feedback is positive, management can establish those products into a baseline. If the feedback is either negative or marginal, management has the option to redirect tasks or reallocate resources to correct those defects that have been identified by the V&V process.

Paradoxically, verification and validation has been both a major contributor and a major solution to the so-called software crisis. The software crisis is associated with the vastly increased complexity of data processing systems coupled with the inability of software practices to deal with this complexity. The record over the past two decades reflects this deficiency: few major systems have been delivered within original cost, schedule, and performance specifications. Inadequate verification and validation practices contributed to the crisis in that it was not recognized that software development was a problem-solving process which, if not performed properly, was a major ingredient of software development failures. Previously, the only verification and validation that occurred was the testing at the end of the development cycle. But this lacked visibility into the quality of the software until that point was reached. Consequently, surprises resulted, many of which were not relished.

The solution to this software crisis began with the recognition of software development as a complex problem-solving process, perhaps due in part to the abstract nature of software as a medium. The solution now recognizes problem avoidance and defect detection as required elements in software development, to be performed by verification and validation, which afford a better prospect of identifying and rectifying problems than does the traditional series of formal tests that accompanied the software at the end of its development cycle.

Over time, the scope of verification and validation has widened considerably. Previously, verification and validation had always considered the following traditional issues:

1. Does the product contain all the required features, and have they been implemented correctly?
2. Does the product design produce the desired accuracies, does it respond in the required time frame, and does it operate within the allocated computational resources?

These questions are still of paramount importance today. They have, however, been supplemented by a number of recent issues. For example, verification and validation now includes producibility. This concerns the question of whether the product can be developed with the allocated cost and schedule resources. Another issue of contemporary concern is that of maintainability, which embraces the issue of whether the product can be continually modified to accommodate changing user needs. Producibility and maintainability collectively reflect an intrinsic concern over the life-cycle cost of the product, including the cost of development plus the cost of operations and maintainance.

Life-cycle cost has always been a troublesome issue. With the recent ability to emphasize certain elements of quality, such as maintainability, expandability, and flexibility, there is promise that some of the problems concerning it can be surmounted.

Part III of the text covers key aspects of verification and validation technology in detail.

Conducting Design Reviews, Walkthroughs, and Inspections

7.1
Introduction

In the previous chaper we identified the three lines of defense in verifying engineering products: review, testing, and independent verification and validation (IV&V). This chapter addresses reviews, the first line of defense in the process. Each of the following types of reviews is explored:

- Formal design reviews
- Internal review cycle
- Walkthroughs
- Inspections

These reviews are presented essentially in the chronological order of their historical emergence, beginning with the formal design review and progressing into the more recently conceived software inspection. Commentary is provided on the mechanics and comparative advantages of each type of review. The general historical pattern has been that each new type of review has rectified many of the weaknesses of its historical predecessor. The strengths and weaknesses of each type are summarized in Figure 7-1 with this rectification of weaknesses highlighted. The final section of the chapter provides guidance on employing these reviews in combination to achieve the desired level of quality.

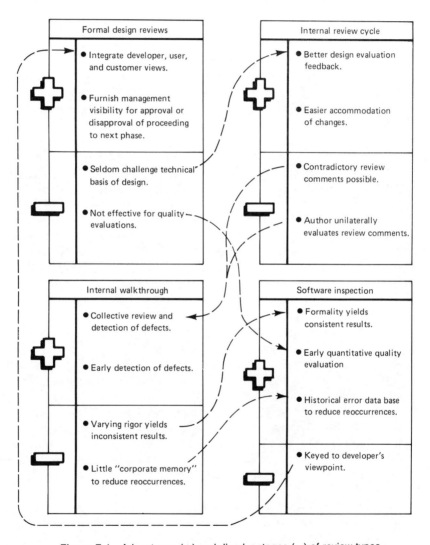

Figure 7-1 Advantages (+) and disadvantages (−) of review types

7.2
Formal Design Reviews

A formal design review is directed toward providing feedback to management on the status of the products under review. A formal design review or audit normally occurs at the conclusion of a life-cycle phase. With visibility into general product quality furnished by feedback from the review, management can determine whether the state of the product merits proceeding on to the next phase of development. If major quality deficiencies are present, management will want to redirect efforts to rework all or part of the candidate products before establishing these products as a baseline point of departure for the next phase of development.

The baseline concept is very important to the quality engineering discipline. Baselining entails "freezing" the products from a life-cycle phase to establish a check-point or stable point of reference. It thus makes clear what is being evaluated during the design review. Before baselining occurs, the products from a particular phase of development are controlled by the engineering organization that created them. After baselining, those products are controlled by management. The act of baselining thus constitutes management's blessing of the state of the product. The formal mechanism that gives management the visibility to make the baselining decision is the design review.

A formal design review is an "ex-process" activity, i.e., it is a review that is performed after the product has been created. This is in contrast to the "in-process" nature of walk-throughs and inspections: these types of review are intended to interact with the product creation process and provide immediate feedback on the quality of the product to the developers. The formal design review may result in either positive or negative feedback. Severe negative feedback, however, is usually awkward to all parties involved and is largely unexpected. The formal design review is really intended to be an affirmation event rather than a defect removal process. This latter exercise is usually the focus of walkthroughs and inspections, and is a point that will be further pursued in Sections 7.4 and 7.5.

The modern concept of a design review is perhaps a decade-and-a-half old; the main aspect of this concept is that responsibility for the design and related products is shared among the major "players" in the system development process: the customer, the user, and the developer. These parties are not necessarily physically distinct and may even overlap or coincide. Nonetheless, each of their roles is invariably identifiable on any project. What is desired from a design review is to achieve a common view of the state of the products under review, whether that assessment be positive or negative. The achievement of this mutual view is likely to involve discussion and negotiation. Thus, the interaction between the developer, user, and customer must be collaborative rather than adversarial. While such a mindset may be difficult to adopt, a failure to collaborate will result in consequences probably even more difficult to absorb.

Even though a common view among the three parties is desired, it is the customer's approval of the design that is the final goal since the customer is the immediate sponsor of the project (the user may be the ultimate sponsor) and holds the purse strings.

The acceptability criteria for the products scrutinized during the review should be reasonably objective. It must be recognized, however, that there will always be room for interpretation among the three parties involved, no matter how precisely such criteria are stated. The two major criteria for acceptability or rejection arising out of the design review are:

1. Do the candidate products for the baseline in question contain what was intended by the previous baseline?
2. Do the candidate products for the baseline in question contain all the features demanded by the requirements baseline?

More detailed evaluation criteria are possible but may not always be workable for a formal event involving anywhere from 10 to 100 people. A formal design review is a confidence-building event, and is a quality evaluation activity only in the most general sense. The results of a previously performed detailed quality evaluation should be presented at the design review in summary form by the developer, who should highlight the major defects discovered that remain uncorrected. The actual quality evaluation is more appropriately performed earlier as an in-process review in conjunction with an inspection, as will be explained in Section 7.5

The resources and materials needed to plan and conduct a design review are as follows:

- A meeting agenda
- Conference rooms
- The design review package
- Presentation materials
- Meeting minutes

The mechanics of a design review, including the flow of these resources, are diagrammed in Figure 7–2. The developer prepares a data package of the products to be reviewed and submits them to the customer and user sometime before the actual review, usually 30 to 45 days. While the customer and user analyze the data package, the developer prepares the design review presentation. The actual review is conducted as a seminar activity, with the presentations made by personnel associated with the developer. The customer and user question the presenters as necessary. The major output of the review is problem reports that document supposed defects. Any of the parties attending the review may write a problem report. After the actual review concludes, there is usually an informal post-review meeting of management representatives of the three "players." One of the topics of this meeting is a brief review of the problem reports. Redundant reports are coalesced, and invalid or trivial reports are deleted. The surviving problem reports are then included in the minutes of the design review prepared by the developer. The minutes will also include an agenda for rectifying the discrepancies.

The customer will provide formal notification to the developer on the adequacy of

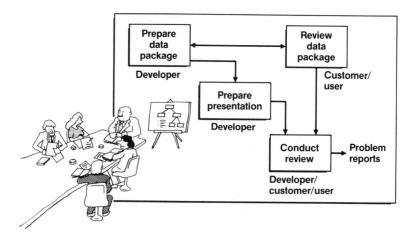

Figure 7-2 Design review mechanics

the review after receiving the minutes[1]. This notification will generally be at one of the three approval levels:

1. *Approval,* to indicate that the review was satisfactory.
2. *Contingent approval,* to indicate that satisfaction of further actions is required before full approval is conferred upon the review.
3. *Disapproval,* to indicate that the products reviewed were seriously inadequate.

Disapproval of the review could require substantial rework and a replay of the design review.

A typical sequence of formal reviews and audits is illustrated in Figure 7–3. Each life-cycle phase culminates with a review and establishes a baseline in most cases. This sequence meets Department of Defense acquisition requirements and is applicable in concept to any large system development effort. The sequence can be compressed for smaller systems associated with a foreshortened series of life-cycle phases. It is the principles illustrated on the figure that are important; the terminology is nominal. The key aspects of each specific review are considered next.

SYSTEMS REQUIREMENTS REVIEW.   The purpose of this review is to establish the overall system concept. This entails identifying the preliminary system and mission requirements and the system configuration, all of which will have emerged from an exploration of alternative system concepts. It is thus a further purpose of this review to

[1]*Military Standard Technical Reviews and Audits for Systems, Equipments, and Computer Software, MIL-STD-1521B* (Washington: United States Department of Defense, 1985), pp. 10–11.

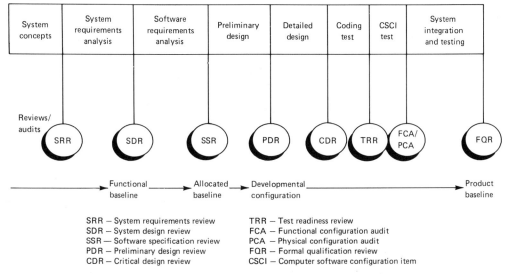

Development phases

System concepts	System requirements analysis	Software requirements analysis	Preliminary design	Detailed design	Coding test	CSCI test	System integration and testing

Reviews/audits

SRR   SDR   SSR   PDR   CDR   TRR   FCA/PCA   FQR

Functional baseline → Allocated baseline → Developmental configuration → Product baseline

SRR — System requirements review
SDR — System design review
SSR — Software specification review
PDR — Preliminary design review
CDR — Critical design review

TRR — Test readiness review
FCA — Functional configuration audit
PCA — Physical configuration audit
FQR — Formal qualification review
CSCI — Computer software configuration item

Figure 7-3 Typical design review and auditing sequence

retrace and explain the selection process. The primary documents included in the data package delivered for the system requirements review are:[2]

- A preliminary system specification
- A preliminary operational concept document
- Various trade study and analysis reports

Typical key items on the agenda for presentation at this review are:

- Risk studies
- Requirements and constraints tradeoffs
- Operational sequences
- Architectures evaluated and tradeoffs
- System partitioning into hardware, software, and operations
- Interface studies

The system requirements review should result in an affirmation of the preliminary system requirements and architecture.

SYSTEM DESIGN REVIEW.   This review provides a further affirmation of the operational (system) and mission requirements and their allocation to hardware, software, or

[2]*MIL-STD-1521B*, pp. 19–22.

operation elements. The review also provides additional confidence in the technical and cost/schedule feasibility of the system design. The primary documents included in the data package delivered for the system design review are:[3]

- An updated system specification
- An updated operational concept document
- A preliminary partial software requirements specification
- A preliminary interface requirements specification
- Various plans, including the software development plan (SDP), software quality program plan (SQPP), and software configuration management plan (SCMP)

Typical key items on the agenda for presentation at this review are:

- Requirements allocation
- Cost-effectiveness studies
- Architecture descriptions
- Quality engineering program and tradeoffs
- Software development procedures
- Results of significant tradeoff studies

The system design review will establish the system functional baseline that acts as a point of departure for the full-scale definition of computer software and hardware configuration items.

SOFTWARE SPECIFICATION REVIEW.[4] This review demonstrates the collective adequacy of the software requirements, interface requirements, and operational concept. The primary documents included in the data package delivered for the software specification review are:

- A completed software requirements specification for each computer software configuration item (CSCI). A CSCI is a major software component.
- An updated operational concept document
- A completed interface requirements specification
- Updated plans, such as the SDP, SQPP, and SCMP

Typical key items on the agenda for presentation at this review are:

- A functional overview of each CSCI

[3]*MIL-STD-1521B*, pp. 23–30.
[4]*MIL-STD-1521B*, pp. 31–32.

- Performance requirements and estimates
- Interface requirements
- Testing methods
- Quality factor requirements for each CSCI, such as correctness, reliability, efficiency, reusability, interoperability, and other requirements applicable to each CSCI.
- Significant updates and changes since the last review.

The software specification review will establish the allocated baseline of requirements to each CSCI.

PRELIMINARY DESIGN REVIEW.[5] This is a review of the basic design approaches for the CSCIs. A separate review is conducted for each CSCI or related group of CSCIs. The reviews prior to the preliminary design review are generally single events at the system or segment level. The preliminary design review should demonstrate that the top-level design of the CSCI satisfies, and that the test plans adequately address, the allocated requirements. The primary documents included in the data package delivered for the preliminary design review are:

- A software top-level design document
- A software test plan
- A preliminary software user's manual
- A preliminary computer system diagnostic manual
- A preliminary computer resources integrated support document
- A preliminary computer system operator's manual

Typical key items on the agenda for presentation at this review are:

- Allocation of requirements to components of the CSCI
- Storage and timing allocations
- The structure of the CSCI
- Implementation of security requirements
- Software development facilities
- Human factors
- Quality factors
- Testing concepts and management

The preliminary design review provides the initial definition of the developmental configuration.

[5]*MIL-STD-1521B*, pp. 33–52.

CRITICAL DESIGN REVIEW.[6]   This is a review of the detailed design solutions for the CSCIs. A separate review is conducted for each CSCI or related group of CSCIs. The critical design review should demonstrate that the detailed design satisfies the allocated requirements, that the detailed design is consistent with the top-level design, and that the test descriptions provide adequate test cases for the test identified earlier in the software test plan. The primary documents in the data package delivered for the critical design review are:

- A software detailed design document
- An interface design document
- A data base design document
- A software test description
- Updates to documents produced for the preliminary design review

Typical key items on the agenda for presentation at this review are:

- A storage and timing allocation report
- A report on the detailed characteristics of interfaces
- A report on the detailed characteristics of the data base
- A human factors report
- A test-case design approach

The critical design review provides a more detailed definition of the developmental configuration than does the preliminary design review.

TEST READINESS REVIEW.[7]   The purpose of this review is to determine whether to begin formal CSCI testing. The goal of the review is to reach a technical understanding on the informal test results, the status of test procedures, and other documentation. The actual CSCI testing may occur incrementally on an integrated basis in combination with increments of other CSCIs. The primary documents in the data package delivered for the test readiness review are:

- A software test procedure manual
- An updated software user's manual and computer system operator's manual

Typical key items on the agenda for presentation at this review are:

- Requirements and design changes
- Test plan/description changes

[6]*MIL-STD-1521B*, pp. 53–68.
[7]*MIL-STD-1521B*, pp. 69–70.

- Testing procedures
- Informal test results
- Test resources and limitations
- The status of software problems
- A testing schedule

The test readiness review further identifies the detailed definition of the developmental configuration.

FUNCTIONAL AND PHYSICAL CONFIGURATION AUDITS.[8] These two audits are usually conducted as a single process. Their purpose is to affirm that the CSCI was successfully tested and meets the requirements of the software requirements specification and interface requirements specification; the audits are also intended to demonstrate that the documentation reflects an up-to-date technical description of the product. These audits may be held incrementally when CSCI testing is performed incrementally as part of system integration. The primary documents in the data package delivered for the functional and physical configuration audits are:

- A software product specification
- A version description document
- A software test report
- A software user's manual
- A computer system operator's manual
- A computer system diagnostic manual

Typical key items on the agenda for presentation at these audits are:

- Test results and findings for each CSCI
- Problem areas and accomplishments
- Auditing of official test data against test plans and procedures
- Software test evaluation
- Discrepancies discovered
- Work plan for resolution of discrepancies

The functional and physical configuration audits identify and establish the product baseline.

FORMAL QUALIFICATION REVIEW.[9] The purpose of this review is to affirm that actual system performance complies with the requirements. The mechanics are identical

[8]*MIL-STD-1521B*, pp. 71–82.
[9]*MIL-STD-1521B*, pp. 83–84.

to the functional configuration audit. Indeed, the two can be combined, particularly when the functional configuration audit is applied to the integrated system.

The formal design review process is summarized by illuminating the strengths and weaknesses of the technique. The major advantages are:

- It provides the visibility to management in determining whether to baseline candidate products and proceed on to the next development phase.
- It acts as a forum to integrate and focus the collective goals of the customer, user, and developer.
- Because of the presence of these three parties, the design review is effective in revealing glaring misconceptions and major requirements-oriented inadequacies.
- Its sequence and content are flexible and can be tailored to the size and criticality of the project.

The formal design review methodology does have weaknesses:

- Its formality lacks the interactiveness to effectively challenge the technical basis of the design, except for obvious conceptual errors.
- Whenever major defects are found, it is often very difficult to rectify them without significantly affecting cost and/or schedule of the project.
- Because of its rigid format, it is not an effective forum for detailed quality evaluations.

Less formal review techniques, including quality evaluations, are more effective for the detection of detailed technical defects. We consider these next.

7.3
Internal Review Cycle

The internal review cycle is the oldest and most fundamental of the informal review techniques. It is a simple iterative process that is illustrated in a somewhat overdramatized fashion in Figure 7–4. The concept is that the originator of a product, perhaps a document, releases a draft version of that product to interested reviewers for scrutinization. The reviewers will individually feed back comments regarding possible defects and/or suggested modifications to the originator. The originator then factors those comments into the next draft of the document. The process iterates until a negotiated level of satisfaction is achieved between the originator and the reviewing parties.

The internal review cycle is an in-process review where the prevalent mentality is to expect and accommodate suggested changes wherever feasible. The process handles purported defects in a more informal, more conversational, and less expensive manner than the formal design review. Because it is an in-process technique, far fewer people

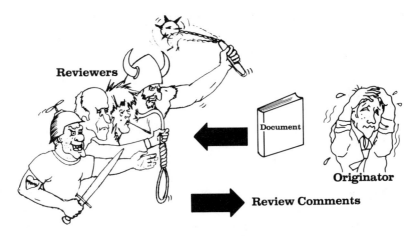

Figure 7-4 Internal review cycle

are affected when changes are made. Note that the customer and user can be and often are included in the internal review cycle.

Although the informality of the internal review cycle promotes feedback, it must be recognized that each reviewer represents a special interest and hence the feedback may be biased. For example, a user reviewing a requirements document may provide comments such as "More definition of the displays should be included!" or "Only a portion of the operability features I originally requested have been incorporated in the specification." Or a test organization reviewer may comment, "Paragraph 3.4.2.1.1 is an untestable requirement," or "With the scope of these requirements, we must develop additional test tools." Or a quality assurance engineer might assert that "The data-flow diagrams do not balance according to the standards." Many of these comments originating from a specialized perspective are valid and useful, but some may not be. Particular culprits are those requests for change that may favor enhancing technical content at the expense of additional cost and/or the schedule. It is also likely that comments from separate reviewers will be contradictory. It is the originator's task to filter these comments, integrate them together, reconcile them with one another, and then improve the product. The drawback is that the originator is called upon to make technical and management value judgments that may be unduly burdensome for a single person or even a small group of people. At such a point, the effectiveness of the technique is impaired.

In summary, the major advantages of the internal review cycle are:

- It is oriented toward receiving negative feedback and making changes.
- Changes involve fewer people and can thus be made less expensively.

The striking disadvantages are:

- Contradictory and/or unreasonable comments may arise as a result of the reviewers acting individually.

- A single party, the originator, must more or less unilaterally evaluate and act on the comments.

7.4
Internal Walkthrough

A more precise internal review process that largely mitigates the disadvantages of the internal review cycle is the internal walkthrough. Rooted more toward collective evaluation and decision making, the walkthrough is basically a peer review conducted within a team environment. It involves the author of a product presenting the salient aspects of the product to a peer review team of anywhere from four to eight people. The objective is to identify defects as a result of focusing the collective mental resources on the product under review. Practically any engineering product—a requirements specification, a design document, code, and even test cases—is a candidate for a walkthrough.

The walkthrough is an informal in-process review aimed at furnishing feedback to the author within the time frame in which revisions are possible and inexpensive. One of the reviewers acts as a moderator, keeping the discussion focused on the review of the product and keeping the walkthrough moving. Another of the reviewers records the defects identified. Where a consensus is not present among the reviewers regarding the presence of a defect, the moderator may have to make the final determination. The written record of defects provides accountability during the walkthrough. The moderator judges, based on the number and severity of defects discovered, whether a further walkthrough is necessary. The ultimate object of the process is not just to hold a walkthrough, but to have a *successful* walkthrough.

Other members of the walkthrough team furnish general opinions regarding the correctness of the items reviewed. Reviewers may also play other specific roles, including

- *The surrogate customer*—usually a system engineer who determines whether all the applicable requirements can be traced into the product.
- *The maintainer*—A critic of the product as regards its readability, understandability, and expandability.
- *The standards enforcer*—A quality assurance engineer who should render a rigid interpretation of development standards. This rigid position is balanced by the typically more liberal interpretation of standards taken by other reviewers.

There are thus few formal rules other than those already stated. Essentially, walkthroughs are informal, and in contrast to the internal review cycle, the author of the product is completely removed from the evaluation and decision-making process.

The major benefit of the internal walkthrough is the early removal of defects. Other ancillary benefits are:

- Better initial product quality as a result of the threat of a walkthrough. Nobody is fond of being embarrassed in front of peers.
- An improved training environment. Junior members of the team learn readily

by observing the experienced methods of their senior associates. The experienced people may also benefit from seeing more modern techniques utilized by the younger people just out of the universities.

- Insurance against the loss of a designer. For any number of reasons, an author may no longer be available. However, because of the exposure of the product to others through previous walkthroughs, another designer can easily fill in for the absent designer.

There are some deficiencies associated with the internal walkthrough that are worth noting:

- Walkthroughs are applied with varying rigor yielding inconsistent results.
- Walkthroughs do not usually add to or utilize a base of historical error data to reduce recurrences of errors.

Several additional guidelines are suggested by Yourdon[10] to make walkthroughs more efficient:

1. Review the product, not the producer. Whenever people interact in group situations, there is the potential for personalities to clash. The moderator should be able to minimize this kind of interplay.
2. The purpose of the walkthrough is error detection, not correction. It is the *author's* job to correct errors. Whenever creative technical people meet, there is always the urge to design by committee. The moderator should be sensitive to this tendency and suppress it.
3. Restrict the walkthrough to a short duration. About an hour is best. The walkthrough team members are being asked to divert some of their time from their primary job assignments. The level of enthusiastic participation will severely diminish if the duration of the walkthrough is unduly lengthy.

A very short written summary of the walkthrough listing the errors detected should be prepared by the recorder and approved by the moderator. The moderator will decide whether the volume and severity of the errors justify holding another walkthrough on the product after the author has implemented corrections.

7.5
Software Inspections

The software inspection is a rigorous in-process review method for detecting errors at their sources. The inspection has similarities to the walkthrough, but its increased formality provides concrete advantages that the other does not, including

[10]Edward Yourdon, *Structured Walkthroughs*, 2nd ed. (Englewood Cliffs, N.J.: Prentice-Hall, 1977), pp. 50–55.

- More repeatable results, derived from the increased rigor of the review.
- A focus on the most likely sources of errors, guided by the "corporate memory" of inspection error history.

The inspection is the vehicle for performing detailed quality evaluation and reporting the results. The inspection technique, coupled with the quality requirements evaluation, furnishes an early quantitative indication of quality, beginning with the requirements and design. Prior to the existence of the software inspection, the first quantitative feedback of quality did not occur until the first test results.

The software inspection was conceived by M. E. Fagan[11] of IBM as a method for efficiently finding errors in design and code. The procedure is of general applicability and can be utilized to review any product of the development cycle. Each design component is normally inspected at the requirements, high-level design, detailed design, and code compilation points. Other products, such as test plans and test cases, can also benefit from inspections. The major features of software inspections are:[12]

- Performing examinations of work products at defined checkpoints.
- Using trained peer inspection teams that review products for errors with a defined five-step procedure.
- Keeping records of errors detected for quality control and process management.

An inspection team consists of three to eight participants. It is most effective when each plays a particular role. The usual roles suggested by Fagan are:[13]

1. *Moderator*—The leader of the inspection. The duties of the moderator include scheduling the meetings, controlling the meetings, reporting the inspection results, and following up on rework.
2. *Designer*—The person responsible for producing the design of the product.
3. *Implementer*—The person responsible for physically implementing the design.
4. *Tester*—A representative of the organization responsible for testing the product.

In addition to these, it is also worthwhile to have the *system engineer* present who is responsible for specifying the requirements for the product.

These five individuals constitute the nominal content of an inspection team. The actual members may vary slightly depending upon the product being examined. For example, if the product has major interfaces, representatives of the interfacing components should be involved in the inspection because interfaces are a major risk area (and a source of errors) in most complex software-intensive systems.

The inspection is designed to determine conformance to each quality requirement

---

[11]Michael E. Fagan, "Design and Code Inspections to Reduce Errors in Program Development," *IBM Systems Journal*, 15 (1976), 182–211.

[12]Fagan, "Design and Code Inspections," 182–189.

[13]Fagan, "Design and Code Inspections," 190.

by a simple ''yes'' or ''no'' answer. Nonconformance, manifested by one or more ''no'' answers, is a measure of departure from quality. This is cause for recording an error and results in subsequent rework.

The inspection includes the following elements:[14]

1. *Overview.* This is a meeting where the designer (or author) of the product under examination describes the salient characteristics of the product to the entire inspection team. These might include, for a design, the architecture or processing logic, the data base, and the interfaces. The objective of the presentation is to educate the inspection team. The meeting concludes upon transfer of the information.

2. *Preparation.* During this phase the participants individually review the documentation to further understand the product. Each participant may study the historical distribution of errors from recent inspections to concentrate on the most prevalent kinds of error during the inspection. The participant may also make a preliminary pass through the quality requirement checklist, which could reveal some glaring errors.

3. *Inspection.* During the inspection meeting, one of the participants is designated as the ''reader'' by the moderator. The ''reader'' paraphrases the design, with the other participants following along and questioning when necessary. The examination is aided by a checklist that includes the quality requirements. The other item on the checklist is the most frequently encountered types of errors as determined by historical data from recent inspections. The designer of the product plays a passive role; he or she is present only to answer questions. Discussion is limited to the identification of errors, and the moderator intervenes only when it is necessary to keep the inspection focused. When an error is recognized, it is recorded and classified by the moderator, who provides a written report of the inspection on special forms within one working day of the inspection meeting.

4. *Rework.* This is what the author of the product does to rectify the errors that were discovered during the inspection meeting.

5. *Follow-up.* This is the action that verifies the rework. Where a small amount of rework is necessary, the moderator may personally verify the rework. Alternatively, the moderator may reconvene the inspection team to reinspect the reworked portion of the product. Where more of the product must be reworked— say, more than five percent, a full reinspection should be carried out. The error reports are recorded in a data base.

The IBM's experience has shown that efficiency in error detection decreases after two hours of inspection. Each inspection session should therefore be limited to no more than that amount of time. Several consecutive sessions may be necessary to fully inspect a product.

[14]Fagan, ''Design and Code Inspections,'' 192–194.

Project: _____ Date: _____

System Name: _____ Unit: _____

Moderator: _____ Room: _____ Phone: _____

Inspection Type:

☐ Requirements   ☐ Design   ☐ Implementation

Location:	Error Description:	Quality Factor	Error Type:	Error Class:	Severity
_____	_____	_____	_____	_____	_____
_____	_____	_____	_____	_____	_____
_____	_____	_____	_____	_____	_____
_____	_____	_____	_____	_____	_____
_____	_____	_____	_____	_____	_____
_____	_____	_____	_____	_____	_____
_____	_____	_____	_____	_____	_____
_____	_____	_____	_____	_____	_____
_____	_____	_____	_____	_____	_____
_____	_____	_____	_____	_____	_____
_____	_____	_____	_____	_____	_____
_____	_____	_____	_____	_____	_____
_____	_____	_____	_____	_____	_____
_____	_____	_____	_____	_____	_____
_____	_____	_____	_____	_____	_____
_____	_____	_____	_____	_____	_____
_____	_____	_____	_____	_____	_____
_____	_____	_____	_____	_____	_____
_____	_____	_____	_____	_____	_____
_____	_____	_____	_____	_____	_____
_____	_____	_____	_____	_____	_____
_____	_____	_____	_____	_____	_____

Figure 7-5 Inspection error list (Reprinted by permission of Robert G. Ebernau, RGE Software Methodologies, Inc.)

An Inspection Error List form used by the moderator to record errors is reproduced in Figure 7–5. This form is for the convenience of the moderator and is not further circulated to management. Note the "Error Class" column on the right of the form, according to which each error is characterized as a missing, wrong, or extra feature. The severity of an error is assessed as either

- *Major*, for an error that does not conform to requirements and/or will cause a product failure, or
- *Minor*, for an error that is not likely to cause a product failure.

The "Error Type" column pinpoints the error as having to do with any of several features: interface, data, logic, input/output, performance, standards, human factors, documentation, syntax, functionality, test environment, or test coverage. The "Quality Factor" column classifies errors according to one or more of the thirteen quality factors in which an item is found deficient: efficiency, integrity, reliability, survivability,

Project: _____ Date: _____

System Name: _____ Unit: _____

Moderator: _____ Room: _____ Phone: _____

Inspection Type:

☐ Requirements   ☐ Design   ☐ Implementation

Error type:	MINOR ERRORS				MAJOR ERRORS			
	M	W	E	Total	M	W	E	Total
Functionality								
Interface								
Data								
Logic								
Input/Output								
Performance								
Maintainability								
Standards								
Documentation								
Human Factors								
Syntax								
Quality Factor								
Other								
Totals								

Figure 7-6 Inspection summary (Reprinted by permission of Robert G. Ebernau, RGE Software Methodologies, Inc.)

usability, correctness, maintainability, verifiability, expandability, flexibility, interoperability, portability, or reusability.

A second report, the Inspection Summary, is shown in Figure 7–6. In this report, the moderator summarizes the list of errors contained in the Inspection Error List, and the information is entered into the historical data base of error data. A third form, the Inspection Report, indicates the disposition of the product submitted for inspection; this form is shown in Figure 7–7. It is this report that is sent to management. If the indicated

Project: _____ Inspection Date: _____

System Name: _____ Unit: _____

Moderator: _____ Room: _____ Phone: _____

Meeting Type

☐ Overview   ☐ Reinspection

☐ Requirements Inspection   ☐ Design Inspection   ☐ Implementation
                                                         Inspection

Number of Inspection Meetings: _____ Inspection Meeting Duration: _____

Total Number of Inspectors: _____ Total Meeting Preparation Time: _____

Total Lines Inspected: _____ Pages of Diagrams: _____

                                        Very Complex ☐ Yes   ☐ No

Unit Disposition: ☐ Accept   ☐ Conditional   ☐ Reinspect

Estimated Rework Effort: _____ (Hours)

Rework to Be Completed by: _____

Reinspection Scheduled for: _____

Inspectors (Please Include Author)

_____   _____

_____   _____

_____   _____

_____   _____

Moderator Certification: _____ Date: _____

Additional Comments: _____

_____

_____

_____

_____

Figure 7-7 Inspection report (Reprinted by permission of Robert G. Ebernau, RGE Software Methodologies, Inc.)

TABLE 7–1: INSPECTION AND WALKTHROUGH PROCESSES AND OBJECTIVES

Inspection		Walkthrough	
Process operations	Objectives	Process operations	Objectives
1. Overview	Education (Group)	—	—
2. Preparation	Education (Individual)	1. Preparation	Education (Individual)
3. Inspection	Find errors! (Group)	2. Walkthrough	Education (Group)
4. Rework	Fix problems	—	Discuss design alternatives
5. Follow-up	Ensure all fixes correctly installed	—	Find errors

Note the separation of objectives in the inspection process.

(Copyright 1976 International Business Machines Corporation. Reprinted with permission.)

TABLE 7–2: COMPARISON OF KEY PROPERTIES OF INSPECTIONS AND WALKTHROUGHS

Properties	Inspection	Walkthrough
1. Formal moderator training	Yes	No
2. Definite participant roles	Yes	No
3. Who "drives" the inspection or walkthrough	Moderator	Owner of material (Designer or coder)
4. Use "How to Find Errors" checklists	Yes	No
5. Use distribution of error types to look for	Yes	No
6. Follow-up to reduce bad fixes	Yes	No
7. Fewer future errors because of detailed error feedback to individual programmer	Yes	Incidental
8. Improve inspection efficiency from analysis of results	Yes	No
9. Analysis of data → process problems → improvements	Yes	No

(Copyright 1976 International Business Machines Corporation. Reprinted with permission.)

disposition of the product is that it be accepted, then the product has met its exit criteria and is considered to be complete.

By keeping the inspection team—especially the designer—intact across all inspections of a product (requirements, high-level design, detailed design, and code), a side benefit is accrued. The designer makes the original estimate of the number of lines of code for the product. Then, through participation in subsequent inspections, the designer is present to see the original estimate evolve and, finally, to verify the actual count at the code inspection. This participation improves the accuracy of the estimation process.[15]

A comparison of inspections and walkthroughs as analyzed by Fagan[16] is shown in Tables 7–1 and 7–2. In Table 7–1, the inspection is shown to be a considerably more rigorous procedure, with a definitive follow-up step to review whatever resolutions are made of the errors uncovered during the inspection. Table 7–2 reveals that the inspection uses error history as a prompting mechanism to improve efficiency in error detection on

[15]Fagan, "Design and Code Inspections," 203.
[16]Fagan, "Design and Code Inspections," 200.

subsequent inspections. IBM has conducted a parallel development of fully comparable components of an operating system in which one development used walkthroughs and the other used inspections. At an identical checkpoint well into the testing process it was found that the product developed with inspections contained 38 percent fewer errors.

Ebenau[17] notes that typical estimates for the cost of inspections range from five to 15 percent of the nonrecurring budget profile for a project. The compensating savings are generally seen in reduced test expenditures. One typical project experienced only a 0.2 percent change in the product during testing; had inspections not been used, a 15 percent change would have been expected. Ebenau reports the following inspection results for three different-size projects:

	Small Project	Medium Project	Large Project
Staff (number of persons)	4	30	100s
Average number of person-hours to detect major defect	0.56	1.2	2.2
Total defects detected	27	33	16

The increased effort required to detect major defects as the project size increases is evident in these data.

In sum, the major benefits of inspections are:

- They are a mechanism for defect detection, resolution, and accountability.
- They provide early quantitative feedback on product quality.
- The formality of an inspection yields repeatable results.
- The historical data base they generate reduces the recurrence of errors and improves the efficiency of subsequent error detection.

The only noteworthy disadvantage of the inspection is that it is entirely keyed to the developer's viewpoint, an expected drawback since the inspection is an internal in-process review. A balanced combination of inspections with formal design reviews will amplify the positive points of each and more than compensate for the negative points they possess.

7.6
Quality Level Guidelines

The review processes can have an influence on the attainment of the four levels of quality: not an issue, average, good, and excellent. Although reviews in themselves do not increase quality, they provide the grounds for a more exhaustive probing for errors to attain higher levels of quality. The errors discovered will signal the need for engineering rework of the product under review. A nominal program of review activities—formal design reviews, the internal review cycle, walkthroughs, and inspections—as a function

[17]Robert G. Ebenau, "Inspecting for Software Quality" (unpublished course notes, 1986), p. 6.

TABLE 7-3 REVIEW ACTIVITIES VS. QUALITY LEVEL

Quality level	Reviews
Not an Issue	• Internal review cycle • Internal walkthroughs
Average	• Internal review cycle • Inspections • Formal design review subset
Good	• Internal review cycle • Inspections • Formal design reviews (full set)
Excellent	• Internal review cycle • Inspections • Formal design reviews • Independent V & V reviews

of quality level is delineated in Table 7–3. A brief explanation of the respective issues is as follows.

"NOT-AN-ISSUE"-LEVEL REVIEWS.   The review activity at this level is informal and internal. The reviews consist of the internal review cycle and internal walkthroughs. These are sufficient because software for which quality is not an issue is not likely to be delivered to an external customer.

AVERAGE-LEVEL REVIEWS.   Software that is of average quality could be delivered to a customer; thus, a formal review forum is necessary. The reviews will consist of a subset of the series of formal design reviews defined in Section 7.2. A nominal subset would be the preliminary design review, critical design review, and functional/physical configuration audit. At this level, the more rigorous inspection substitutes for the walkthrough.

GOOD-LEVEL REVIEWS.   Software that is of good quality will use the internal review cycle, inspections, and the complete set of formal design reviews outlined in Section 7.2. The design review series may be moderately truncated if a small system is involved.

EXCELLENT-LEVEL REVIEWS.   The review processes at this level include all the reviews of the previous level plus a full life-cycle review of the developer's products by an IV&V contractor. IV&V is the subject of Chapter 9.

Chapter 8

Validating Requirements and Design

8.1
Why a Good Statement of the Problem
Is Important

It is a clear, noble goal to achieve confidence in the statement of requirements before proceeding with the design, implementation, and eventual installation of a software-based system. The quantitative benefits of containing requirements problems to the early phases of the life cycle have been evident for some time, e.g., in the relative-error cost profile presented by Boehm.[1] The data show, for example, how the relative cost of an error regarding requirements geometrically escalates as compared to what it would have been if it had been contained in the requirements phase of the project. In general, a considerable portion of the schedule and budget for large, complex high-technology projects is consumed in understanding and stating the problem that is being solved. If

[1]B. W. Boehm, "Verifying and Validating Software Requirements and Design Specifications," *Computer*, Vol. 1, January 1984, p. 76.

the process goes on past the requirements definition phase of the project, it can lead to the consequences just noted. In some cases this is unavoidable: it is just not possible to completely understand complex problems that have not been solved before. System definition and development in these situations becomes partially a trial-and error process, and while some aspects of the matter can be controlled through validation of requirements and design, they cannot be fully eliminated.

It would be expedient to believe that a requirements specification constitutes all the information necessary to design and develop a system. However, this "stone tablet" perspective is flawed. A requirements specification can describe functional behavior, interfaces, performance parameters, computational constraints, and the types of information that flow through the system. But the requirements usually do not effectively communicate the broader context in which the system will operate. This overall context may include further issues, such as the end-to-end activities to be performed, operational sequences, the role of people in the system, interactions with outside systems, and other items that are important to the eventual users of the system. But then this suggests that no complex problem is expressible in a single form and that a complete problem statement therefore entails more than the requirements specification. These key notions are set out in Figure 8–1.

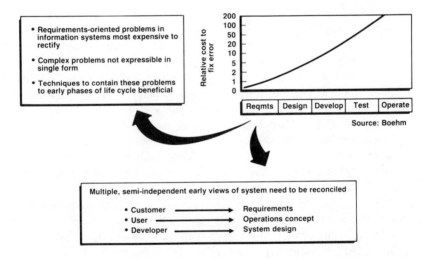

Figure 8-1 Software requirements validation and allocation technology

Multiple views of a system derive directly from the people involved in the system development project. Generally, there are three such parties—a customer, a user, and a developer. Each of these may exist as a physically separate organizational entity, as, for example, in a large Department of Defense software system acquisition. It is also possible for all three parties to coexist in the same company or organization. The development of a telecommunications switching system is a typical case where the customer, user, and developer could all be part of the same company. Regardless of their physical dispositions, the customer, user, and developer are the players—each with a different view—

who frame the system problem statement. Each party relates to the problem statement for a system in a somewhat different coordinate system: the customer will define the problem in terms of functional and performance requirements; the user thinks of the system problem in the frame of an operational concept of dynamic activities and resulting products; and the developer is inclined to picture the problem definition primarily as a system-level design solution in reaction to the customer's requirements. These multiple views of the system are thus "natural" problem statements derived from, and cognitively matched to, the roles of the three parties.

In current practice, these views of the system are developed semi-independently (wholly independently in a few pathological cases) as an inherent consequence of the juxtaposition of the three parties involved. Note that this does not have an entirely negative connotation: there is no single pragmatic methodology in today's repertoire of technology that *can* integrally represent all three of these views. The requirements view depicts mainly functions and their respective inputs and outputs; the operations concept view emphasizes procedures or sequences of functions; and the system design view identifies the interconnected physical components that will implement the system. There are certain methodologies more powerful than others relative to each of these views. For example, structured analysis is a powerful method for defining individual functions and interfaces, but is weak in explaining procedures.

This tripartite statement of the system problem, having been put together semi-independently, will likely contain inconsistencies. It will also be redundant to some degree, and it may have omissions. The three elements of the problem statement must accordingly be knit together or reconciled. In this sense, redundancy, manifesting itself in the different views of the system, is a positive attribute. It can be helpful in identifying discordances among the three views or, even better, in preventing these mismatches from occurring. We should look upon this triadic view of the system as an asset or opportunity to validate the problem statement rather than a shortcoming in present practices. A concrete methodology for reconciling these views is suggested in Section 8.3. For now, the major point to be derived is that a good problem statement is composed of a requirements specification, a system design, and an operations concept that are mutually consistent.

The operations concept is a key component of the problem statement. It describes a system from the user's view. A definition of a system's operational concept would typically include descriptions of the mission, the operational support environment (including the software), the system's operational sequences, and the allocation of the steps of each operational sequence to the physical components of the system to the degree that these components are visible to the user of the system. The operations concept closes some of the gaps in the broad system context not directly addressed by the requirements and design specifications. In effect, it explains how the system is utilized to fulfill its mission. This is particularly important for systems with concurrent multiple sequences.

The attributes of a good problem statement can be somewhat application specific. If the problem statement is viewed as a set of specifications, the following generic set of adequacy criteria can be applied:[2]

[2]Boehm, p. 78.

1. *Completeness.* All parts of the specification are present.

2. *Consistency.* The contents of the specification do not conflict either internally or externally, e.g., the requirements do not conflict with the design or operations concept.

3. *Feasibility.* The system can be realized technically and economically.

4. *Testability.* There is an economically viable method of determining whether the final product meets its specification.

Framing a problem statement in terms of these attributes makes it more likely that we can build a product that emphasizes such quality factors as verifiability, maintainability, reliability, and usability. The attributes essentially provide a model of form and structure that will avoid the occurrence of generic problems. Whether or not the actual content of the problem statement is appropriate then becomes largely a matter of engineering judgment.

The balance of this chapter explores technologies and methods for requirements and design validation that take into account the issues that have been raised in this introductory section. The following specific topics are presented:

- Example manual and automated requirements/design technologies (Section 8.2).

- An application requirements/design validation case study (Section 8.3).

- An application of performance requirements validation with simulation (Section 8.4).

- Use of prototyping including an example application (Section 8.5).

- A guideline for application to levels of quality (Section 8.6).

8.2
Requirements and Design Validation Technology

Systematized technology for requirements and design validation was a largely ignored topic until the mid-1970s. This fits the overall chronological pattern in the evolution of software engineering, which has occurred "inside out" beginning with structured programming and finally advancing to requirements analysis.

The essential process of requirements validation is intrinsically iterative. The process consists of two basic types of activities:

1. Activities interleaved and parallel with the generation of the requirements that will create such desirable properties as completeness, consistency, feasibility, and testability.

2. Activities performed after a draft requirement specification has been published.

This basic requirements validation technology approach is diagrammed in Figure 8–2. Typical parallel activities include systematic methods, such as structured analysis, that emphasize human reasoning and automated simulation models that help in prescribing

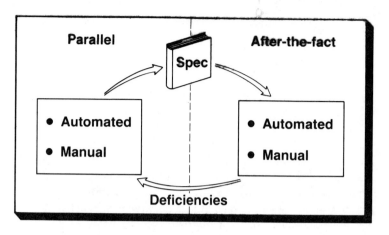

Figure 8-2 Requirements validation: Basic technology approach

performance requirements. Some after-the-fact activities might be reviews and inspections. The process iterates until all known deficiencies are corrected and no new ones are discovered. Any deficiencies found would be rectified in the next release of the draft specification.

On larger systems it is customary to go through a concept definition phase before the customer commits to a full-scale development. The objective is to define and validate the system requirements and design. The concept definition phase can be viewed as a partial mini-development cycle that precedes the full-scale development. The methodology that is generally applied is the iterative process just described. By penetrating forward to a system design, the technical and economic feasibility of the system requirements can be established to a higher degree of confidence than would be possible by considering only the candidate requirements.

Within a period of less than five years centered about 1975, a number of advances in requirements analysis emerged. Some of the more significant ones included structured analysis, the problem statement language/problem statement analyzer (PSL/PSA), the system verification diagram (SVD), and the software requirements engineering methodology (SREM). Structured analysis was introduced by Ross[3] and refined by DeMarco,[4] and is a broad methodology directed toward a progressive logical definition of the elements that play a part in the system, functions, and data. It employs a graphical communication schema called the data-flow diagram that synchronizes the functions and data. The Teichrow group[5] at the University of Michigan developed the PSL/PSA, which is a computer-aided requirements analysis tool centering on a formal-style requirements language coupled with a consistency analysis of the problem statement delineated in that

[3]D. T. Ross, "Structured Analysis (SA): A Language for Communicating Ideas," in *IEEE Transactions and System Specification*, Vol. SE-3, January 1977, pp. 2–5.

[4]T. DeMarco, *Structured Analysis and System Specification* (Englewood Cliffs, NJ: Prentice-Hall, 1979).

[5]D. Teichrow and E. A. Hershey, III, "PSL/PSA: A Computer-Aided Technique for Structured Documentation and Analysis of Information Processing Systems," in *IEEE Transactions on Software Engineering*, Vol. SE-3, January 1977, pp. 41–48.

language. The SVD, which originated at Computer Sciences Corporation,[6] is a graphical technique for analyzing a requirements specification by mapping the text into stimulus-response elements that are connected into a directed graph. Alford[7] conceived the SREM at TRW under U.S. Army sponsorship. SREM employs a graphical technique called an R-NET and a textual requirements language; the R-NET depicts how a stimulus or input message is transformed into a response message. SREM also has an embedded simulation capability for verification of performance requirements.

Each of these methodologies and their variants fits within one of two formal foundations: (1) a data-flow model, or (2) a stimulus-response model. Structured analysis and PSL/PSA are examples of the first, while the SVD and SREM are examples of the second. The data-flow model is advantageous in showing the synchronization of functions with the data paths that flow between them, as well as being an excellent mechanism for progressive system decomposition from the most to the least abstract levels of detail. The strength of the stimulus-response model is in charting the procedure or scenario that transforms a stimulus into an eventual system response; its effectiveness is basically limited to a single level of abstraction.

Several example tools and methods employed in requirements and design validation technology are now illustrated.

8.2.1 COMPUTER-AIDED DESIGN AND SPECIFICATION ANALYSIS TOOL (CADSAT)

CADSAT renders automated assistance to the structured analysis methodology. Its major output is a consistent and complete structured specification. The tool is a direct descendant of PSL/PSA.

CADSAT provides the facilities to define requirements in a formal language with a precise syntactical structure. The requirements specification is thus expressed in a machine-readable data base. The analyst defines the objects that play a part in the system, functions, and data by means of input language statements. A more recent version of CADSAT uses a graphic data-flow diagram interface to replace most of the textual inputs. CADSAT automatically checks the precision and consistency of the input syntax and analyzes the semantics of the described inputs by checking the relationships between data and functions for consistency. These capabilities are valuable in cross-checking the inputs of several individuals working on a requirements specification. CADSAT provides reports that assist the analyst in better understanding system flow, system structure, data structure, and data derivation.

The substantive output of CADSAT is a formatted statement of functional requirements that can be incorporated directly into a deliverable requirements specification. An extract from a requirements document produced by CADSAT is shown in Figure 8–3. In it, the function CONTROL SPEED is specified in three subparagraphs: inputs, processing description, and outputs. Each of the data items delineated in the input and

---

[6]R. Carey and M. Bendick, "The Control of a Software Test Process," in *Proceedings of the Computer Software and Applications Conference—1977*, IEEE No. 77 CH1291-4C, November 1977, pp. 327–333.

[7]M. Alford, "A Requirements Engineering Methodology for Real Time Processing Requirements," in *IEEE Transactions on Software Engineering*, Vol. SE-3, January 1977, pp. 60–69.

CADSAT Output Example

3.4.4.3.2 Control Speed.

A. INPUTS

DATA NAME	UNITS	RANGE	PRECISION	SOURCE
ANG_X	DEG	+180 TO −180	0.0055	Attitude_Ref (3.4.4.1)
QAO_EL_T11 XDCHRH_20	FEET	10,000 TO 0	0.5	Attitude_Ref (3.4.4.1)
RATE_GAINS	N/A	N/A	N/A	Ctrl_Surface_Cmd (3.4.4.3.1.2)

DATA NAME IDENTIFICATION

ANG_X	: This is data element 1 in the test data base. It flows from : F1 to F32.
QAO_EL_T11 XDCHRH_20	: This is data element 7 in the test data base. It flows from : F1 to F32.
RATE_GAINS	: This is data element 22 in the test data base. It flows from : F312 to F32.

B. (U) PROCESSING

1. (U) Angle of attack to trim, ALPHA, the three components of SPEED, U, V, W, the four components of FIN_POS, LSCC, LPCC, USCC, UPCC, and the pitch rate and yaw rate components of FILTERED_BODY_RATES FILT_Q, FILT_R, shall be extracted from the DYNAMIC_STATUS table and the EL_T31 component of DIR_COS shall be extracted from the NAV & ATT_DATA table every 20 milliseconds.

2. (U) The speed boost augmentation factor DRAG shall be computed every 20 milliseconds if FINAL_WIRE_CLEARANCE = COMPLETED

$$DRAG = KT*[-EL\_T31]*BUOY+ADMS*(W*(FILT\_Q)-(V*(FILT\_R)]+ANG\_X$$

C. OUTPUTS

DATA NAME	UNITS	RANGE	PRECISION	DESTINATION
ENG_SPEED	RPM	100,000 TO 0	5	Smooth_Depth (3.4.4.2.1)
FINAL_WIRE_ CLEARANCE	STATUS	NOT CLEAR, CLEAR	N/A	Ctrl_Surface_Cmd (3.4.4.3.1.2)
REM_FUEL	LBS	10,000 TO 0	0.5	Smooth_Depth (3.4.4.2.1)
TACT_YAW_RATE	RAD/SEC	+0.5 TO −0.5	1.5E-5	Ctrl_Surface_Cmd (3.4.4.3.1.2)

DATA NAME IDENTIFICATION

ENG_SPEED	: This is data element 11 in the test data base. It flows from : F32 to F21.
FINAL_WIRE_	: This is data element 20 in the test data base.

Figure 8-3 Requirements document extract

output subparagraphs are qualified by several attributes that are analyst supplied and alterable for each individual function. The processing subparagraph defines the process that transforms the inputs into the outputs. Note that certain keywords representing data items are printed in uppercase, a signal to CADSAT that these keywords should be consistency checked for exceptions.

The result of exception checking is captured in Figure 8-4. The data item TACT__YAW__RATE appears either in the input subparagraph (subparagraph A) or the output subparagraph (subparagraph C), but not in the processing description subparagaph (subparagraph B). Similarly, the data item FIN__POS appears in subparagraph B, but fails to appear either in subparagraph A or subparagraph C, and so on down the list. All these exceptions indicate obvious flaws or oversights that have been detected for subsequent correction.

```
Exception list for paragraph 3.4.4.3.2
      TACT_YAW_RATE appears in A (or C) but not in B.
      FIN_POS appears in B but not in A (or C).
      FILTERED_BODY_RATES appears in B but not in A (or C).
      FILT_Q appears in B but not in A (or C).
DYNAMIC_STATUS
      FILT_R appears in B but not in A (or C).
      DYNAMIC_STATUS appears in B but not in A (or C).
      EL_T31 appears in B but not in A (or C).
      DIR_COS APPEARS IN B but not in A (or C).
      ATT_DATA appears in B but not in A (or C).
      TACT_YSW_RATE appears in B but not in A (or C).
      REQ_SPEED appears in B but not in A (or C).
```

Figure 8-4 CADSAT exception check

CADSAT is an example of the degree that automation can assist functional requirements validation. While the exceptions detected are probably significant, they are flaws in form or structures alone; this type of technology cannot directly analyze the actual content of the requirements.

8.2.2 SYSTEM VERIFICATION DIAGRAM (SVD)

The SVD is primarily a manual technique that is intended to focus attention on the content of functional requirements. Formulated from the requirements specification, the SVD represents the requirements graphically as a sequence of stimulus-response elements. The form of a representative SVD is contained in Figure 8-5.

Each stimulus-response element is associated with specific requirements from the specification and hence is labeled with the requirement number or paragraph references. The stimulus consists of an input event and any associated conditional qualifiers of the state of the system at that point. The response is similarly composed of output events plus conditional qualifiers occurring as a result of the input event. An example of the generation of a thread from requirements is displayed in Figure 8-6. The figure shows an input event entailing a new hostile track detection and a conditional qualifier, that the track files are not full, combining from paragraphs 3.7.1.1.4 and 3.7.3.1.5 of the speci-

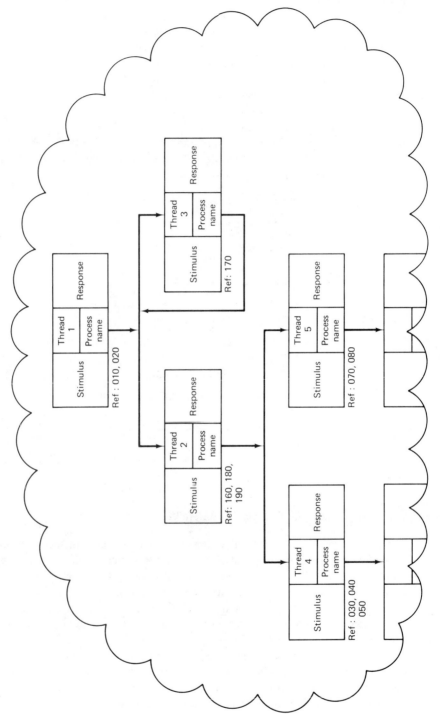

Figure 3-5 Representative form of system verification diagram

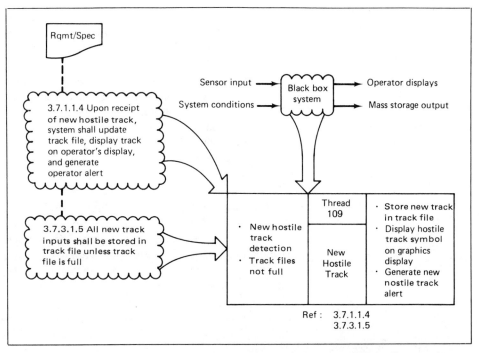

Figure 8-6 Identifying a thread from the requirements (Source: Robert Carey and Marc Bendic, "The Control of a Software Test Process," *Proceedings of the Computer Software and Applications Conference 1977* [New York, N.Y.: IEEE, Inc.], IEEE Catalog No. 77CH 1291-4C, Copyright 1977 IEEE.)

fication to form the stimulus of this thread. The response is also derived from information offered by these two paragraphs. The threads representing the requirements specification are concatenated with arrows which denote the flow of the thread sequence to form the SVD.

An effect that aids in the validation of the requirements occurs as a result of the discipline of the SVD procedure. The process of constructing the SVD causes the requirements to be viewed in a parallel context because of the graphic medium. By contrast, simply reading the text of the specification would allow only a serial assimilation of the information. Also, the SVD procedure focuses additional attention on the content of the requirements. The net effect is that inconsistencies, redundancies, and omissions may be revealed that would otherwise have gone undetected at this point. An effective sequence of events in applying the SVD approach would be as follows:

- Construct the SVD immediately upon availability of the requirements specification draft.
- Document errors and suspicious areas.
- Consult with the customer and user, if necessary, and develop revisions to erroneous areas.
- Incorporate revisions into the next draft of the requirements specifications.

- Update the SVD.
- Repeat the preceding procedure until no more flaws in the requirements are evident.

As an example of a requirements flaw that would be exposed by the SVD approach, consider again the hostile-track thread of Figure 8–6. The conditional qualifier of the stimulus is that the track files are not full. Accordingly, it is natural to expect that, after dealing wih this thread, the requirements analyst will create a parallel thread consisting of the same input event and a corollary qualifier—that the track files are full. This thread, identified as thread number 110, is illustrated in Figure 8–7. What is the flaw here? Simply this. Inspection of paragraphs 3.7.1.1.4 and 3.7.3.1.5 provides no indication of what the system reaction should be to a new hostile track under the condition that the track files are full (assuming that there are no other paragraphs in the specification that address this issue). So the response to this stimulus cannot in fact be signified on the SVD at this time. Perhaps the new track should be dropped, or perhaps it should displace an existing track of lesser importance. The analyst may wish to discuss this point with the customer or user before arriving at a conclusion. In any case, the requirements specification must be revised to clear up this significant omission.

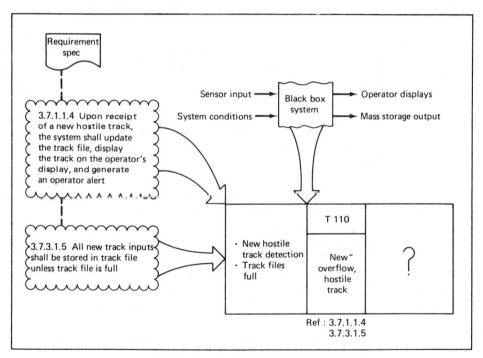

Figure 8-7 Identifying a requirement flaw

The SVD is an informal device for the validation of requirements. Its main thrust is to represent the text of the requirements in graphical form and, in so doing, to direct the analyst's attention to possible inconsistencies, redundancies, and omissions. The use of the SVD in a broader context is examined in Section 8.3.

8.2.3 AUTOMATED INTERACTIVE SIMULATION SYSTEM (AISIM)[8]

Whenever there are questions concerning the timing and capacity of a system, simulation or modeling should be considered as a mechanism for determining the feasibility of candidate performance requirements. A model is a simplified representation of an object; simulation entails the interaction of a model with its enviroment to determine the dynamic properties of a system. A simulation model is also called an analytical prototype. Whenever the size and complexity of a system exceeds the ability to do a "pencil and paper" analysis, a machine-executable simulation can overcome the complexity to evaluate the performance characteristics of the system prior to implementation. This will be particularly necessary when a system's operation is composed of concurrent processes and activities.

A discrete event simulator models the functional and physical elements of a system and, usually, some part of the system's operational environment. The dynamic behavior of the system is predicted by interjecting a representation of an operational scenario or sequence of events into the system model. The performance characteristics are determined by observing the response of the model to the scenario. The feasibility of attaining postulated performance requirements is inferred from the simulation results. Simulation techniques are useful in assessing the following types of performance characteristics:

- Accuracies of parameters
- Durations of system responses to specific inputs
- CPU utilizations
- Storage utilizations
- Ability to meet operational time constraints
- Man/machine interactions and responses

Simulation development can be an expensive and time-consuming affair. Historically, the results of simulations have not generally been available at the key decision-making deliberations that take place in the early conceptual phase of a project. The need to overcome this deficiency and develop simulations in a short period of time inspired the development of the Automated Interactive Simulation System (AISIM). AISIM is a discrete event simulator whose major distinguishing characteristic is its graphic interactive interface requiring no actual programming. This allows analysts to develop simulations without becoming immersed in programming details. AISIM is particularly adept at modeling such activities as network communications, operational loading, procedural operations, parallel processing, process communications, and shared resources.

[8]The Automated Interactive Simulation System (AISIM) was developed by Hughes Aircraft Company, Ground Systems Group, under sponsorship by the U.S. Air Force Electronic Systems Division.

Figure 8-8 Construct model quickly with AISIM

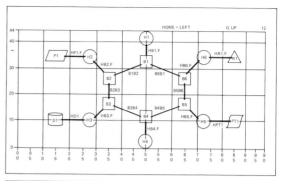

(1) Specify architecture and paths

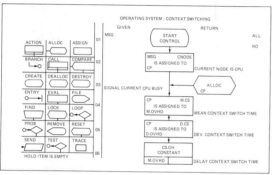

(2) Define activities and scenario

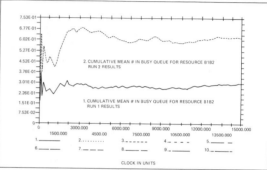

(3) Simulate and view analysis results

The graphical interactive features of AISIM are demonstrated by the photographs of the graphics screens shown in Figure 8–8. The photos explain how a simulation using AISIM is rapidly constructed in three major steps. In the first step, the analyst literally draws a picture of the system architecture on the screen. Pictured here are the processors, storage devices, and communications channels. The analyst is then prompted by a form to fill in the loads and capacities for each element of the architecture. On the second screen, the analyst defines the functional activities or processes that are performed within the architecture. This is done by drawing a flowchart of each process. The analyst selects, from the menu on the left of the screen, the type of function to be performed at each step of the flowchart; quantitative data is specified by filling in forms. The analyst then constructs a scenario. Since AISIM is a discrete-event simulator, the times of occurrence of each event are specified deterministically, or else one of the several preprogrammed statistical distributions may be utilized. The model is then compiled and executed against the scenario. AISIM provides automatic management of each system resource using a first in–first out scheme. If another resource management algorithm is needed, the analyst may define an overriding process embodying the desired algorithm. The analytical results of the simulation are presented graphically for understandability. The normal format shows the values of an analyst-determined parameter as a function of time. The simulation results of the same parameter for two or more simulation runs may be displayed simultaneously on the same graph, the better to highlight, for example, the impact of the design alternatives on system performance. The graphical interactive interface of AISIM is analyst oriented rather than programmer oriented and supports the development of simulations in a much shorter schedule than would otherwise be possible using traditional methods.

8.3
An Application of Functional Requirements
and Design Validation

This section presents a requirements and design validation methodology and a pilot case study that are based upon the integration of three models of a system: the functional requirements view, the operations concept view, and the system design view. The methodology, which relies heavily on the SVD, identifies mismatches among these views, focusing on the interleaving of the models.

The three models are cross-correlated manually by the engineer. When a single person or a very small group associates three separate and potentially uncoordinated system views, it is likely that human judgment will be effectively prompted either to discover explicit errors or to be guided to a better statement of the problem. The associations of the views will be applied iteratively in conjunction with the refinement and modification of the problem statement in all three coordinate systems.

The traditional sequential, feed-forward model of the software life cycle is widely recognized as an ideal that is barely approximated by the human problem-solving cycle, which is necessarily iterative in nature. Communications among people are imperfect, mistakes are made, and there is a continual need to accommodate new inputs. These factors conspire to cause analysts to revert to previous life-cycle phases to modify earlier work. This is particularly evident in the early concept, requirements, and preliminary design phases of the life cycle. Controlled and minimized, reversion to previous cycles can be employed advantageously to validate requirements.

The requirements definition and preliminary design stages of the life cycle can be regarded as controlled experiments in search of a good problem statement. The system-level design solution is an experiment to validate the system-level requirements. Iteration between the two transpires until a comfortable level of confidence is accumulated in both of them. Operational procedures and constraints are then envisioned, and any inconsistencies in the design are resolved. In this context, system design is considered part of the requirements definition stage of the life cycle: it is a necessary step to establish the technical and economic feasibility of implementing the requirements. There is thus a level of design analogous to each level of requirements. This life-cycle view envisions requirements validation as an intrinsic ingredient of the requirements definition activity and not as a separately identifiable overlay. According to it, requirements validation operates in parallel with requirements definition to become a preventive mechanism rather than just an after-the-fact evaluative mechanism.

8.3.1 THE METHODOLOGY: CONSOLIDATING THE THREE VIEWS

The thrust of the aforementioned methodology is to establish equivalency between the requirements view, the operations concept view, and the system-level design view. The overall flow of the methodology is sketched out in Figure 8–9. The circles or bubbles in the diagram represent the various functions involved, while the arrows between the

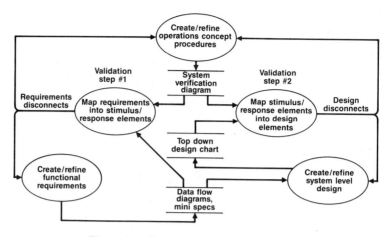

Figure 8-9 Reconciling three system views

functions denote data flow; labels juxtaposed to the arrows name the data elements. The validation process illustrated results in the creation of the following products:

- *Requirements* represented by a systems data-flow diagram (DFD) and textual specifications of logical operations for each function on the DFD.
- *The operations concept*, represented by an SVD that graphs the stimulus-response elements. The SVD is derived from and summarizes the operations concept which exists originally in whatever natural format it was created. Each stimulus-response element represents an operational scenario in abbreviated form.
- *The system-level design*, displayed by a top-down hierarchical diagram or any alternate representation that depicts the physical components and their interconnections.

Equivalency or validation is accomplished by detecting inconsistencies between the products and refining the products until continuity and consistency are achieved.

The actual procedure entails two validation steps. The first associates each requirement paragraph in the textual specifications with a comparable stimulus-response element in the SVD. The association generally fits several requirement paragraphs to each stimulus-response element. A stimulus-response element then represents an aggregation of several logically related requirements. This step may reveal inconsistencies between the products in the form of a stimulus in the requirements without a response, a response without a stimulus, or any number of other inconsistencies and redundancies.

The second validation step maps each stimulus-response element (now also representing the requirements as a result of the first validation step) into the sequence of design components which, when strung together, instantiate the behavior demanded by the stimulus-response element. The process is similar to that described by Carey and

Bendick, but is used here in a much broader context in which the SVD is employed as an abstraction of the operations concept. Inconsistencies may be discovered in the form of a missing stimulus or response in the design components, the presence of an unrelated stimulus and response, or unassociated design elements with no apparent linkage to the requirements or scenarios. These inconsistencies form the basis for refining the operations concept, design, and requirements until equivalence occurs and validation is consequently accomplished. The present knowledge base of rules, empirically derived, for discovering inconsistencies is provided in Table 8-1. The 1.n series of rules comprises the first validation step, and the second validation step is controlled by the 2.n series of rules.

The SVD, which is derived from the system operations concept, acts as the pivot of this requirements validation method. Each stimulus-response element defines a single scenario or procedure and, when linked with other elements, forms a model of the system operations concept. The natural statement of the envisioned operations is transformed into an SVD, thus presenting a formatted representation of the operations concept.

Figure 8-9 presents mainly the data flow of this methodology. The procedure involved, i.e., the sequence of the functions, is as follows:

1. The requirements and operations concept are generated approximately in parallel, with the latter usually lagging slightly in time. The operations concept is abstracted into an SVD.

2. The first validation step is performed, establishing equivalency between the requirements and operations concept.

3. A system-level design is produced.

4. The second validation step is performed, establishing equivalency between the operations concept (including the requirements obtained as a result of validation step 1) and the system design.

Whenever inconsistencies are discovered, an iteration occurs.

It is important to recognize that this validation procedure should recur a number of times over the development cycle. The system problem statement is created once and then refined, modified, and upgraded over and over again. In doing so, it is essential to ensure continuing equivalency between the three system views each time a requirements change occurs. In reality, there will be persistent open requirements issues and resultant requirements changes well into the implementation stages of the life cycle. It is therefore appropriate to maintain a living, up-to-date record of the validation. The validation can be charted relationally as shown in Figure 8-10. The relationships between the requirement paragraphs, stimulus-response elements, and design elements are upgraded with each iteration of the validation procedure, and the relationship pattern can form the basis for later testing and integration of the system.

To summarize, this requirements validation methodology is oriented toward stimulating human judgment to discover the inconsistencies among the requirements, operational concept, and design of the system. The pairwise mapping of the three products

[9]Carey and Bendick, pp. 327–330.

TABLE 8-1: PRESENT KNOWLEDGE BASE OF RULES

Rule no.	Natural representation	Procedural Representation	Predicate Calculus Representation
1.1	Each requirement (ireq) must be singly correlated with a scenario (condition: CORRELATED) except when multiple scenarios involve the same stimulus with different existing states (condition: DIFSTATE).	IF CORRELATED(ireq) THEN RETURN(OK) ELSE IF DIFSTATE(ireq) THEN RETURN (OK) ELSE RETURN (BAD)	$\{$CORRELATED(ireq)$\Rightarrow$OK$\}$ V $\{[\sim$CORRELATED(ireq) Λ DIFSTATE(ireq)$]\Rightarrow$OK$\}$ V $\{[\sim$CORRELATED(ireq) Λ $\sim$DIFSTATE(ireq)$]\Rightarrow$BAD$\}$
1.2	It is best that each scenario (iscen) correlate with anywhere from two to eight requirements (condition: COR2–8), but if not, each must correlate with one requirement (condition: CORRELATED).	IF COR2–8(iscen) THEN RETURN(GOOD) ELSE IF CORRELATED(iscen) THEN RETURN(OK) ELSE RETURN(BAD)	$\{$COR2–8(iscen)$\Rightarrow$GOOD$\}$ V $\{$CORRELATED(iscen)$\Rightarrow$OK$\}$ V $\{[\sim$COR2–8(iscen) Λ $\sim$CORRELATED(iscen)$]\Rightarrow$BAD$\}$
1.3	The stimulus (stim) and response (resp) of the scenario must both be identifiable (condition: PRESENT) in the requirements.	IF PRESENT (stim,resp) THEN RETURN(OK) ELSE RETURN(BAD)	$\{$PRESENT (stim,resp)$\Rightarrow$OK$\}$ V $\{[\sim$ PRESENT(stim) V $\sim$ PRESENT(resp)$]\Rightarrow$BAD$\}$
2.1	Each design module (module) must correlate with at least one scenario (condition: COR__GE__1).	IF COR__GE__1(module) THEN RETURN(OK) ELSE RETURN(BAD)	[COR__GE__1(module)$\Rightarrow$OK] V [$\sim$COR__GE__1(module)$\Rightarrow$BAD]
2.2	Each terminal module (termod) must be singly correlated with a scenario (condition: CORRELATED)	IF CORRELATED(termod) THEN RETURN(GOOD) ELSE RETURN(BAD)	[CORRELATED(termod)$\Rightarrow$GOOD] V [$\sim$CORRELATED(termod)$\Rightarrow$BAD]

	Description	Code	Formula
2.3	Each step in the scenario (step) should correlate optimally with a single design module (condition: CORRELATED), but it is acceptable for a step to correlate with two modules (condition: COR2MOD)	IF CORRELATED(step) THEN RETURN(GOOD) ELSE IF COR2MOD(step) 　　THEN RETURN(OK) 　　ELSE RETURN(BAD)	{CORRELATED(step) $\Rightarrow$ GOOD} V {[~ CORRELATED(step) $\wedge$ COR2MOD(step)] $\Rightarrow$ OK} V {[~CORRELATED(step) $\wedge$ ~ COR2MOD(step)] $\Rightarrow$ BAD}
2.4	Each scenario (scen) should correlate with anywhere from one to five new design modules (condition: COR1__5), but it can correlate with more if the modules are members of the same subtree under a single transaction center (condition: SUBTREE).	IF COR1__5(scen) THEN RETURN(GOOD) ELSE IF NOT CORRELATED(scen) 　　THEN RETURN(BAD) 　　ELSE IF SUBTREE(scen) 　　　　THEN RETURN(OK) 　　　　ELSE RETURN(BAD)	{COR1__5(scen) $\Rightarrow$ GOOD} V { ~ CORRELATED(scen) $\Rightarrow$ BAD} V {[~ COR1__5(scen) $\wedge$ SUBTREE(scen)] $\Rightarrow$ OK} V {[~ COR1__5(scen) $\wedge$ ~ SUBTREE(scen)] $\Rightarrow$ BAD}
2.5	Each scenario (scen) should correlate optimally as a vertical path through the design hierarchy (condition: VERPATH), but it is acceptable for it to correlate within the same subtree (condition: SUBTREE).	IF VERPATH(scen) THEN RETURN(GOOD) ELSE IF SUBTREE(scen) 　　THEN RETURN(OK) 　　ELSE RETURN(BAD)	{VERPATH(scen) $\Rightarrow$ GOOD} V {[~ VERPATH(scen) $\wedge$ SUBTREE(scen)] $\Rightarrow$ OK} V {[~ VERPATH(scen) $\wedge$ ~ SUBTREE(scen)] $\Rightarrow$ BAD}
2.6	The stimulus (stim) and response (resp) of the scenario must both be identifiable (condition: PRESENT) in the design and be on a continuous path (condition: CONTINUOUS).	IF PRESENT(stim,resp) THEN IF CONTINUOUS (stim,resp) 　　THEN RETURN(OK) 　　ELSE RETURN(BAD) ELSE RETURN(BAD)	{[PRESENT(stim,resp) $\wedge$ CONTINUOUS(stim,resp)] $\Rightarrow$ OK} V {[~ PRESENT(stim) V PRESENT(resp)] V ~ CONTINUOUS(stim,resp)] $\Rightarrow$ BAD}

Stimulus/ Response Elements		Requirement Paragraph	Design Component IDs
	XXXXX	XXXXX,XXXXX, XXXXX	XXXXXXXXX,XXXXXX XXXXXXXX
	XXXXX	XXXXX,XXXXX, XXXXX,XXXXX	XXXXXXX,XXXXXX, XXXXXXX,XXXXXX
	XXXXX	XXXXXX,XXXXXX	XXXXXXX,XXXXXX, XXXXXXX
	XXXXX		

Figure 8-10   Documenting requirements validation

provides the illumination or prompting for the engineer to make deeper inquiries into the consistency among the three views of the system. Thus, the stimuli are sure to be stronger and more numerous than if each product were reviewed individually. The success of the method does depend on a single person or a small tightly knit group of persons integrating the three views. It has been found that the most appropriate individual to play this role is the test engineer, who is a disinterested party with no vested interest in any of the products involved. By being the key personality in this process, the test engineer gains a much more informed understanding of the requirements, operational overview, and system design, an understanding that is not likely to accrue otherwise. The technique may also be effectively employed by a verification and validation contractor operating independently of the developer, if the customer has elected to retain such a contractor.

8.3.2   A PROJECT APPLICATION

The method just described has been recently employed in a pilot project, with positive results. The project was the development of a local area network communications system. The system provides narrowband and wideband communications services to a large number of users with devices as shown in Figure 8–11. The major architectural elements are a narrowband network, over which small to medium-sized files and messages are transmitted, and a wideband network, over which very large, dense files are transferred. All devices are connected to the narrowband network through concentrators, while only a subset of devices interface with the wide-band network. The system required the development of approximately $\frac{1}{4}$ million lines of embedded software for communications protocols, access controls, and network management.

The communications system and its applications utilize a very large data base. The applications devices make various queries on the data base, which then conveys files to the requesting devices over both networks. The applications devices then prepare intermediate and final products that are transmitted back to the data base over the commu-

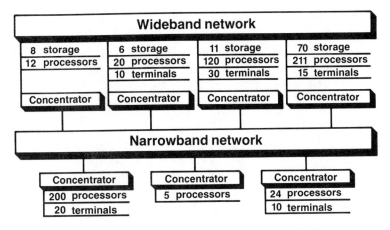

Figure 8-11 Communications system architecture

nications network for storage and then eventually distributed to remote locations over long haul lines.

The customer's requirements were documented in a specification issued at the beginning of the project which contained functional, performance, and interface requirements. The functional requirements were defined in the following areas:

- Network interface
- Narrowband data transfer
- Wideband data transfer
- Internetworking
- Access management
- Network management
- Electronic mail

The three system views that were derived from the customer's problem statement are described next along with an excerpt from the validation process.

The requirements view is contained in the data-flow diagram of Figure 8–12, which was derived directly from the customer's requirements specification. The bubbles represent each of the seven functional areas contained in the specification, and the arrows show the data that flow between the functions. Users of the system interface with the communications services through the network interface function. The access management function allows authorized users to have access to the system and denies access to unauthorized users. Authorized users can access narrowband transfer, wideband transfer, internetworking, and electronic mail services. The network management function sets up the physical network connections and monitors the performance of the system. The data-flow diagram adds a graphical clarity that is not present in the completely textual original specification. Both the specification and the data-flow diagram depict functions

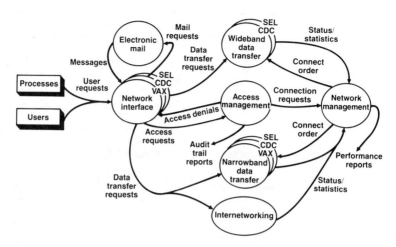

Figure 8-12   Communications system data flow

and interfaces, but say little about the sequences of functions or procedures that the system must support.

A section of the "natural" statement of the operations concept in the form of an input-process-output diagram is displayed in Figure 8-13. Illustrated are the procedures or scenarios of a user attempting to access the system and, if successful, selecting an applications function. These scenarios were abstracted onto the SVD shown in Figure 8-14. In the figure, stimulus-response elements L1.0, L1.1, and L2.0 represent the login scenarios shown originally in Figure 8-13. Three additional related scenarios are also illustrated on the SVD that define process accesses (L4.0, L4.1) and function termination (L3.0).

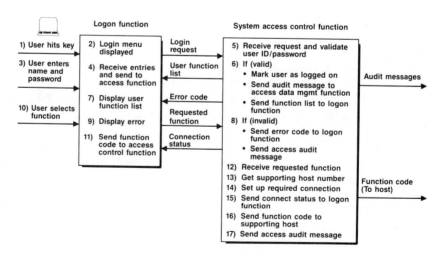

Figure 8-13   "Natural" statement of operations concept

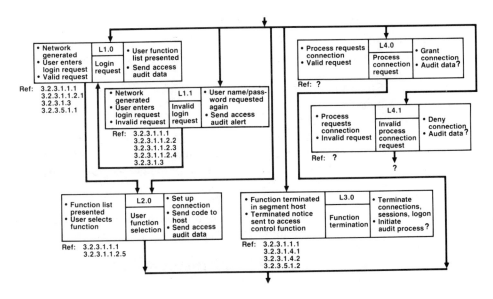

Figure 8-14 System access stimulus-response elements

The SVD in Figure 8–14 takes a snapshot after the first validation step that has correlated the requirements with the operations concept. The references below and to the left of each stimulus-response element identify the requirements paragraphs that supply the behavior demanded by each operational scenario. Several problems are immediately evident at this stage, as indicated by the question marks on the SVD. First, access requests for the automated processes given by elements L4.0 and L4.1 have no requirements antecedents in the specification. Second, there is no mention of the need to record audit message data for these elements, as well as for element L3.0. Finally, for element L4.1, the operations concept provides no clue as to what procedure is invoked when an unauthorized automatic process is denied access to the system. A list of inconsistencies uncovered as a result of the first two validation steps is shown in Figure 8–15.

Regarding the second validation step, each stimulus-response element is associated with the string, or thread, of design components that provides the behavior demanded by the stimulus-response scenario. The thread scenario for stimulus-response element L1.0, the login request, is detailed in Figure 8–16. The stimulus and response are indicated at the top; under each design component is a description of the function performed by the component at that step taken from the original operations concept notation in Figure 8–13. The boxes with dashed outlines indicate the use of a prepackaged communications service that is actually another thread in the system. The stimulus-response mapping of this scenario into the system access control software configuration item design structure is illustrated in Figure 8–17. The shaded boxes indicate the software modules shown in the scenario of Figure 8–16 that must be executed for this thread.

Thread L1.0
- One operations concept step correlates with four design modules.

Thread L2.0
- Cannot find design module that sends connection status to login module.

Threads L1.0, L2.0
- Module strings in design not in vertical slice, scattered horizontally—stimulus and response not continuous, or very complex design.
- Access control design batches audit messages, OPS concept shows event-by-event transfer.

Threads L4.0, L4.1
- Process accesses do not have antecedent in segment specification.
- No audit data requirements specified for process connection requests.
- What is next step after invalid process request is denied connection? Unspecified.

Thread L3.0
- Requirement para 3.2.3.1.4, logoff not in OPS concept material.
- Requirement para 3.2.3.1.4.1, fuzzy "appropriate audit process" and not in OPS concept.

Thread L1.1
- Requirement paras 3.2.3.1.1.2.3 and 3.2.3.1.1.2.4, what is OPS concept for handling >5 unsuccessful logons? Not mentioned at present.

Requirement para 3.2.3.1.1.1
- Correlated with three thread scenarios.

Figure 8-15 Multiple view analysis sample problems

These modules are scattered widely over the control structure, suggesting that the stimulus and response may not be connected as a continuous path. A continuous path would normally be represented by a straight vertical slice through the hierarchy. If present at all, stimulus-to-response continuity would have to be established by an elaborate chain of flags. This would indeed be a complex, error-prone design, and in fact it was reevaluated. The thread scenario for stimulus-response element L2.0, the user function selection, is mapped out in Figure 8–18. A clear problem was the inability to find the module in the design that performed the function of sending the connection status to the login module.

The errors mentioned in the preceding paragraph further establish the value of correlating different views in the same system. The figures demonstrate the power of graphical presentations to focus human attention on inconsistencies, omissions, and complexities that require correction or refinement. It is possible that even without this

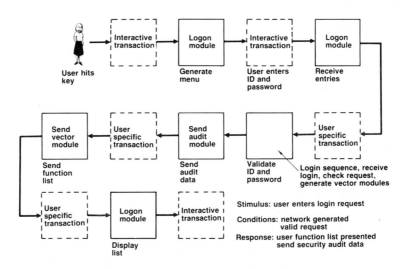

Figure 8-16 Login request, Thread L1.0

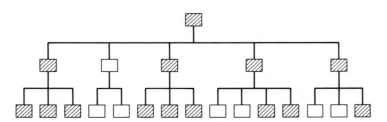

Figure 8-17 Mapping of thread into software design

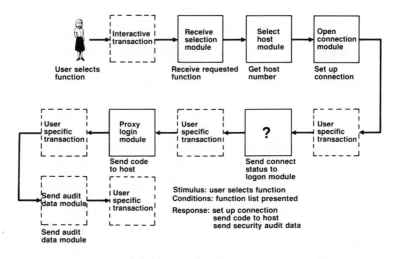

Figure 8-18 User function selection, Thread L2.0

technique some of the errors listed in Figure 8–15 would have been noticed, but probably not until some later time.

The system that was the subject of the pilot application in question consisted of approximately 25 thread scenarios. Overall, the average error detection rate using this paradigm was two errors per thread scenario. Conservatively speaking, this is twice the detection rate that would be expected using conventional review techniques.

There is an additional benefit to be obtained from the delineations of the thread scenarios such as those shown in Figures 8–16 and 8–18: each functional step denoted beneath the design component in the thread scenario is a detailed requirement allocated to that component; so the union of all the functional steps assigned to a design component over all the thread scenarios is an initial detailed requirements allocation to that design component.

Requirements validation performed by this technique runs in parallel with and is inseparable from the main requirements definition activity. It is an iterative process that considers the functions, interfaces, procedures, and top-level design as an experimental process. The act of reconciling the requirements, operations concept, and system design is intended to lead to deeper levels of insight into the system definition and thereby reveal inconsistencies that should be rectified. Ideally, if the technique is applied iteratively in concert with the generation of these three products, most major explicit errors should be avoided, and the main result is the building of confidence in the problem statement of the system. Note that the reconciliation process should be repeated each time a requirements change is proposed.

8.4
Validating Performance Requirements:
An Application

This section describes an application in the validation of performance requirements. The same communications system as in the functional requirements validation example in the previous section is used here to extend the case study. The reader should refer to the project application discussion in Section 8.3 for a description of the system application. The system was simulated using the AISIM tool explained in Section 8.2. The key performance attributes involve the time required to transfer certain types of files. This time is measured from the point of user request until receipt of the requested file by the user device. The simulation model is first outlined, followed by an explanation of how key design decisions were made based upon feedback from the simulation. Performance profiles for several file-transfer scenarios are illustrated.

The first step in modeling the communications system depicted in Figure 8–11 is to set up a model of the traffic that flows through this architecture. This entails understanding the applications that use the communciations system and characterizing the traffic produced by the applications. The traffic demands are then described in the model in terms of scheduling and data management requests. These, in turn, result in a detailed scenario of file/block transfers and virtual circuit control-handling signals to manage the transfers. The communications scenario is then overlaid on candidates for the communications architecture of the system. Alternatives in the architecture are then evaluated against performance parameters such as file-transfer response times.

A multiple-layer system traffic model that was constructed to simulate the said communications system is shown in Figure 8–19. The details of this model were filled in incrementally, proceeding top down using the AISIM tool. Both the system and the model are event driven: communications transfers, many of which occur in parallel, are actuated by the applications users of the communications system. This is indicated on the top level of the diagram. In performing an analysis of a support system such as a communications system or a data management system, the key thing to keep in mind is that *we must understand the larger system structure whose applications are the users of the support system.*

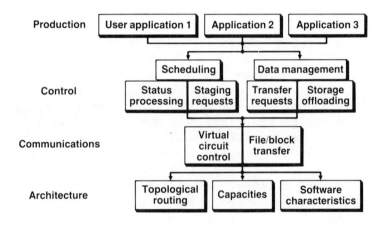

Figure 8-19 System traffic model

The results obtained from this simulation model supported a number of design decisions pertaining to the definition of the communications system. These decisions proceeded from a consideration of the fundamental architecture trade-offs to deliberations at a more detailed level. There were three major architectural alternatives:

1. Use a communications bus for both the wideband network and the narrowband network.
2. Use a communications switch for both networks.
3. Use a hybrid with a switch for the narrowband and a bus for the wideband. (In general, switches are better for networks with a large number of interconnections with small individual volume transfers. Buses are usually better for very large volume transfers with a small number of device interconnections.)

These three basic architectures were modeled (at the bottom layer of the model) and simulated against a benchmark scenario of applications usage over an eight-hour period. The response-time profiles for this scenario and for each of the three architectural

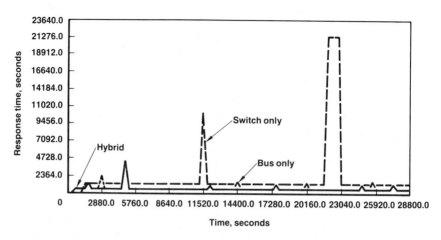

Figure 8-20 Somparative architectural analysis

alternatives produced directly by AISIM, are shown graphically in Figure 8–20. The switch-only configuration displays an inferior performance profile in comparison to the other two when considered over the eight-hour period. The hybrid alternative is superior in performance to the other eight-hour reference scenario, except for a short burst in the early part of the period. The hybrid configuration was selected because of its overall better performance and resiliency to burst communications traffic demand. This is the configuration shown in Figure 8–11.

Another key design decision for this system concerned the data-staging strategy, which the AISIM model helped analyze. There were essentially two choices for this strategy:

1. Provide data to users (operators or automated processes) on demand, or
2. Prestage the data on local data storage devices during an off-shift. (The data demand pattern was largely predictable a day in advance.)

Each of these choices entailed performance, hardware cost, and software cost considerations. A larger contingent of hardware is required for the on-demand option to meet a specific response-time requirement. The larger network size requires more software for network management and more complex protocols. Intuitively, it was clear that the prestaging option was the cheaper one. However, such an option is associated with a higher level of risk connected with the predictability of the data demand and the uncertainty of the availability of off-shift time for staging the data. It was therefore necessary to determine what the actual cost penalty was for the on-demand option, and weigh that against the risk. Some of the data for that decision were provided by the AISIM model and are assembled in Figure 8–21. The graph shows the dependencies among response time (left ordinate), hardware system size (abscissa), and overall relative cost (right ordinate). Two curves show the trade-off across this space for the prestage option and the on demand (nothing prestaged) option. For an average response time requirement of 420 seconds, it can be seen that the on-demand option required a system over four times

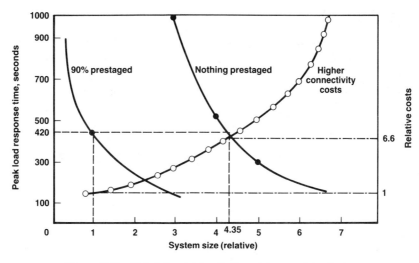

Figure 8-21   Simulation trade-off: Oversizing vs. data staging

as large in terms of hardware. The curve labeled ''higher connectivity costs'' integrates the cost of the larger system size with the added software costs and other per-device hardware costs. As shown, it costs 6.6 times as much to meet the 420-second requirement for the on-demand option as against the prestaged option. Because of this enormous cost differential, it was decided to accept the operational risk of the prestage option.

Another performance validation confirmed by the AISIM communications system model is presented in Figure 8-22. Here, the 130-second response-time requirement for a specific type of file transfer is evaluated. An eight-hour simulation reveals that this requirement is comfortably met. The graph is an actual direct output from AISIM.

A final trade-off decision concerns whether to place a transmission-control protocol–internetwork protocol (TCP/IP) in an applications host computer or in an

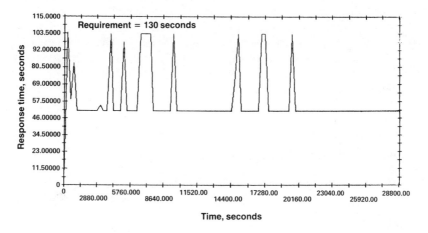

Figure 8-22   Simulation response-time validation

outboard network interface unit. It is plain that the protocol located in the applications host computer will take away some computation cycles from the application. Will it, however, hoard enough cycles to justify the cost of external network interface units? Each alternative was considered and evaluated using the AISIM model. A simplified representation of the modeling results are outlined in Figure 8–23. The graph shows the percentage of processing cycles consumed in the host that is required to support the protocols for each of the two cases. Surprisingly, it was revealed that up to 50 percent of the processing capacity of the host could be consumed in communications processing if the protocols were totally allocated to the host. This was not acceptable, and the decision was made to allocate the protocols to a network interface unit.

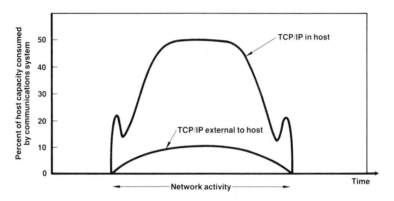

Figure 8-23　Software protocol trade-off simulation

The preceding discussion has illustrated how a relatively sophisticated simulation model supported major design decisions for an architectural definition of a major system. The results of models should, of course, not be blindly applied; there will always be residual questions concerning the adequacy of a model and the correctness of its implementation. Indeed, it may be necessary to validate a model. This is sometimes done, for example, by constructing two parallel models: a simulation model could be validated by an analytical model, and vice versa. A more general guideline is that the results generated by a model should more or less fall within the limits of engineering intuition. If they do not, then it is necessary to either find a defect in the model or revise the perception of the intuitive boundaries.

8.5
Prototyping to Validate Requirements and Design

Prototyping is a proof-of-concept technique directed toward the validation of requirements, the product design, and interfaces before making a commitment to the final product. It embodies all three quality techniques: engineering, reviewing, and testing.

The discussion here involves an example of prototyping as applied to the communications system of the previous two sections.

Prototyping is primarily a risk-reduction technique for large systems, particularly those with embedded applications, where much of the risk is embodied in the interfaces. The prerequisite for successful prototyping is, first, to recognize that risk is present, and second, to be willing to invest time and money to reduce that risk. The alternative is, of course, to be willing to accept the consequences of failure. Prototyping must result from a systematic analysis of the risks and must be regarded as just one of all the potential mechanisms that are available to reduce risk. Once prototyping is decided upon, we must be able to isolate the areas that are candidates for prototyping.

Prototyping reflects a deviation from the standard feed-forward life-cycle model (Figure 7-3). A revised life-cycle model is called the ''spiral'' life-cycle model. The spiral model, which readily incorporates prototyping into its formal foundation, is an iterative model as shown in Figure 8–24. One of its major features is a continual and iterative analysis of risks. A potential prototyping cycle follows each risk analysis iteration. It can readily be seen, then, how prototyping fits into the repetitive risk review process of the spiral life-cycle model. Each prototyping event leads to a more informed and more confident assessment of the requirements and design before final commitment to the product building cycle occurs. This is shown as the last iteration on the outside of the spiral. The spiral model illustrates the potential areas where prototyping can be useful in risk mitigation. It is unlikely that any given system will exploit prototyping in all of these areas; the actual employment of prototyping on any given project will depend on the specific risks involved, the schedule, the costs of prototyping, and the weighing of all of these against the consequences and costs of failure. There are two types of

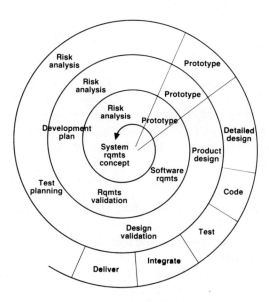

Figure 8-24 Spiral life-cycle model

prototypes: operational prototypes and analytical prototypes. An operational prototype can be a software element, a hardware element, and/or a procedure that operates in place of a real system element as part of a system. An analytical prototype, on the other hand, is an analogy to a system element. This can be a paper model, a simulation, an analysis, a straw man, a benchmark, a breadboard, or a brassboard. Such a prototype is constructed strictly for analytical purposes and does not operate in place of the actual system element in the system. In Section 8.4, the analytical prototype was in the form of a simulation model.

One practical example of operational prototyping in a large-scale system development uses the communication system diagrammed in Figure 8–11. The overall general risk area of this system is the narrowband network. This is because of the large number of devices that must be interconnected and also because the communication system is being built in parallel with the applications that actually use the communication capabilities. That is, we have a multiple-segment development, of which the communication system is just one segment. The primary thrust of the prototype is to provide early validation of the interface against the application segments of the system. The plan involves taking the prototype and providing it to the applications segment developers fairly early in the development cycle before full system integration takes place. Should there be major problems in either the interfaces or the functionality of the communication system, they should be revealed as a result of the early release of the communication prototype for the narrowband data transfer capabilities.

A key consideration in defining and developing the prototype is to isolate the candidate areas of the system by means of the SVD. The SVD provides a model of both the requirements and the operations concept of the system. The threads are natural operationally oriented partitions. One candidate thread is illustrated in Figure 8–25. This thread supports an intrasegment narrowband data transfer. Below the stimulus-response element that characterizes this transfer scenario are the specific requirements from the specification that are supported by the said scenario. By providing the capabilities of thread number 11 to the other segments that are in use, an early test of the interfaces to the system can be performed to stabilize those interfaces before the eventual final system integration. Also shown in Figure 8–25 is the expanded stimulus-to-response thread scenario. This scenario shows the linear sequence of events that must occur between the point where a host processor requests a file and the point where that file is transferred to and stored back in the requesting host. The functional steps involved in this transformation are shown beneath each block of the scenario, within which is indicated the physical components of the system, both hardware and software, that are executed serially to provide the transformation of the stimulus into the response. This thread scenario identifies the components that must be at least partially built to prototype thread number 11. It entails the reception of the host request by the narrow-band network through the hardware to a symmetrical version of the narrowband network CPCI that resides in the data-base processor. The data-base processor receives that request, initiates a file transfer through its file transfer service, and begins sending the narrowband data from the storage controller across the narrowband network hardware. The data are received incrementally by the narrowband network configuration item in the originating host. The host file transfer service then stores the file in its local storage.

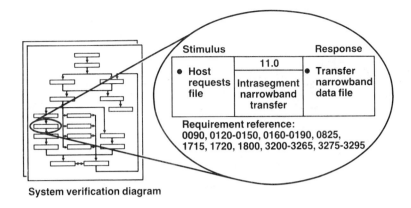

System verification diagram

Scenario:

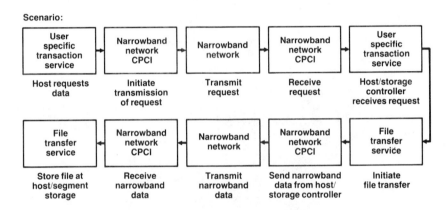

Figure 8-25 Isolating candidates for prototyping

The overall hardware and software configuration of the support package prototype that was eventually sent to the other developers is illustrated in Figure 8–26. The hardware elements of the prototype consist of several terminals, one interface frame for the narrowband network, and a processor that acts as both the originating host and the data-base storage controller. The software components consist of the narrowband network computer program configuration items and the network interfacing computer program configuration items. The latter includes the user-specific transaction service and the file transfer service that were indicated in the thread scenario of Figure 8–25.

The overall role played by the support package prototype in the total communication system development plan is illustrated in Figure 8–27. Each of the circles indicates a thread completion point; the squares consist of the aggregation of threads into builds. The support package prototype consists totally of early versions of threads 11, 7, 10, and 12. These threads contain a significant portion of a narrowband transfer capability, which is the major area of risk that was identified in the system. The support package provided an early interface demonstration in conjunction with the application segments of the system. The objective, again, was to stabilize a potentially risky interface. The

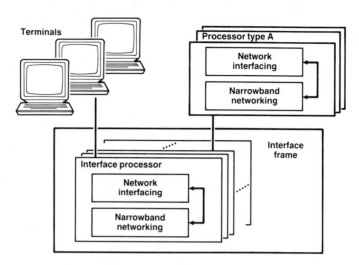

Figure 8-26 Support package prototype

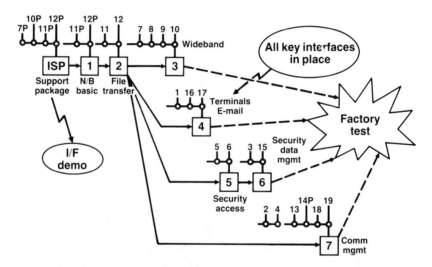

Figure 8-27 Integration plan based on thread scenario

order of the buildup was to build the major interfaces of the system first. This began with the narrowband capability in the support package build and the narrowband basic build, and then progressed into the file transfer build and the wideband interface build. The next build implemented the electronic mail and terminal interface functions. At build number 4, a logically complete system consisting of all the major interfaces of the communication system was in place. The remaining builds, 5 through 7, and their associated threads fleshed out the skeleton of the system.

After the completion of all builds, the communication system was integrated in the factory, tested, and then sent to the operational site for integration with the other application segments. The support package prototype was provided to the developers of the other application segments at their factories for an early integration of the narrow-band communications interface, before shipment of all segments to the operational site. Problems that developed at the operational site during the integration process would be more complex and expensive to correct in contrast to the discovery and rectification of these problems before on-site integration. The building and provision of the prototype to the other developers is a major risk-avoidance step that leads to an eventual successful integration.

The example just discussed has provided an illustration of how prototyping is effectively used as a risk-mitigation device. In this particular case, the perceived risk involved the interfacing of a complex system among a number of separate development contractors. In general, prototyping should be directed at the perceived risk on any given system. For large embedded system applications, this is often, but not always, concentrated at the interface points of the system. It is also possible that major risks can be present in regard to performance and functionality.

To recount, the success of a prototyping effort depends upon identifying the areas where risk is present, isolating those areas that are candidates for prototyping, and developing prototypes for them. The development of a prototype should at least be a controlled, informal process, although there may be times when a totally formal development process is called for. Feedback from the prototype, particularly if problems are uncovered, should lead to a refined statement of the requirements and possibly the design.

8.6
Levels of Application for Quality

The requirements and design validation activities that should be applied to achieve each discrete level of quality—not an issue, average, good, and excellent—are summarized in Table 8–2. There are basically three ''tracks'' of activities: (1) functional requirements and design validation, (2) performance validation using modeling or simulation, and (3) prototyping. Each track escalates in intensity by quality level.

The level of activity at which quality is not an issue is characterized by informality. Functional requirements are traced to design components, but are generally reported upon only verbally. Simulation and modeling may include modeling of algorithms if algorithm performance is an issue.

At the level of average quality, function requirements are traced to design and documented in a written report. Performance requirements may be validated analytically with a ''pencil-and-paper'' analysis. Further algorithm modeling may also be relevant.

A major escalation takes place at the level of good quality. Functional requirements are traced into the design using stimulus-response threads, and system performance is modeled with an executable simulation. Test cases are created by a simulation of input scenarios, and key risk areas become candidates for prototyping.

TABLE 8-2 REQUIREMENTS/DESIGN VALIDATION
ACTIVITIES BY QUALITY LEVEL

Quality level	Requirements/design validation activities
Not an issue	• informal/verbal traceability analysis • algorithm modeling
Average	• traditional requirements/design traceability (documented) • "pencil-and-paper" performance modeling
Good	• stimulus-response analysis with system verification diagram • moderate system performance simulation • input scenario simulation for test cases • prototype critical areas
Excellent	• detailed stimulus-response analysis • detailed system performance simulation • detailed input scenario simulation for test cases • prototype more critical areas

The same set of activities is performed at the level of excellent quality, except more detailedly and intensely.

It should be recognized that these are general guidelines: each system development may have characteristics that will require deviations.

Employing Independent Verification and Validation

9.1
Background and Origins of IV&V

Independent verification and validation is employed when added systematic insurance for the functioning and performance of the system is required. An independent agent, other than the developer, applies reviews and/or testing to further assess the product of the developer.

IV&V is usually said to have arisen in the early days of the U.S. Air Force's Space and Missile Systems Organization, when it was applied to missile software, space vehicle launches, and activation and control of nuclear weapons and guidance systems. The IV&V process evaluates critical and complex software, not necessarily to avoid all errors, but to eliminate, with a high degree of certainty, those errors that can have catastrophic results. Such results might be loss of life or mission failure, or even less compelling repercussions such as equipment damage or significant economic loss. The process should be conducted with disinterest in the outcome of the validation, i.e., the agent performing the validation should have no stake in the results and should be free of influence from those who do.

We generally think of IV&V as involving the use of an independent contractor only. However, there are several valid possibilities for IV&V:

- Use of an independent testing organization
- Customer performs the validation
- Use of an independent contractor

An independent testing organization centralizes the testing function in an organization that is separate from the developers. The testing organization still reports to the same program manager as the developing organization, but a high degree of independence is achieved. The scope of this organization is limited to testing. This has both advantages and disadvantages: the independent test organization is probably the lowest cost of these three options; this is linked to the limited scope of its activity. This approach by itself is consistent with the needs of low to medium risk programs. The liability of the approach is that both development and testing are under the control of the same contractor and program manager. There can be pressures to disguise embarrassing discoveries.

When the customer performs the validation, he or she assumes all responsibility for IV&V. This also has its advantages and disadvantages. On the one hand, it reduces the number of contracts that have to be monitored as compared to the use of an independent contractor. Also, there is better coordination with the user, because the customer is usually closer to the user than in either of the other two kinds of IV&V. On the other hand, it may be difficult for the customer to staff the verification and validation function: most customers, at least in the government community, find it much easier to obtain financial resources for a verification and validation function than to acquire scarce personnel resources.

The employment of an independent contractor to perform verification and validation overcomes the disadvantages of the other approaches. The independent contractor can be used for the entire life cycle of the system, or only a portion of it. The contractor is not at all involved with the development activity. Independent contractors are generally used for larger systems possibly involving high technology, and with a probable high cost of failure should problems develop in the deployment of the system. Of the three IV&V options, this can be the highest in cost. By way of compensation, it has the highest degree of commitment and scope and is also the most objective of the three. It is this approach that is generally referred to when the term *independent verification and validation* is mentioned.

Independent verification and validation is the third line of defense of software quality. The first two lines are reviews and testing performed by the developing contractor. IV&V entails attributes of both reviews and testing.

The following sections will explain the levels of application of independent verification and validation activities as a function of quality, the profile of an IV&V organization, a framework for determining the need for independent verification and validation, and a recount of an unsuccessful IV&V effort.

9.2
Levels of Application for Quality

The IV&V effort associated with the four levels of quality is as follows (see also Figure 9-1):

- Not an issue—No IV&V effort.
- Average—System engineering support is provided to the customer for a constructive critique of the developer's products, including identification and recommendation of solutions to problems.
- Good—A more extensive effort is maintained over the development cycle, with emphasis on analysis and testing of critical areas.
- Excellent—A full life-cycle parallel analysis is provided, including system-level testing and integration.

Each of the quality levels is, of course, associated with an increased level of cost.

Requirements	Design	Construct	Test/Integration
● Prepare IV&V management plan	● Review design specifications	● Issue IV&V test plan for selected functions	● Test selected functions
● Review requirements specifications	● Issue deficiency reports	● Issue full IV&V test plan	● Evaluate critical test results
● Document review comments	● Attend design reviews	● Issue code status report	● Issue IV&V test report
● Attend design reviews	● Spot-check critical design areas		● Perform system test
● Independently analyze requirements	● Evaluate developer's test program		● Evaluate system test result
	● Confirm overall design adequacy		● Integrate products
			● Conduct stress tests

Average quality

Good quality

Excellent quality

Figure 9-1 Independent verification and validation activities.

The IV&V activity for the average quality level is essentially a passive review of the developer's products. This occurs mainly during the requirements and design phases of the life cycle. The product of the effort is usually a set of discrepancy reports and recommendations for the solution to any major problems detected during the review process.

For the good quality level, the scope of the IV&V expands significantly, including all of the same efforts at the average level plus additional activity. Initially, it entails the independent analysis of requirements in particular critical areas. The aim is to concentrate on critical areas that have the most potential for mission failure, equipment damage, or economic loss. This emphasis extends into the design phase, where there are checks on critical design areas. Also included is an evaluation of the developer's test program in these areas. During the coding or construction phase of the project, the IV&V contractor will develop a test plan for selected critical functions. During the testing and integration phase, the IV&V contractor will manage and execute the testing of those functions selected, evaluate the test results in those areas, and issue an IV&V test report.

For the excellent quality level, an IV&V contractor is employed over the entire development cycle. The contractor performs an analysis of the development activities parallel to that of the developer. This includes an independent analysis of the full requirements set, a confirmation of the overall design adequacy, and an evaluation of the developer's test program. At the excellent level, the IV&V contractor is more involved with testing than at any of the other levels. Detailed test plans and procedures are developed, and during the coding phase the code will be incrementally analyzed against the quality requirements recorded in the requirements specifications. The IV&V contractor will usually perform most of the system-level testing and integration, especially if more than one developer is involved. The IV&V contractor will be responsible for the execution of the integration and system test and will evaluate the test results. A test report will be issued by the IV&V contractor. The integration and system testing will emphasize off-nominal and stress testing.

9.3
Profile of an IV&V Organization

The activities performed by an IV&V organization can be quite challenging, requiring[1]

1. Significant experience
2. A base of personnel skilled in the technology required
3. A repertoire of qualified and transferable tools

In addition, the organization should not be a threat to the development contractor.

A good IV&V contractor should thus have independent verification and validation as a major business concern, together with priority management attention to this area. On any particular project, the IV&V agent should not be a natural competitor of the

---

[1]*Management Guide for Independent Verification and Validation (IV&V)* (Los Angeles: U. S. Air Force Space Division, 1980), p. 4–3.

development contractor. This is important in order to maintain the integrity of the IV&V process: there should be absolutely no reason for the IV&V contractor to make the developer appear inept. Sometimes, for very large system development efforts, only a very large organization is capable of performing IV&V. In that case, when another large organization is the developer, it may be impossible for it not to perceive the IV&V contractor as a threat.

There is a tendency for small and medium-sized companies to emphasize IV&V as a specialty. There is also a tendency for government organizations to set aside IV&V contracts exclusively for these small and medium-sized companies. The use of these specialty houses has both advantages and disadvantages for any given project. On the positive side, a smaller company is likely to be able to perform the work with a lower overhead than a larger company. Smaller companies are also likely to be able to approach the job with a higher degree of commitment and responsiveness because an individual contract represents a higher percentage of their business base. Smaller companies are also likely to be able to interface more naturally and effectively with the developer, being less likely to be a threat or competitor to the developer than larger companies are. On the negative side, small companies, by their very nature, have resource limitations and may not be able to respond to unanticipated demands, particularly if major problems develop. Also, small companies may have only a small inventory of tools available because of their inability to invest heavily in this area. Furthermore, the stability of small companies is always of some concern. Finally, the breadth of expertise as regards large systems may be somewhat limited in a small company because its business is not primarily in that area. In any given situation, these characteristics represent a trade-off that has to be considered in contracting for IV&V.

A typical allocation of IV&V activities, listed by function and percentage, is as follows:[2]

- Requirements analysis, 12–17%
- Design analysis, 14–18%
- Code analysis, 18–22%
- Testing, 18–26%
- Tool preparation, 2–15%
- Management and reporting, 15–25%

This distribution is by no means the same profile that one would expect for a development contract. Particularly noteworthy is the high percentage of management reporting, 15–25 percent. In a development contract, this percentage would be in the range of perhaps 8–15 percent. This general profile of the IV&V job is composed of a significant amount of problem reporting, coordination of plans and schedules, adjudication of problems, and coordination meetings. It is thus a management-intensive task. Of course, this is precisely the intent of the customer in employing an IV&V contractor—to have the contractor assist in the management of the program.

[2]R. Dean Hartwick, "Software Verification and Validation," in *Software Management: Implementation and Results* (Los Angeles: AIAA, TMSA, DPMA, 1978), p. 80.

The relationship of the IV&V contractor to the other participants in the software project is depicted in Figure 9-2. The IV&V agent is employed in parallel with the software developer, both being managed by the customer. Although the IV&V contractor interacts with the developers on an informal level, formal communication of evaluation results is the prime objective and is conveyed through the customer and with the customer's approval. The activities of the IV&V contractor are most intense at the beginning and end of the development cycle; the mid-part of the cycle is characterized mainly by the passive review process.

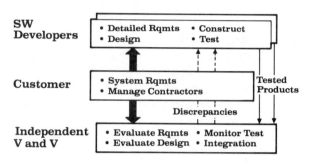

Figure 9-2 Relationships of IV&V contractor.

At the beginning of the program, the IV&V contractor will assist the customer in developing the system requirements, and perhaps even the requirements specification. The IV&V contractor will generally run the system requirements reviews and prepare the system-level-interface control document and the integration and test plan. At the end of the life cycle, the IV&V contractor will manage the integration of the products of all the software developers and will effect the planning, execution, and analysis of the system tests. During the mid-part of the development process, the IV&V contractor concentrates on reviewing the developer's products; the detailed planning of integration and system testing also occurs during this period.

9.4
Determination of Need for IV&V

Independent verification and validation should be considered when software errors could result in loss of life, injury, mission failure, damage of equipment, or wasted economic resources. This section establishes a framework for quantitatively evaluating the need for independent verification and validation. The method explained here characterizes this need over a spectrum of four discrete levels. Each of these levels is directly analogous to the four levels of quality. This technique is adapted from the methodology promulgated by the U.S. Air Force Space Division[3]. The method consists of evaluating the probability of occurrence of a number of criticality factors, each of which is in turn

---

[3]*Management Guide for Independent Verification and Validation (IV&V)*, Appendix I.

analyzed to predict what would happen should a failure occur within the criticality factor. The major criticality factors are loss of life, mission failure, equipment damage, and economic impact. Other such factors are safety, interface complexity, technical complexity, required technical innovation, real-time properties of the system, software size, scope of use, and security implications. Not all of these factors will be pertinent to every system, and only those criticality factors important to a given project are evaluated.

Four IV&V levels are considered in the evaluation: no need, C, B, and A. These are directly analogous to the four required quality levels. The scoring mechanism that determines the IV&V level is illustrated in Figure 9-3. Each criticality factor is rated and aggregated with other factors to produce an IV&V value ranging from 0 through 12. Rule-of-thumb guidelines for correlating score with IV&V level are shown; the scoring involves the cross-product of the probability of occurrence with the impact of failure for each criticality factor. The probability of occurrence is selected from four discrete values (impossible to frequent) and is quantitatively expressed as an integer from 0 to 3. The criticality class, or impact of failure, ranges from negligible to catastrophic. An integer value from 1 through 4 is correspondingly assigned. The cross-product of the two factors gives the IV&V value for each criticality factor.

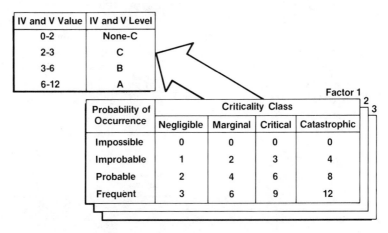

IV and V Value	IV and V Level
0-2	None-C
2-3	C
3-6	B
6-12	A

Probability of Occurrence	Criticality Class			
	Negligible	Marginal	Critical	Catastrophic
Impossible	0	0	0	0
Improbable	1	2	3	4
Probable	2	4	6	8
Frequent	3	6	9	12

Figure 9-3 Determination of need for IV&V.

Next, the analysis is extended by scoring the pertinent factors against the major components of the system. First, an IV&V value is computed for each of the system components; Figure 9-4 shows an example in which four criticality factors have been scored against each of the subsystems of a missile flight control system. Each subsystem is then evaluated for each criticality factor, and the total score is summed and then averaged to produce a net IV&V value for each subsystem. This IV&V value is then used to compute an IV&V level for each subsystem based upon the guidelines in Figure 9-3. Once an IV&V level is obtained from this analysis, Figure 9-1 can be consulted to delineate the specific activities that are nominally appropriate for that level.

Factor / Subsystem	Loss of Life	Mission Failure	Equipment Damage	Economy Impact	Total Score	IV&V Value
Ground checkout	4	6	8	6	24	6
Launch	8	8	8	8	32	8
In-flight operation	0	8	8	8	24	6
Command Control	4	6	8	8	26	6.5
Telemetry	0	6	6	8	20	5
Ground data reduction	0	2	2	2	6	1.5

Figure 9-4   IV&V needs analysis example.

Averaging across the factors is not the only way of determining the net score. A more sophisticated evaluation would assign weights to each of the factors. As an additional embellishment, IV&V need might also be determined for detailed components below the subsystem level.

As Figure 9–3 shows, a score from 0 to 2 usually requires no IV&V; a score of 2 to 3 merits minimum IV&V to attain an average level of quality; a score of 3 to 6 suggests more IV&V activity needed for a good level of quality; and a score of 6 to 12 merits full life-cycle verification and validation, commensurate with an excellent level of quality.

The IV&V values obtained from this technique are also used to initially assess IV&V costs at a macroscopic level. A rule of thumb for determining this cost is displayed in Figure 9–5, which is derived from data accumulated by the U.S. Air Force.[4] The IV&V value for a system component is registered on the curve and then extended to the ordinate to estimate the IV&V cost, which is expressed as a percentage of the devel-

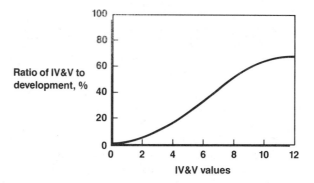

Figure 9-5   IV&V/development relative effort.

[4]*Management Guide for Independent Verification and Validation (IV&V)*, Appendix I.

opment cost. For example, the IV&V needed to achieve an excellent level of quality would require an additional 65 to 70 percent of the development costs. On the other hand, a somewhat less critical component requiring only an average level of quality (with an IV&V value of 3) might cost only 10 percent of the development costs. The methodology thus provides a mechanism for isolating those components of the system requiring high levels of IV&V from those requiring lower levels.

The general method outlined in this section brings rigor to the analysis of need for independent verification and validation. It clearly is no substitute for sound engineering and management judgement. It does provide a quantitative and objective framework for that judgement to be applied.

9.5
An Unsuccessful Application of IV&V

Independent verification and validation is not necessarily appropriate for every project or every organization. The following material briefly documents an instructive failure of an experimental application of IV&V that bears this assertion out.

IV&V was experimentally applied to two satellite command and control system projects at Goddard Space Flight Center. The results of these projects were compared with those of two past projects of a very similar nature where IV&V was not performed.[5] The evaluation was based on six parameters: the number of ambiguities and misinterpretations in the requirements, number of design flaws, cost of system and acceptance testing, early discovery of faults, early operations and error rates, and overall cost of the project.

The results of the comparison are summarized in Figure 9–5. At best, they were

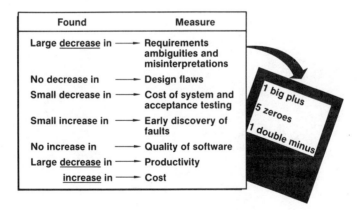

Figure 9-6   Results of IV&V experiment.

[5]Jerry Page, ''Methodology Evaluation: Effects of Independent Verification and Integration on One Class of Application,'' (NASA/GSFC Sixth Annual Software Engineering Workshop, unpublished notes, 1983).

mixed. The one major positive finding was a large decrease in ambiguities and misinterpretations in the requirements. There was little difference between the two sets of projects in number of design flaws, cost of system and acceptance testing, early discovery of faults, and quality of the software (operations and maintenance error rates). A major negative finding was an 85 percent higher cost for the projects that used IV&V. This was an unacceptable result because the expectation was that the use of IV&V would result in an improvement in all of these categories.

Some further explanation is illuminating. The second set of projects represented the first applications of IV&V in the given environment. The people involved were inexperienced in the applicable technology, and the systems were relatively small. From the failure, Goddard staff learned that if IV&V is to be effective at all, it will be so only for larger systems that require somewhat higher levels of reliability.

A lesson learned from this application is that instant success should not be expected. Key factors in establishing success are proper project analysis and the use of an organization experienced in IV&V.

Special Techniques for Achieving Exceptional Quality

Thus far, we have centered on four levels of quality: not an issue, average, good, and excellent. Excellent quality is normally required only in exceptional circumstances, such as nuclear power station control, air traffic control, space flights, patient monitoring systems, and electronic banking applications. The quality-related characteristics of these systems are that failures can lead to loss of life, severe financial loss, property damage, liability, and the like. The exceptional nature of failures in these systems demands exceptional techniques to prevent them. Prominent among these techniques are the following:

Correctness proofs, a mathematical technique for proving the correct functional content of software design and/or implementation.

Multi-version software, a multiple development approach designed to ameliorate the effects of latent design defects.

Software-reliability modeling, a software reliability prediction technique based on historical failure data that aids in determining when enough effort has been expended in testing.

Software fault tree analysis, an analytical technique to uncover and provide recovery for software-caused events that could lead to a system-level safety hazard.

10.1
Correctness Proofs

In the view of some analysts, the correctness of software programs can be certified in a static manner by using mathematical proofs of correctness, also called program proofs. The proof concept employs the program source statements to prove mathematical theorems about program behavior. The expected behavior is characterized by a set of assertions which reflect the intentions of the designers with respect to the relationships of variables at the beginning, end, and, optionally, intermediate points of the program. The annotated program can be converted into a theorem and the theorem proved.

Correctness proofs are intended to verify programs on a more global foundation than testing, which checks the performance of programs on the limited basis of a set of sample test data. Among the major obstacles that limit the use of these proof techniques are the difficulties in developing the assertions that are to be proved and the length of the computations involved.

The major application of correctness proofs is in the verification of data protection mechanisms to safeguard confidential data. The major goal of correctness proofs is to demonstrate the consistency between the formal specification of a security model and its design and implementation. A typical security model consists of a set of rules to determine whether a particular subject should be given access to a particular object.[1] This is important when a system is holding information at various levels of security classification.

Correctness proofs offer support for the correctness and integrity of the system. Correctness deals with the extent to which the design and implementation conform to the stated requirements as articulated by the assertions in the proof. The proofs themselves directly address the completeness, consistency, and traceability criteria associated with the given correctness factor. Integrity deals with security against either overt or covert access to programs or data bases and is associated with the single criterion of system accessibility, which connotes complete control over who, when, what, and how data and software are accessed from either a user or application system.

Several first-generation automated verification environments have been developed to aid in mathematical proofs. The most prominent are:

Gypsy, developed at the University of Texas.

Hierarchical Development Methodology (HDM), developed at Stanford Research Institute.

Ina Jo, developed by System Development Corporation.

AFFIRM, developed by the University of Southern California.

[1]Maureen Cheheyl, Morrie Glasser, George A. Huff, and Jonathan K. Millen, ''Verifying Security,'' *Computing Surveys*, Vol. 13, No. 3, September 1981, pp. 282–283.

While these systems differ markedly in approach and style, components common to all of them can be identified. These components include a specification language processor, a verification condition generator, and a theorem prover.[2] Yet, even with these automated support environments, a current practical limit on the volume of code verified is on the order of hundreds of source lines. Furthermore, devising proofs and using the related tools require a great degree of mathematical expertise.[3]

More recent, second-generation views of verification environments concentrate more on an integrated overall development process. The interactive transformational paradigm designed by Applebaum and Keeton-Williams is one example.[4] This system centers around a knowledge-based or expert system approach, suggesting the features of ''automatic programming.'' Second-generation approaches are intended for less skilled users on large-scale problems involving much larger volumes of code. These systems are in their infancy at present, and their utility remains to be demonstrated.

10.2
Multiversion Software

The goal of multiversion software is very high reliability. Multiversion software is especially useful in applications in which results may lead to loss of life, property damage, or liability—for example, electronic banking transactions, nuclear power control, missile guidance, and air traffic control. The approach is to develop more than one version of the same program to minimize the detrimental effect on reliability of latent defects.

In the hardware world, a technique called triple modular redundancy (TMR) is used to build very high-reliability hardware systems. Using this technique, a hardware function is replicated three times, performing identically on identical inputs. A voter function then makes a majority decision, based on the outputs from the three replicated functions, whether to produce a final output. If one of the hardware functions has failed, TMR will still produce a correct result. The TMR technique is illustrated in Figure 10-1.

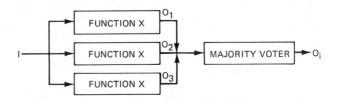

Figure 10-1 Hardware TMR (triple modular redundancy).

[2]Cheheyl et al., p. 280.
[3]Cheheyl et al., p. 336.
[4]C. H. Applebaum and J. Keeton-Williams, *PVS-Design for a Practical Verification System*, MITRE Corp., MTR 8936, May 1983.

Triple modular redundancy achieves its very high reliability through the use of fault tolerance (i.e., anomaly management). In the hardware world, where components wear out over time, TMR will be able to recover without failure when one of the three components fails.

Multiversion software (also known as n-version programming) is the software analog of TMR. Although software does not wear out over time, multiversion software can be used to mask the effect of latent design defects. A direct analog of TMR would have three identical programs (perhaps on three different machines) executing on the same inputs and a majority voter to decide on the output. Since the defects would be identical in the three replicated programs, erroneous outputs would also be identical. This technique is not of much use in software because the voter would vote for the majority even when the majority was in error. So instead, multiversion software is the *independent development* of multiple versions of the same program.

It has been suggested that using a single requirements specification, n versions of a program (for TMR, $n = 3$) developed by n independent programming teams will result in n independent sets of latent design defects. Thus, when the n programs operate on the same input, it is statistically unlikely that all of them will produce the same erroneous output. Hence, this modified software approach to TMR should result in more reliable software than the use of only one program.

There are two basic strategies for using and voting on the independently developed, multiple versions of software:

1. *Recovery blocks.* (See "System Structure for Software Fault Tolerance," B. Randell, *IEEE Transactions of Software Engineering*, Vol. SE-1, June 1975.)

2. *N-version programming.* (See "The N-version Approach to Fault Tolerant Software," A. Avizienis, *IEEE Transactions of Software Engineering*, Vol. SE-11, No. 12, December 1985.)

The basic flow in the recovery block technique is shown in Figure 10–2 for $n = 3$. Before processing begins, the state of the machine is saved. Then, given input I, program version number 1 is executed to produce output O_1. Output O_1 is then subjected to an acceptance test. If it is accepted, processing is completed for this function. Otherwise, version 1 is in error, the starting state of the machine is restored, version 2 of the

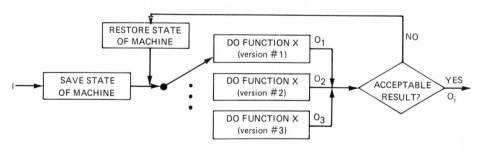

Figure 10-2 Multiversion programming using recovery block approach.

program is executed using input I, and output O_2 is subjected to an acceptance test. The process continues until an acceptable result occurs. This type of multiversion programming is especially suited to applications in which different algorithms are needed depending on the domain of input. It is important to note that the logic used to determine the acceptability of the result is unique with respect to a given application.

The basic flow for *n*-version programming is shown in Figure 10–3 for $n = 3$. As in TMR for hardware, all versions of the program are executed using input I and produce outputs O_1, O_2, and O_3. The different outputs are subjected to a consensus voter which determines the final outcome. The voter can use application-independent logic to choose among its inputs (e.g., majority rules).

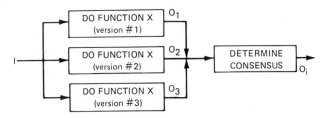

Figure 10-3 Multiversion programming using NVP approach.

Two requirements for *n*-version programming to be effective are:

1. A complete and accurate requirements specification must be available at the beginning of the programming effort.
2. The *n* versions of the design efforts must be functionally and physically independent.

One caveat in using this technique is that it has not been proven that independent design teams will in fact produce statistically independent defects. Indeed, as reported in one journal article,[5] certain intellectually difficult problems will result in similar defects no matter how independent the program designs are.

10.3
Software Reliability Modeling

The goal of software reliability modeling is to determine whether more development or testing of a program is needed to achieve an acceptable level of reliability. (The reliability of a program is the probability that the program will operate correctly in a specified environment for a specified period of time.) As in multiversion software, applica-

[5]J. C. Knight and N. G. Leveson, "An Experimental Evaluation of the Assumption of Independence in Multiversion Programming," *IEEE Transactions in Software Engineering*, Vol. SE-12, No. 1, January 1986, pp. 96–109.

tions especially suited to reliability modeling are those in which loss of life, property damage, or liability are at stake. However, any software that may require "proof" of reliability can benefit from this technique. The approach used is to predict the reliability of the software based on data regarding past failures.

Software reliability modeling originated out of hardware reliability modeling. In hardware, where components are manufactured in quantity and warranted for reliability (i.e., MTBF), reliability modeling involves the arithmetic product of the probability of correct operation of all components in a system to determine the overall system MTBF. Unacceptable reliability is dealt with by choosing higher reliability components or using exotic techniques such as TMR.

But software does not wear out like hardware, so the MTBF analogy is not applicable. However, software does have latent design defects which can cause a system to fail. Even though it is impossible to know how many defects are remaining in a program that could lead to a failure, the theory behind reliability modeling is that the MTBF caused by latent design defects can be predicted. Unacceptable software MTBF is dealt with by testing further or redesigning.

There are three basic types of reliability metrics used for modeling:

1. Time between observed failures
2. Observed failure counting
3. Fault seeding

The metric for time between observed failures is based on the time elapsed between two failures. Given the failure history for n failures, this type of metric predicts when failure $n + 1$ will occur. Testing and redesigning can be stopped when the time interval between failures n and $n + 1$ reaches an acceptably high value.

The metric for observed failure counting is based on the number of failures occurring during a fixed interval of time. Testing and redesigning can be stopped when the cumulative number of observed failures occurring during the given interval has reached an acceptably low value.

The metric for fault seeding is based on predicting the number of faults remaining in a program. Some number of faults, say N, are seeded (purposefully inserted) in a program, and tests are then run to validate the program. The tests will result in finding n seeded faults and m indigenous faults. Given the ratio N/n of seeded faults to seeded faults found, the theory asserts that we can say something about the ratio M/m of indigenous faults predicted to indigenous faults found. Testing and redesigning can be stopped when M becomes acceptably small.

The interested reader is referred to the following sources:

1. *IEEE Transactions on Software Engineering*, Volumes SE-11, Number 12 (December 1985) and SE-12, Number 1 (January 1986).

2. *Draft IEEE Standard P982*, *Software Reliability Modeling*, June 1985.

3. P. Y. Chan and B. Littlewood, *Parametric Spline Approach to Adaptive Reliability Modeling*, Centre for Software Reliability, The City University, Northampton Square, London, ECIV OHB, U.K.

The first reference is to two special issues of the *IEEE Transactions on Software Engineering* that deal exclusively with software reliability. The second reference contains some 40 different reliability metrics that can be used for reliability modeling. The third reference is given as an aid for matching candidate reliability metrics to a specific application, since the reliability of any given metric is dependent on the application.

10.4
Software Fault Tree Analysis

Software fault tree analysis is one of many special techniques dealing with the need for safe software (see [6] for a more complete treatment). The goal of software fault tree analysis is to verify that there are no defects that could lead to a safety hazard and to pinpoint software parts to give special attention to during development and testing to avoid hazardous conditions. Fault tree analysis is especially useful in applications where a system failure could lead to loss of life, property damage, or liability, such as in patient monitoring systems, air traffic control, nuclear power station control, and manned space flights. The approach is analytical, tracing system hazards backwards through program logic to find those software conditions that could cause or avoid the hazards.

Software fault tree analysis fits into the following overall safety hazard analysis procedure:

1. Identify the system hazards that are to be avoided.

2. Given the system hazards, determine the software-functional hazards that could lead to a system hazard—for example:

    Failure to perform a required function

    Performing a function that is not required

    Timing or sequencing problems

    Failure to recognize or correct a hazardous condition

    Producing the wrong response to a hazardous condition

3. For each software-functional hazard, use fault tree analysis to work backwards through the program logic to determine the set of possible causes of that hazard, or show that they cannot be caused by the logic of the software.

4. Use the results of the analysis to guide further design, pinpoint critical functions and test cases for them, guide the placement and content of run-time checks, and determine the conditions under which fail-safe procedures should be initiated.

Fault tree analysis gets its name from the logic diagrams that it employs. At the root of the tree is the hazard to be avoided. The branches that emanate from the root go out to those software conditions immediately preceding the hazard that could lead to it.

[6] N. G. Leveson, "Software Safety: What, Why, and How," *ACM Computing Surveys*, Vol. 18, No. 2, June 1986, pp. 125–163.

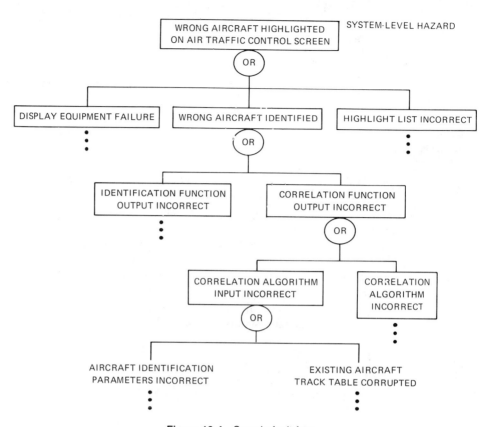

Figure 10-4 Sample fault free.

These branches may be connected to the root by either an AND node (all branch conditions must be present to cause the hazard) or an OR node (any branch condition can cause the hazard). Each second-level condition is then resolved into third-level conditions in the same manner, and so on. The final diagram is a tree-like structure of conditions that are necessary to cause the system-level hazard. At the bottommost level, the potential software causes of system-level hazards will have been identified. An example of a software fault tree is shown in Figure 10–4.

Testing

_____

11.1
Where Testing Fits In

Each tier of the three-tier quality model citing engineering, reviewing, and testing represents activities that are progressively more expensive in achieving quality software. The ideal objectives of the process are:

1. To engineer in quality as perfectly as possible right from the start.
2. As the next most desirable alternative, to remove all errors by means of reviews.

Careful engineering is requisite to achieving quality software, and comprehensive reviews and requirements/design validation provide further value to the evolving product. The reality of the state of the art is, however, that we will still need to test the software product, usually extensively.

There is nothing in the near future that will change this conclusion radically. Testing has undergone a considerable amount of modernization over the last decade, and there has been a recognizable tendency to move it farther upstream in the development process as well. Another favorable movement is toward incremental integration testing and systematized regression testing. Although undesirable from an economic standpoint, testing remains a very important and relied-upon technology for identifying errors in the software product and then referring those errors back to the engineering process for rectification.

A total reliance on testing to achieve a quality product is unrealistic and foolhardy. Historically, validation originally consisted of a traditional series of acceptance tests that were applied to the software product at the very end of the development cycle. As systems became more complex and larger, this strategy resulted in a lack of visibility into the quality of the software until the very end of the development. A number of surprises were forthcoming, among them costly fixes and late deliveries. Unfortunately this lesson had to be learned through direct experience. As a further penalty, the approach also left few options in dealing with major problems revealed by testing. Sad but true, the economic impact of errors uncovered by testing is much greater and affects more people than errors uncovered and dealt with in the review process.

The goal of quality engineering is to reveal as many errors as possible before testing is introduced. In reality, this is not completely possible. However, large numbers of residual errors left to be uncovered by testing introduce high cost and schedule penalties. Hence, a balanced program of review and testing activities becomes the most effective technology approach to the verification and validation aspect of quality engineering.

The chapter begins the discussion of testing technology. The broad concepts of testing are addressed by the following topics:

- A definition of the basic testing problem,
- A multiple test data domain approach,
- An exploration of the independent test organization, and
- A template for testing activities by quality level.

Succeeding chapters refine these concepts into concrete methods for the control of development, testing and integration using threads.

11.2
The Basic Testing Problem

Testing is defined as the controlled execution of the software product in order to expose errors. It is said that normally, when, according to preestablished criteria, the number and severity of errors fall below a specified threshold, proper operation of the software has been demonstrated. However, the accuracy of this statement depends heavily on the framework in which proper operation is defined. Thus, testing requires a great deal of forethought and design.

Ideally, testing a software system completely requires a set of all possible inputs. However, this is impractical and economically infeasible for all but the most trivial of systems. A practical strategy involves the selection of a subset of the possible inputs that can establish a statistically significant high probability of correctness of the system within economic constraints. The major testing problem then becomes the issue of trying to accommodate opposing goals: we would like to test the system with as many test cases as possible to demonstrate correctness with a higher probability; and at the same time, we also wish to minimize the number of test cases because of the effort involved in designing and generating test cases. Test engineering, then, remains somewhat of an art, lacking the rigor of the scientific process.

The selection of a subset of all possible test inputs is accomplished by partitioning testing into a number of domains and levels, each with a different set of goals. Each level of testing addresses the software at a different level of completeness or integration, culminating with the entire integrated system. Each level has both common and distinct testing goals. At each level a requirements-driven "black box" approach to testing is paramount, i.e., testing should demonstrate that the system performs according to the intentions of its architects as articulated by the requirements specification (correctness). The "black box" approach is often supplemented by a "white box" strategy: supplement the original requirements-oriented test cases with additional inputs so that all the internal structure of the software are executed.

Goal differentiation is a very important element in contriving an economically feasible testing strategy. Some goals are feasible at one level, but difficult at another. Clearly, at least two levels of testing can be delineated: (1) unit-level testing and (2) integration-level testing. As the name implies, unit-level testing entails the execution of a single software component, or a small number of components, with test stimuli. It emphasizes the demonstration of functions, coverage of the internal structure of the software, and demonstration of the accuracies of individual algorithms. A secondary emphasis is on the determination of computational performance. Integration-level testing, by contrast, emphasizes the execution of the interfaces between the units and the execution of the software to show conformance to computational performance requirements. A lesser emphasis is on the demonstration of functionality.

Unit-level testing is usually planned and executed by the engineering organization that has developed the software. Integration-level testing, for all but very small systems, is normally performed by an organization that is independent of the software developers. An independent organization is more likely to design and implement a testing program that is thorough, complete, and objective. There is no reason for such an organization to either exaggerate or disguise problems that are discovered. This is the overall rationale for the use of an independent testing organization for integration-level testing.

11.3
Engineering Software Test Data in Multiple Domains

The basic testing issue has been identified as an engineering issue consisting of trying to accommodate opposing goals. The process is thus highly constrained and will, in general, result in a significant departure from the full-coverage ideal testing theories often advanced. A well-designed testing approach, then, must be bound by cost and schedule constraints.

An empirically derived approach to accommodate these constraints is built around the definition of multiple test coverage domains. This approach consists of identifying, in order of priority, a number of domains and then successively devising and enhancing, by increments, a set of tests to meet the objectives of each domain. The following useful and practical list of domains of coverage has been compiled by Redwine:[1]

1. Function coverage domain, which tests software as it is specified, i.e., by functions.
2. Input coverage domain, where each input type—especially the extreme conditions—is included in the test cases.
3. Output coverage domain, where the software is stimulated to produce each type of output by at least one test.
4. Function interaction domain, which checks the interactions among functions.
5. Code execution domain, where previous test cases are expanded to traverse previously unexecuted portions of the software structure.

The function test data domain derives its test data requirements from the requirements specification. Software is most naturally specified according to function and its associated inputs and outputs. A typical checklist for function test data would include the following types of cases:

- External inputs
- External outputs
- Invalid inputs
- Singularities or special values
- Combinations of inputs
- Likely errors

Testing with a combination of these inputs would very likely present a difficult combinatorial problem. Engineering judgment and experience are required to overcome this challenge. While there is no universal algorithm that can be applied, pairs or triplets of test cases are often useful to consider. The approach is a good one for executing individual functions, but unfortunately, it can produce an unconscious complacency. The major problem is that it overlooks the operational interactions among multiple functions: function domain testing can be sufficient for unit tests, but it is insufficient for higher levels of integration testing. This issue will be discussed further shortly.

The input test data domain expands the test case data base of the previous domain. The intent is to test the extent of the data domain upon which functions can successfully

[1]S. T. Redwine, Jr., "An Engineering Approach to Software Test Case Design," *IEEE Transactions on Software Engineering*, Vol. SE-9, March 1983, pp. 191–200.

operate by focusing attention on extreme input values. Typical items that would appear on a checklist in this domain are:

- Extreme numeric ranges
- All record types
- Various data overcapacities
- Interrupt overcapacities
- Anomalous patterns such as missing data

Anomalous patterns that are overlooked in the initial software design have been a major cause of rework during the maintenance phase of certain, mainly real-time, systems.

The objective of the output test data domain is to generate each type of output that is possible for the system. The output section of the requirements specification should be examined, and a test case contrived to generate all outputs addressed in the specification. A typical checklist would include the following types of output test data cases:

- All diagnostics
- All error messages
- All types of reports
- All types of files and record types
- All input/output transfers
- All interrupt types
- All possible termination modes

Clearly, testing all combinations of possible outputs is generally practically impossible. However, by judgmentally selecting pairs or triplets of possible outputs, a full variety of output behavior can be demonstrated.

The function interaction test data domain is based upon the realization that the behavior of one function can affect another. The interactions are generally not well addressed by a requirements specification. The purpose of using this domain is to test the software as it will execute in operation.

Some system developments generate an operations concept document. For these systems, the function interaction scenarios can be derived from this operations concept. Otherwise, an informal operations concept can be derived using the thread analysis methodology described in Chapter 8. A typical checklist for this type of testing would include:

- All stimulus-response scenarios
- Illegal inputs not covered by other test data domains
- Inputs/system state combinations

- Outputs/system state combinations
- "Vertical slices" through the design hierarchy

The vertical slice technique would be achieved by using the stimulus-response thread scenarios. Function interaction coverage also presents a potential explosive combinatorial problem. An operational thread analysis using engineering judgment can avoid this by delineating the most important linear sequences. Experience has shown that individual function testing is insufficient; it is necessary to get to this type of function interaction testing as early as possible in the test program to exploit a very fertile area of potential errors, viz., the interactions among functions.

The code execution test data domain targets in on untested portions of the software structure not previously covered by other test data domains. The overall goal is to achieve coverage of all sections of the software structure. This full-coverage testing goal can be brought under effective economic control through proper definition of full-execution objectives and the use of proper automated technology to support the testing.

The practical applicability of the various test domains requires some further explanation. Each of the five domains has a different applicability to both unit-level testing and integration-level testing. Unit-level testing usually concerns itself with testing a single software component. Integration-level testing is directed toward integrating several or more software components or portions of those components. In terms of specifications, unit-level testing is oriented toward testing functions specified within a component-level requirements specification. Integration-level testing is oriented toward testing full system behavior as specified within the system-level requirements specification. A more practical list of successive test domains for unit-level testing is, in order of priority:

1. Function domain
2. Function interaction domain
3. Input domain
4. Output domain
5. Code execution domain

This revised priority introduces consideration of function interactions at a much earlier point in the testing. The hierarchy of coverage domains for integration-level testing is:

1. Function interaction domain
2. Input domain
3. Output domain

Note the enhanced importance assigned to the function interaction domain at both unit- and integration-testing levels in comparison to the original list proferred by Redwine.

This section has explored a practical agenda for test data design based upon domains of coverage. Although this approach provides some rigor to the test design process, it must be supplemented with sound engineering judgment backed up by considerable experience.

11.4
The Independent Testing Organization

A very important aspect of a testing approach is who has the organizational responsibility for testing. In general, the independent test organization (ITO) is responsible for the planning and conduct of all formal testing of the software products. This embraces both the integration-level testing and system acceptance testing. Unit-level testing, on the other hand, is generally performed by the engineering organization that developed the software. This informal testing results in a partially validated product that is then handed off to the ITO for formal integration testing.

On the modern software project, the testing organization is independent of the development organizations. The reasons for establishing the testing organization as an independent entity are that (1) the engineering of a test program is a major task, and (2) an independent testing organization preserves objectivity. Planning and execution of the testing effort requires an investment of time and labor which can exceed that of the actual software development. In order to assure that testing represents more than an afterthought to the development, a parallel effort is necessary to properly engineer the test program. A group of people not involved with the implementation of the system is likely to do a more thorough and objective job of planning and executing the tests. System implementers would be more likely to generate a trivial series of test cases.

The development organization codes and assembles units of the software components that are then informally tested. Control of the testing is then transferred to the independent test organization. The ITO integrates incremental units of software from two or more components in a process known as integration testing, for which the ITO is solely responsible. Design of the test program generally occurs in parallel with that of the product.

Test planning actually commences with activities oriented toward validation of the requirements and design as described in Chapter 8. The thread scenarios resulting from this validation form the first phase of the plans. Each test is designed in successive steps of refinement. A typical series of documentation representing the test program design is as follows

- System test plan
- Individual test plan
- Individual test procedure
- Individual test report

The system test plan details the approach taken to demonstrate that the software system meets the functional, design, and performance requirements. A draft of this plan is prepared during the requirements analysis phase of the project and is updated during subsequent phases of the development cycle. The content of a representative system test plan is shown in Figure 11-1. The preparation of the system test plan is a major undertaking that has profound influence on the quality and eventual cost of the delivered system. The plan addresses the activities that take place during the period when delays and complications are quite costly to the project. Considering the influence this plan has

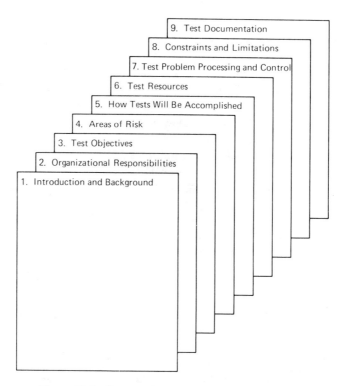

Figure 11-1   Content of representative system test plan.

on the success of the project, a modest investment to produce a good plan is quite justified. An early concentration on the testing and integration approach will minimize the surprises that will arise in later, more vulnerable stages when the options for resolution are drastically limited.

The basic content of a representative individual test plan is delineated in Figure 11–2. The test description provides a detailed description of the test in a logical flow diagram showing the elements being tested and their internal and external interfaces. The test implementation section includes descriptions of the baseline configuration control procedures, test personnel requirements, test simulation data requirements, and operational data requirements. The test environment should be described in terms of equipment, software, documentation, data, and limitations associated with the eventual conduct of testing. The test requirements consist mainly of a requirements/evaluation allocation matrix for the requirements being tested. The analysis plan defines the method for determining pass/fail criteria for each test requirement and should address test data recording, the evaluation approach, and acceptance criteria.

The individual test procedure decomposes the test plan into a step-by-step procedure that is required to execute the test. The content of the procedure includes required actions, system responses, and steps required to initialize, maintain, terminate, and restart the software being tested. The test procedure also identifies nondeliverable software and hardware that are to be employed during the test.

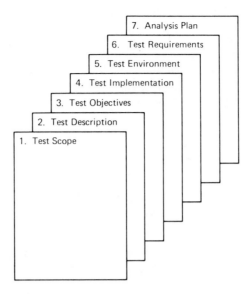

Figure 11-2 Content of individual test plan.

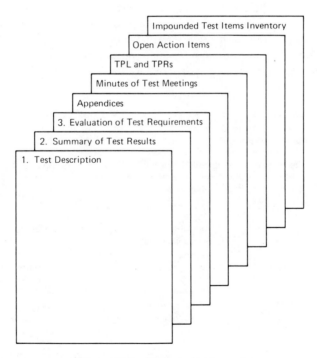

Figure 11-3 Content of test report.

An individual test report is prepared for each major test to formally document its results. The report is usually issued within 30 days of completion of the given test. The overall content of a representative test report is shown in Figure 11-3. The summary of test results describes chiefly the requirements met or not met and associated liens. The evaluation of test requirements contains the following information for each requirement in the test plan:

- Statement of requirements
- Data collected
- Analysis performed
- Comparison of performance against acceptance criteria
- Deviations from the plan or procedure

Any changes, if necessary, to the test procedure and plan should be incorporated and issued at the same time as the release of the test report.

11.5
Testing by Quality Level

The level of quality required will directly influence the intensity, focus, and organizational responsibilities of the testing approach for an individual system. Table 11-1 lists the testing activities required to achieve the usual four quality levels tabulated against both unit-level testing and integration- or system-level testing. The quality level is determined primarily by the required quality level goals for correctness and reliability.

TABLE 11-1 TESTING ACTIVITY BY QUALITY LEVEL

Quality Level	Unit Testing	Integration/System Testing
Not an issue	Programmer unit tests	Programmer integration(informal)
Average	Programmer unit tests	Independent test organization Formal plans and procedures
Good	Programmer unit tests 90–95% path structure coverage	Independent test organization Formal plans and procedures Thread/build testing Stress/anomaly testing Critical areas tested by IV&V agent
Excellent	Programmer unit tests 100% path structure coverage	Independent test organization Formal plans and procedures Thread/build testing Extensive stress/anomaly testing System acceptance test by IV&V agent

QUALITY NOT AN ISSUE. Testing at this level is almost entirely programmer performed. There is little, if any, written test planning. Systems at this level are small and simple enough to permit this informality.

AVERAGE QUALITY. Systems at this level are usually in the deliverable category, i.e., there involves a developer who has a contract, either formal or informal, to provide a product to a customer or user; the parties may reside in the same organization. The main contrast between this and the previous level involves the use of the ITO for integration and system testing. Testing is based upon formal written plans and procedures.

GOOD QUALITY. At this level, more structure is introduced into all tests. Threads and builds partition the system into more manageable, functionally oriented sections and orient the testing toward the operations concept of the system. A modest amount of stress and anomaly testing is also performed. Stress testing determines the response of the system to overload; it is generally expected that there are adaptive mechanisms to deal gracefully, although possibly with degraded performance and functionality, to overload stimuli.

Also, at the good-quality level, particularly critical application functions will be tested by an IV&V agent and path structure goals at the unit-testing level will be gauged for about 90–95 percent of the path structure. A practical path-testing scheme will be described in Chapter 12.

EXCELLENT QUALITY. Testing at this level entails approximately the same technological approach as that done at the previous level, but more comprehensiveness is involved. Key additions are:

- Increase of the path structure goal to 100 percent
- More extensive stress/anomaly testing
- Use of the IV&V agent to perform the system acceptance test

Excellent quality is usually required only for portions of systems, and the testing approach need not be totally homogeneous.

Control of Software Development and Testing[1]

12.1
Basic Approach

This chapter describes a method of software development and testing that

- Segments a complex software development into more manageable functional elements.
- Demonstrates key functional capabilities early in the testing activity.
- Maintains a visible connection between testing and software requirements, thus formalizing the testing process.
- Forms the basis of a very effective project planning and control strategy.

[1]This chapter is adapted from Michael S. Deutsch, *Software Verification and Validation: Realistic Project Approaches* (Englewood Cliffs, N.J.: Prentice-Hall, 1982).

The approach described is derived from the threads methodology originally developed at Computer Sciences Corporation and introduced here in Chapter 8. The threads technique has undergone refinement in its application at Hughes Aircraft Company. The concept exerts a powerful influence on the organization of software development and testing because of its combined technical and managerial merits.

Development is narrowly defined here to include software coding and informal programmer functional checkout. Testing, on the other hand, is a more formal activity that is guided by prepared plans and/or procedures. The tested product normally forms a baseline against which changes are controlled. At the earliest levels of testing, the product developer conducts the tests and controls the baseline.

The coding and checkout activities have habitually constituted the ''dark'' period of the development cycle. During this stage, there has been a lack of adequate metrics to define the status of the project, and thus development has seemingly gone ''underground.'' The approach we will consider ameliorates this deficiency by providing a rigorous means of segmenting complex software development into the small, functional chunks called *threads*, individually scheduled and used to monitor completion status. The latter is updated frequently and displayed, thus providing visibility into the condition of the project at any stage of its development.

Figure 12–1 depicts a software testing procedure that is visibly connected to the requirements. The procedure is driven by the system verification diagram (SVD) derived directly from the software requirements specification. The SVD consists of stimulus-response elements that are associated with an identifiable function and specific requirements. Each such element can be mapped into the design to identify the specific software modules which, when executed, perform the function of that thread. A highly detailed relationship, then, exists between the functional requirements (represented by the SVD) and the design (the modules) that combine to form threads. This relationship is the primary means by which the software development can be accurately defined and closely controlled. Each thread will be tested individually by the development team in such manner that the modules corresponding to the thread are exhaustively tested with each path segment being executed at least once. The mechanisms for accomplishing this objective are explained in Section 12.5.

The next step of the planning process is to allocate specific threads to specific *builds*. Each build represents a significant partial functional capability of the system, and each incremental build demonstration is a partial dry run of the *final acceptance test*. Each successive build demonstration regressively tests the capabilities of the previous builds. Thus, the demonstration of the full system is the natural culmination of integrating the final build into the accumulation of previous builds.

12.2
Defining the Threads

The objective of the SVD is to represent the software requirements as a series of stimulus-response pairings in a complete, consistent, and testable manner. Inconsistencies, redun-

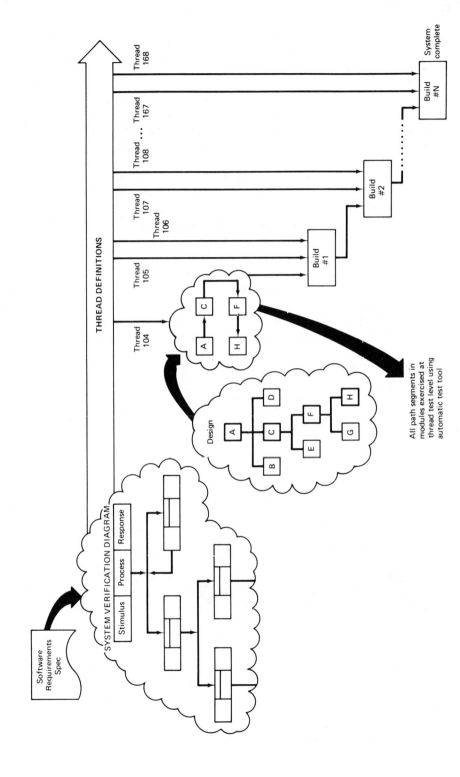

Figure 12-1 Software test/development procedure visibly connected to requirements.

dancies, and omissions may be revealed while developing these stimulus-response pairings.[2]

Each stimulus consists of one or more inputs plus any conditional qualifiers; each response consists of one or more outputs plus conditional qualifiers generated as a result of the inputs.[3] Each stimulus-response element represents an identifiable function or subfunction, has a direct relationship to one or (usually) more software requirements, and can later be associated with the modules in the software design architecture which will then form the thread. The SVD is normally generated from the requirements specification before the software architecture is designed; alternatively, it can be derived from sequences specified in an operations concept document and then validated against the requirements specification.

The entire requirements specification can be represented by a set of stimulus-response elements which are logically connected to each other by arrows which denote sequence. Quite often, a conditional qualifier associated with the input event of an element is the successful completion of the function represented by the previous thread in the sequence. Complete functional testing of the software is attained if all paths through the SVD are traversed during the test program.[4]

The stimulus-response elements of the SVD may be viewed as qualitative assertions of system behavior specifying, in an informal language, the state of the system before and after each processing transformation. In this context, it is the objective of testing to demonstrate that actual system behavior is the same as the asserted behavior that is specified by the SVD.

The SVD is also a unified depiction of the testing requirements in graphical form and may be included in the requirements specification document. The threads represent the functions that must be tested, and the paths through the SVD are the sequences of functions that are to be tested.

A portion of an SVD that was used for a recent software development is shown in Figure 12–2. This SVD addresses a set of interactive functions in which the operator is presented a display containing a set of default initialization parameters. The operator may accept the default set of parameters or enter manual overrides for any or all of these initialization parameters. The requirement numbers that each thread satisfies are denoted below and to the left of each thread block.

Thread 1.0 begins the processing sequence by presenting a display consisting of the initialization parameters and default values. One of seven paths from stimulus-response element 1.0 is possible depending on the operator input event and system condition:

1. Element 2.0 involves the operator's accepting all the default parameters without modification. This is followed by element 9.0, which accepts the stimulus of element 2.0 and sets all the control parameters to the default values.

[2]Robert Carey and Marc Bendic, "The Control of a Software Test Process," *Proceedings of the Computer Software and Applications Conference 1977*, IEEE Catalog No. 77CH1291-4C (New York: IEEE, 1977) pp. 327–333.
[3]Carey and Bendic, pp. 327–29.
[4]Carey and Bendic, pp. 331.

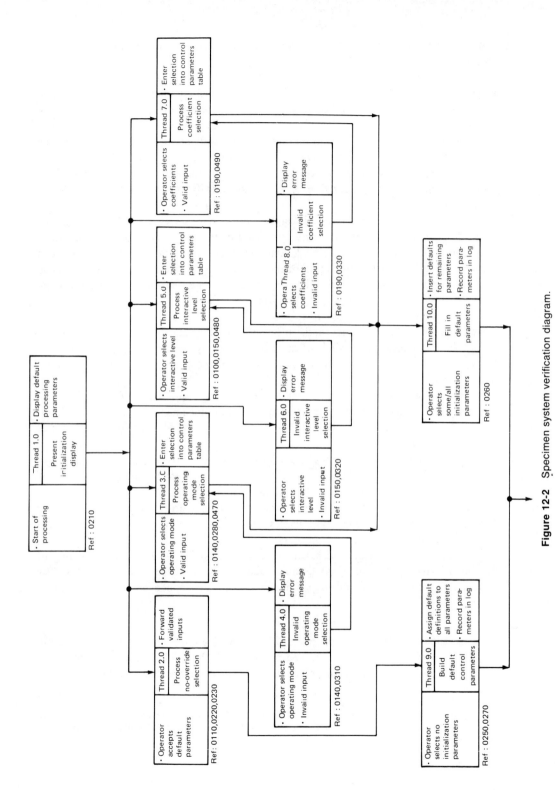

Figure 12-2 Specimen system verification diagram.

216

2. Element 3.0 is stimulated by the operator's manually selecting a valid operating mode. The response is to set this selection in the control parameters table.

3. Element 4.0 occurs when the operator enters an operating mode selection that is invalid. The response is to feed back an error message to the display. The eventual succeeding event is a valid operating mode selection, element 3.0.

4. Element 5.0 is stimulated by the operator's manually selecting a valid interactive level. The response is to set this selection in the control parameter table.

5. Element 6.0 occurs when the operator enters an interactive level selection that is invalid. The response is to feed back an error message to the display. The eventual succeeding event is a valid interactive level selection, element 5.0.

6. Element 7.0 is stimulated by the operator's manually selecting a valid set of coefficients. The response is to set these selections in the control parameter table.

7. Element 8.0 occurs when the operator enters one or more invalid coefficient values. The response is to feed back an error message to the display. The eventual succeeding event is a valid coefficient input, element 7.0.

The common succeeding event of elements 3.0, 5.0, and 7.0 is element 10.0. This element fills in default values for those parameters not set by the operator. The paths from element 9.0 and 10.0 then converge to another element not shown in the figure.

The example highlights the logical association of stimulus/response events derived from the functional requirements. The SVD is the key factor that subsequently drives the planning effort for test and buildup.

12.3
Planning the Testing and Buildup Process

Detailed test planning can begin when the software architecture defining the structure of the modules is available. This normally occurs, in software developments sponsored by the Department of Defense, by the time of the preliminary design review (PDR). The test planning approach requires a modular software architecture developed from structured design precepts; less organized designs of diluted modularity will reduce the effectiveness of the planning because the relationship between the stimulus-response elements and the software modules will then be indistinct. Experience shows that the technique works well with a structure density of, on the average, 100 higher order language source lines per module (which later may be subdivided further into subroutines).

In this concept, software testing and construction are intertwined; they do not occur separately and sequentially. The order in which the software is coded, tested, and synthesized is essentially determined by the SVD, which defines the test procedure. Through the SVD's segmentation of the system into threads that are ordered by date, the modules associated with each thread are coded and tested commensurately with the thread ordering. The threads are synthesized into builds, each of which incrementally demonstrates a significant partial functional capability of the system. This culminates in a demonstration of the full system, which occurs as a natural conclusion to integrating the last build into the aggregate of previous builds. The approach provides an orderly means of segmenting complex software development into smaller, functionally oriented sections.

A convenient mechanism for recording the relationships between the stimulus-response paths, requirements, and modules which implemented the thread is the thread functional allocation chart shown in Figure 12-3. The information contained in this chart is derived from the SVD of Figure 12-2 and the software design architecture for these interactive functions.

Requirement IDs	Thread ID	Thread Title	Complexity Units	Module IDs
0210	1.0	Present initialization display	3	1.1, 1.1.1, 1.1.1.1, 1.1.1.2
0110, 0220, 0230	2.0	Process no override selection	2	1.1, 1.1.2, 1.1.2.1, 1.1.2.1.1, 1.1.2.1.2
0140, 0280 0470	3.0	Process operating mode selection	2	1.1, 1.1.2, 1.1.2.2, 1.1.2.2.1
0140, 0310	4.0	Invalid operating mode selection	2	1.1, 1.1.2, 1.1.2.2, 1.1.2.2.2
0100, 0150, 0480	5.0	Process interactive level selection	2	1.1, 1.1.2, 1.1.2.3, 1.1.2.3.1
0150, 0320	6.0	Invalid interactive level selection	2	1.1, 1.1.2, 1.1.2.3, 1.1.2.3.2
0190, 0490	7.0	Process coefficient selection	2	1.1, 1.1.2, 1.1.2.4, 1.1.2.4.1
0190, 0330	8.0	Invalid coefficient selection	2	1.1, 1.1.2, 1.1.2.4, 1.1.2.4.2
0250, 0270	9.0	Build default control parameters	2	1.1, 1.1.2, 1.1.2.1, 1.1.2.1.1
0260	10.0	Fill in default parameters	2	1.1, 1.1.2, 1.1.2.6

Figure 12-3 Specimen thread functional allocation chart.

The architecture of the software modules is represented by the structure diagram shown in Figure 12-4. Each module is assigned an identification number located in the upper left corner of the box that locates that module hierarchically in the system. The structure decomposes into two basic branches: those modules which build and output the display picture to the display terminal, and those modules which process the operator inputs after presentation of the display on the terminal. In a well-structured design, all of the basic processing work is done by the modules at the terminal, or lowest, level of the hierarchy. All of the parent modules are control modules—that is, the function of

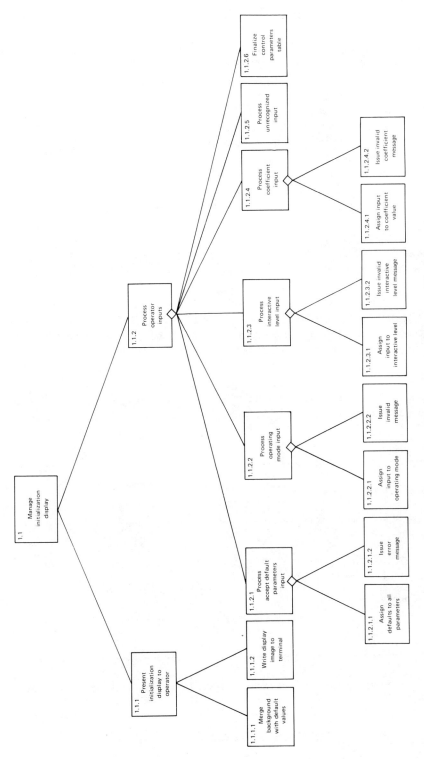

Figure 12-4 Sample software architecture.

these modules is to properly invoke the subordinate modules and arrange them in order of priority.

The information contained on the thread functional allocation chart of Figure 12–3 under the headers "Requirement IDs," "Thread ID," and "Thread Title" is transferred directly from the SVD. The header "Complexity Units" represents an estimation on a linear scale from 1 to 5 of the person-effort required to code, check out, test, and integrate each thread. A rating of 5 means "most complex," and a rating of 1 means "simplest." This subjective measure is based on the volume of code to be constructed, the code complexity, and the complexity of the interface with other threads that have already been integrated. The threads under examination in the chart contain a moderate volume of code, involving relatively uncomplicated interfaces; the ratings of 2's and 3's reflect this evaluation. The Hughes Aircraft Company application largely supports Computer Science Corporation's experience that this estimation parameter is useful and linear.

Under the header "Module IDs" are the modules, referenced to the structure diagram of Figure 12–4, which implement each thread. For an individual thread, the serial execution of the modules listed performs the function of the stimulus-response element and its associated requirements. In the case of thread 1.0, since all of its modules are new, they must be coded in order to implement the thread. Subsequent threads involve a combination of new and previously coded or tested modules. Usually, the higher level control structure is implemented as a result of the first two or three threads, and the subsequent threads add new modules to the structure at lower levels of the architecture hierarchy.

The execution sequences of the modules correlated with three threads—1.0, 3.0, and 4.0—are illustrated in Figure 12–5. All of the modules of thread 1.0 will be newly coded. For thread 3.0, module 1.1 has previously been implemented as a result of thread

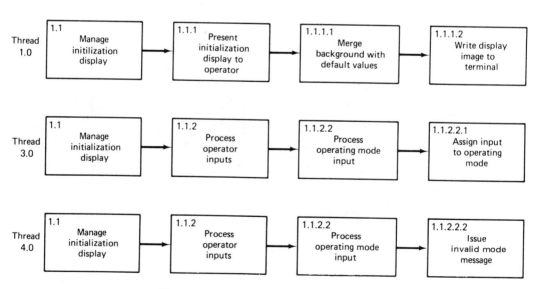

Figure 12-5 Execution sequences of threads.

1.0, and module 1.1.2 already exists courtesy of thread 2.0. Modules 1.1.2.2 and 1.1.2.2.1 must be coded and then integrated with modules 1.1 and 1.1.2 to form thread 3.0. In the case of thread 4.0, modules 1.1, 1.1.2, and 1.1.2.2 are existing modules. Module 1.1.2.2.2 is a new unit that must be constructed and then integrated with modules 1.1, 1.1.2, and 1.1.2.2 to constitute thread 4.0.

A complication occurs in fully testing module 1.1.2.2 in thread 3.0. Note in Figure 12–4 that this module acts as a control module with an alternation construction: it will direct processing of a valid operating mode input by ordering execution of module 1.1.2.2.1, or it will handle an invalid operating mode input by executing module 1.1.2.2.2 to issue an error message to the operator. The invalid input case is not within the scope of thread 3.0. Nevertheless, in order for the modules of thread 3.0 to link properly and to fully test module 1.1.2.2, some modification of module 1.1.2.2.2 must exist. The remedy for this situation is to substitute a *stub* for module 1.1.2.2.2. A stub is a dummy component that simulates the functioning of the module in question. Stubs will have varying levels of functionality. In this case, the stub need only consist of the subroutine name and the proper termination control statements; no functional statements are necessary. Thus, the insertion of a stub for module 1.1.2.2.2 is an expediency that permits us to test thread 3.0. For testing of thread 4.0, this stub will be replaced by the actual functional code written for the module referenced.

With the threads approach, the order of implementation of the modules in the design structure is in sequential order of execution, as illustrated in Figure 12–5. This implies that, for each thread, the order of construction commences at the top of the hierarchy and penetrates to the lowest level until all the modules that are required to perform the function of the thread are coded and integrated. This sequence corresponds to the order of execution of the modules of the thread. Thus, the implementation is neither top down nor bottom up. Top down and bottom up are strictly structural concepts without a rigorous association to functions. Top-down implementations implement all the modules at higher levels in the invocation structure before penetrating to the lowest levels. Bottom-up implementations, of course, proceed from the lowest level on up. The threads approach is concerned with the implementation of functions; it utilizes structure only as a means of achieving that end. Thus, within the threads approach we reject both top-down and bottom-up implementation in favor of execution-order implementation for each thread. This is not an indictment of top-down design; it is assumed that this is one of the methods for formulating a structured design.

The next step in the process is to assign threads to builds and designate completion points over the schedule period. Two considerations are paramount: it is normally in the interest of the project to implement the threads which comprise the highest technical risk early; and a logically complete system, although not functionally complete, should be the objective as early in the buildup schedule as possible.[5] This is basically an implement-to-schedule strategy: if, despite the best efforts of all concerned, the entire system has not been completed by the scheduled date, there will still exist the nucleus of a system that performs functions which are demonstrable and operationally useful. Undoubtedly, the customer will be displeased, but the extent of the displeasure will probably be far less than with a less organized approach which may have completed the

[5]Carey and Bendic, pp. 332–33.

same volume of code but which would consist of diverse software units not yet orderly sequenced into operational functions.

One of the objectives of this strategy is to furnish both management and the customer with alternatives should it become clear that the full product that has been contracted for cannot be delivered by the scheduled date, or cannot be built within the originally allocated budget, or both. The customer would like full latitude in dealing with the situation, including being able to exercise any of the following options:

1. Accept delivery on the originally scheduled date with only a subset of the required functions.
2. Extend the delivery date so that the system will contain all the required functions or a fuller subset thereof.
3. Provide more funding to obtain a fuller set of functions.
4. Do both (2) and (3) if necessary (as is usually the case).

As has been pointed out, the customer will always be unhappy with schedule slippages or cost overruns. This displeasure is undoubtedly compounded if the choices available to resolve the situation are strictly limited to extending the schedule and, in all likelihood, absorbing a cost overrun. A schedule slip could have far-reaching repercussions. Other systems that in some way interface with the local system may be prevented from reaching operational status as a result of the delay. The customer can escape these consequences, or at least some of them, if he or she is able to accept, by the original date, a partially completed system that logically functions while containing a subset of the original capabilities that is operationally useful. As a result of these circumstances, the contractor's reputation will no doubt be blemished; however, by having a fallback position available for the customer, the extent of the damage will at least be limited. There is, of course, never any substitute for on-time, on-budget performance. Yet the contractor can still maintain a reputation for rational project management under adverse conditions with proper planning.

A logically complete system is one that can accept input data, process the data, and provide a useful set of outputs or partial outputs while applying an operationally useful subset of functions. The main thrust of this concept is attaining an overall flow from the front end to the back end of the system with, perhaps, only a subset of functions implemented in between. The approach to defining a logically complete system is highly dependent on the individual application. One almost universally applicable rule of thumb is that the logically complete system should be defined around its key interfaces.

The results of the planning effort are displayed on a *build plan*—a diagram, ordered by date, of the sequence of construction and testing events, including

- The sequence of the builds
- The relationship of the builds to each other
- The allocation of threads to builds
- The sequence of the threads

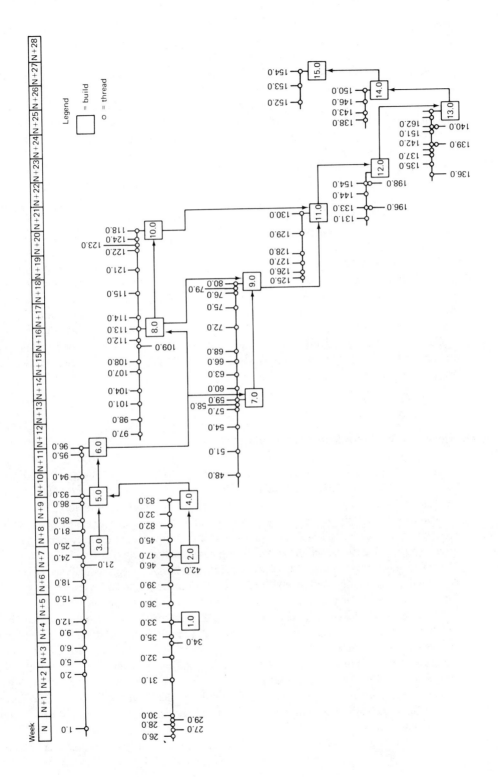

Figure 12-6 Sample build plan.

A sample build plan from a recent software development project is illustrated in Figure 12–6. Implementation of an end-to-end data flow is achieved at build 6.0, which occurs less than halfway into the scheduled implementation period; this constitutes a logically complete system for this project. Builds 7.0 to 15.0 add additional functions which supplement the basic data transformations and provide operator interactive control over the processing sequence. Each build adds new functions (threads) to the system and, to the extent indicated by the connecting arrows on the build plan, contains the cumulative capabilities of previous builds. Each build demonstration tests the new capabilities and regressively tests the capabilities aggregated by previous builds. The final acceptance test of the total system occurring at build 15.0 is merely a natural culminating event of this succession. Because a thread is directly linked to software modules, the build plan also defines the order of construction of the modules. Each thread is also tested informally, and the build demonstration tests may be viewed as natural culminating events in a succession of thread tests.

Because, by their very nature, threads represent useful operational functions, a measure of thread completion also represents a measure of project completion. By using the number of complexity units assigned to each thread, the build plan may be summarized into a *thread production plan*, shown in Figure 12–7, for the same software development project as in Figure 12–6. The solid line represents the planned production rate against which the actual production rate, in dashed lines, may be plotted. Thus, the thread production plan provides an easily understood means of reporting actual progress vs. planned progress.

12.4
The DC Network Analysis Software System

In order to further clarify the utility of the threads approach, let us consider an example. The DC network analysis system analyzes the input description of an electrical network and calculates the node voltages plus other electrical parameters. Probably, the development of a small, straightforward system such as this does not require elaborate planning procedures; that is, because of the system's simplicity, it is "intellectually manageable" on an informal basis. Nonetheless, the threads approach can apply.

The functional requirements specification for the DC network analysis system is contained in Figure 12–8. The data-flow diagram furnishes an overall view of the system functions and functional interfaces. Three major processing functions are specified: an input processing and control function, a central transform, and an output processing function. *Input processing and control* accepts parameters describing the requested system output products. The *central transform* determines the node voltages by calculating the element parameters, forming the elements into matrices, and computing the voltages from the matrices. *Output processing* furnishes a printed report of the node voltages and calculates and outputs certain ancillary electrical parameters if they have been requested. Section 3.0, *Requirements*, of the specification contains the processing requirements for each of these functions. In addition, a section containing capacity requirements limits the size of the network that the system can accommodate. An identi-

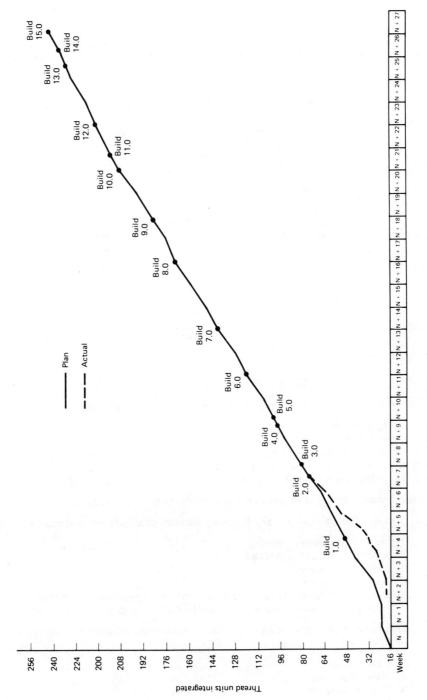

Figure 12-7 Sample thread production plan.

225

1.0 Introduction

This computer program accepts inputs describing the dc electrical network, generates the network equations, and solves the equations to determine the unknown voltages and currents.

2.0 Interfaces

A data flow diagram of the three major processing functions is presented here:

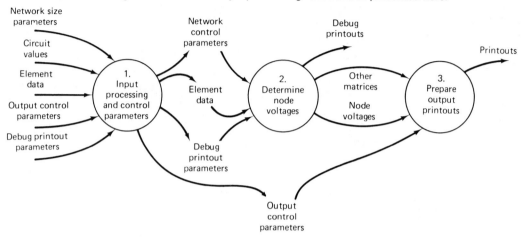

3.0 Requirements

3.1 DC Network Analysis Capacity Requirements

The system shall be able to process a network of the following size:

(C010) a. Up to twenty nodes
(C020) b. Up to fifty branches
(C030) c. Up to fifty passive elements including independent voltages and current sources
(C040) d. Up to fifty dependent current sources
(C050) e. Up to fifty dependent voltage sources

3.2 Requirements for Input Processing and Control Parameters Function

(I010) a. This function shall accept the following network configuration parameters as input:

(I020)   1. Number of network nodes
(I030)   2. Number of network branches
(I040)   3. Short circuit value
(I050)   4. Open circuit value
(I055)   5. Element data for each branch consisting of branch type, branch number, initial node, final node, branch element value, and branch number for dependent source

(I060) b. This function shall accept as input control parameters requests for hardcopy output of any or all of the following data sets:

(I070)   1. Node voltages
(I080)   2. Branch voltages
(I090)   3. Element voltages
(I100)   4. Element currents
(I110)   5. Branch currents

Figure 12-8 Functional requirements specification for DC network analysis system.

(I120) c. It shall be possible, if requested by input control parameter, to obtain debug printouts of the following data sets:

(I130) 1. Nodal conductance matrix
(I140) 2. Equivalent current vector
(I150) 3. Nodal incidence matrix
(I160) 4. Branch conductance matrix
(I170) 5. Dependent voltage source matrix
(I180) 6. Independent voltage source vector
(I190) 7. Independent current source vector

3.3 Requirements for Determine Node Voltages Function

(V010) a. The following elements shall be computed for each branch:

1. Resistance
2. Conductance
3. Capacitance
4. Inductance
5. Independent voltage source
6. Independent current source
7. Transconductance
8. Transfluence
9. Transpotential
10. Transresistance

(V020) b. A nodal incidence matrix A shall be constructed consisting of resistance, conductance, capacitance, and inductance elements for each branch.

(V030) c. An independent voltage source matrix E shall be constructed consisting of independent voltage source elements for each branch.

(V040) d. An independent current source matrix J shall be constructed consisting of independent current source elements for each branch.

(V050) e. A branch conductance matrix G shall be constructed consisting of resistance, conductance, capacitance, inductance, transconductance, transfluence, and transresistance elements for each branch.

(V060) f. A dependent voltage source matrix D shall be constructed consisting of transpotential and transresistance elements for each branch.

(V070) g. If requested, debug printout of the nodal incidence, independent voltage source, independent current source, branch conductance, and dependent voltage sources shall be provided.

(V080) h. A nodal conductance matrix G_n shall be calculated using the following equation:

$$G_n = A(GD^{-1})A^T$$

(V090) i. An equivalent current source vector J_n shall be calculated using the following equation:

$$J_n = A(J\text{-}GE)$$

(V100) j. If requested, debug printout of the nodal conductance matrix and equivalent current source vector shall be provided.

(V110) k. A solution vector V_n containing the node voltages shall be calculated using the following equation:

$$V_n = G_n J_n$$

3.4 Requirements for Prepare Output Printouts Function

(P010) a. A printout of the output node voltages shall be provided.
(P020) b. If requested, a branch voltage vector shall be computed and printout provided.
(P030) c. If requested, an element voltage vector shall be computed and printout provided.
(P040) d. If requested, an element current vector shall be computed and printout provided.
(P050) e. If requested, a network branch current vector shall be computed and printout provided.

Figure 12-8 (Continued)

227

fication number, indicated in parentheses, has been assigned to each requirement in order to facilitate traceability of the satisfaction of each requirement.

The requirements of this specification have been synthesized into stimulus-response elements. The resulting SVD is depicted in Figure 12–9. This SVD is fairly straightforward and without complications. Some salient observations are:

1. Stimulus-response element 3 occurs when debug data set 1 has been requested as an input parameter. This element combines requirements from Sections 3.3 and 3.2.

2. Because both of elements 3 and 4 occur on condition that the matrices have been set up, they are depicted in parallel on the diagram.

3. Element 6 occurs when debug data set 2 has been requested by an input parameter. The requirements associated with this element have been combined from Sections 3.3 and 3.2.

4. Elements 6 and 7 are both invoked when the equivalent current vector is computed. Hence, they are depicted in parallel on the diagram.

5. Elements 9, 10, 11, and 12 are stimulated by the printout of the node voltages, which occurs in element 8. These elements will be executed in any combination based upon requests for the appropriate data sets in the input parameters. All of these elements combine requirements from physically separate portions of the specification.

With the completion of the SVD, the test procedure for the DC network analysis system has been defined. We are now in a position to relate these test requirements to design elements that implement the stimulus-response paths identified in the SVD. Accordingly, let us consider the modular structure of the system. A structure chart defining the architecture of the DC network analysis system is displayed in Figure 12–10. At the first level of abstraction, the system decomposes into three modules: a module that inputs the control parameters, the central module that computes the nodal voltages, and an output module that provides printed output of the circuit quantities. Note that this structure conforms to the classical structured design arrangement of an input branch, a central transform, and an output branch. The central transform module VOLT consists of two major functions: a module that formulates the network equations, and a module that solves them.

The thread functional allocation chart for the system is shown in Figure 12–11. In most cases, the modules relied upon for any given thread reflect the capabilities of previous threads plus new modules unique to the present thread. Thus, each thread regressively tests the capabilities of the previous threads in the sequence.

The thread complexity units assigned range from 1 through 4. Because the interfaces of the system are of approximately identical difficulty, the complexity unit assignments are primarily based on the volume of code on the individual thread. Thread 2 requires the implementation of a fairly large number of new modules; hence, it has been assigned a complexity unit rating of 4. Since thread 4 also involves a considerable number of modules, it has been allocated a rating of 3 units. Thread 5, 6, and 7 involve a slightly

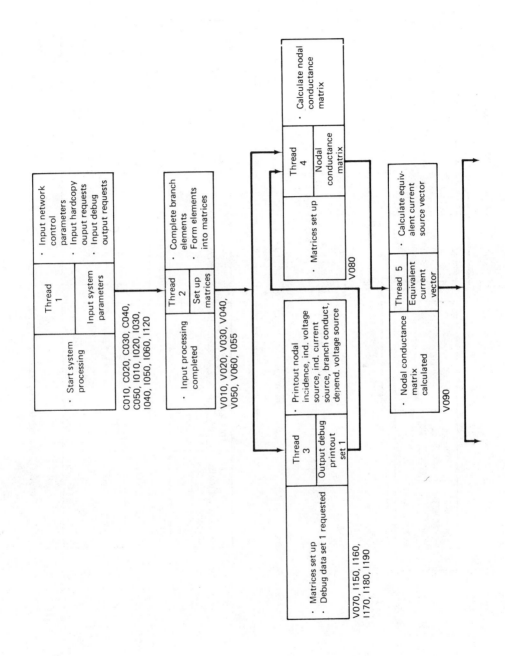

Thread 1

- Start system processing

Input system parameters

- Input network control parameters
- Input hardcopy ouput requests
- Input debug output requests

C010, C020, C030, C040, C050, I010, I020, I030, I040, I050, I060, I120

Thread 2

- Input processing completed

Set up matrices

- Complete branch elements
- Form elements into matrices

V010, V020, V030, V040, V050, V060, I055

Thread 3

- Matrices set up
- Debug data set 1 requested

Output debug printout set 1

- Printout nodal incidence, ind. voltage source, ind. current source, branch conduct., depend. voltage source

V070, I150, I160, I170, I180, I190

Thread 4

- Matrices set up

Nodal conductance matrix

- Calculate nodal conductance matrix

V080

Thread 5

- Nodal conductance matrix calculated

Equivalent current vector

- Calculate equivalent current source vector

V090

229

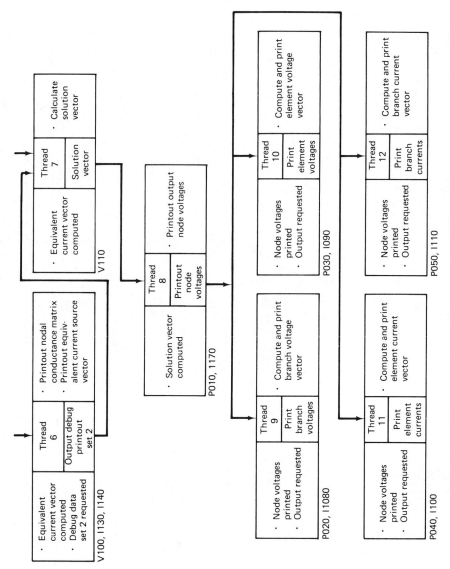

Figure 12-9 System verification diagram for DC network analysis system.

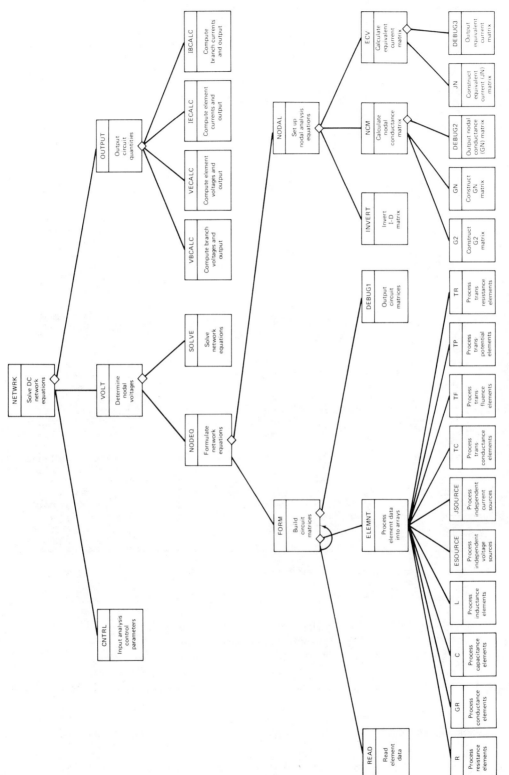

Figure 12-10 DC network analysis system architecture.

Requirement IDs	Thread ID	Thread Title	Complexity Units	Module IDs
C010, C020, C030, C040, C050, I010, I020, I030 I040, I050, I060, I120	1	Input system parameters	1	NETWRK, CNTRL
V010, V020, V030, V040, V050, V060, I055	2	Set up matrices	4	NETWRK, CNTRL, VOLT, NODEQ, FORM, READ, ELEMNT, R, GR, C, L, ESOURCE, JSOURCE, TC, TF, TP, TR
V070, I150, I160, I170, I180, I190	3	Output debug printout set 1	1	THREAD 2 MODULES + DEBUG1
V080	4	Nodal conductance matrix	3	THREAD 2 MODULES + NODAL, INVERT, NCM, G2, GN
V090	5	Equivalent current vector	2	THREAD 2 MODULES + NODAL, ECV, JN
V100, I130, I140	6	Output debug printout set 2	2	THREAD 4 MODULES, THREAD 5 MODULES + DEBUG2, DEBUG3
V110	7	Solution vector	2	THREAD 6 MODULES + SOLVE
P010, I070	8	Printout node voltages	1	NETWRK, OUTPUT
P020, I080	9	Print branch voltages	1	THREAD 2 MODULES + OUTPUT, VBCALC
P030, I090	10	Print element voltages	1	THREAD 2 MODULES + OUTPUT, VECALC
P040, I100	11	Print element currents	1	THREAD 2 MODULES + OUTPUT, IECALC
P050, I110	12	Print branch currents	1	THREAD 2 MODULES + OUTPUT, IBCALC

Figure 12-11 Thread functional allocation chart for network analysis system.

smaller amount of code and, accordingly, have been allotted unit ratings of 2. The remaining threads are associated with a fairly trivial volume of code and have been assigned 1 complexity unit per thread. The rationale used for these ratings is only semiquantitative; in a real project environment, it is likely that a more rigorous algorithmic mechanism would be used for enumerating and assigning complexity units.

Next, the threads are allocated to builds, and specific completion dates are assigned to each thread. The result of this exercise is recorded on a build plan with the following three builds:

1. *Build 1: Basic input and output.* This build contains threads 1 and 8 and implements the basic input interface and the basic output interface early in the development. In order to accomplish thread 8, a contrived set of nodal voltages must be provided. The availability of this output interface will facilitate the evaluation of the results from build 2.

2. *Build 2: Solution processing.* Threads 2, 3, 4, 5, 6, and 7 constitute this build, which formulates the network equations and solves them. The build also outputs certain debugging printouts that allow for the evaluation of intermediate results.

3. *Build 3: Supplementary output parameters.* Threads 9, 10, 11, and 12 are contained in this build, which furnishes the capability to compute and output certain supplementary circuit quantities. Each of these quantities is provided only if requested by an input control parameter.

This development approach is laid out on the build plan shown in Figure 12-12. Two programmers could be assigned to work together as a team to construct and test the system. Experience indicates that on a system this size, approximately eight hours per thread complexity unit is a reasonable estimation on which to plan the scheduled duration. This rate of production is reflected on the build plan. In general, the amount of effort required per complexity unit is dependent upon the size and complexity of the system, the number of people applied to the problem, and the overall ability of the organization to develop the system in question.

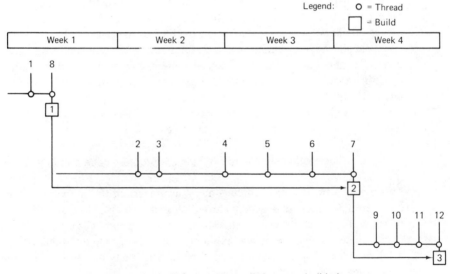

Figure 12-12 DC network analysis sytem build plan.

12.5
Full-Exercise Testing

Unit testing, of which low-level thread testing is a specific example, presents a fortuitous opportunity to economically test the entire software functionality. The reason such wholesale testing is economical is because the number of paths through the software is of reasonably small volume since only a small amount of code is executed at any one time. The threads technique is a perfect functional partitioning mechanism that assists full-exercise testing. Full exercise testing is explored in this section, in conjunction with the threads technique, through discussion of these topics:

- Full exercise test goals and measures
- Attributes of test coverage analyzer tools
- An example application of full coverage testing using the RXVP8O™ test coverage analyzer tool, and
- An analysis of life cycle cost benefits provided by this methodology.

12.5.1 TEST GOALS AND MEASURES

The objective of all verification and validation activities is to ensure that the delivered software product satisfies all the requirements specified. If test cases are selected strictly with these high-level objectives in mind, then the set of test cases will probably not be representative of the anticipated operational usage. Thus, the reliability of the software is not necessarily demonstrated or guaranteed. Indeed, frequently software errors are found during operational use that were not discovered during testing because no test case ever executed certain sections of code.

Delivery of reliable systems necessitates a testing activity that thoroughly executes the entire system. This could involve the construction, execution, and evaluation of such a huge number of test cases that, in all likelihood, the task will be economically as well as practically beyond human capacity. Accordingly, automated tools are often relied upon to evaluate test results, to measure the extent of the software exercised, and to assist in generating test cases that will execute those portions of the software not previously covered.

The following statement appeared in the statement of work included in a recent request for proposal from a govenmental agency:

The testing shall fully exercise the program code and data base.

This requirement is typical of customers' awareness of the software reliability problem and their unwillingness to accept partially tested systems. More and more, such requirements will apear as provisions in software procurements. Clearly, however, the means of compliance with them, unless explicitly stated, is open to interpretation. For example, a fully exercised system could mean one in which any one of the following, listed in descending order of difficulty, is executed.

- All permutations of control paths through the program
- All paths from outcomes of decision statements
- All statements in the program

Testing all possible combinations of paths through a program will probably require thousands of years or more of computer time even for common structures that appear simple. Thus, this test goal is not practical.

Testing all program statements at least once can usually be attained without particular difficulty, but is not considered to be sufficient. For example, doing so does not test all outcomes of decisions. Accordingly, many errors that involve erroneous transfer of control will be missed.

Testing of all path segments derived from outcomes of decision statements has been demonstrated to be achievable in practical software development environments. In defining decision paths, a loop structure would normally consist of two paths—the loop execution and loop escape.

Thus far we have learned that testing will never fully validate program correctness. That is, testing confirms only the presence of errors, not their absence. The line of reasoning behind these statements is that an economically feasible number of test cases is an insufficient statistical base from which to infer program correctness and, hence, the absence of errors. On a theoretical basis, it is hard to contest this argument. As a realistic matter, however, testing is the only practical device available to ascertain the likely correctness of the physical software product for any but the most trivial of software systems. In other words, the only pragmatic approach is to use testing efficiently to increase the *probability* of program correctness. This is done by carefully selecting test inputs to fully traverse as many path segments of the program control structure as possible.

Testing all decision paths, then, emerges as a goal that is achievable, beneficial, and economically practical. We define a decision path as consisting of the sequence of statements lying between the outcome of a decision up to and including the next decision. This sequence is immediately executable, once the initial decision outcome has been evaluated, and is the basic logical segment of the control structure. We can formally call it a *decision-to-decision path* and abbreviate it as ''DD-path.'' Figure 12–13 shows the partitioning of a typical flow sequnece into the following DD-paths:

- DD-path 1 is from module entry to the first decision element.
- DD-path 2 is the true branch from the first decision element.
- DD-path 3 is the false branch from the first decision element.
- DD-path 4 is a loop iteration.
- DD-path 5 is from the loop escape to the module exit.

By defining a set of inputs that execute all five DD-paths with successful results, there is a high probability that the module depicted is correct.

12.5.2 TEST COVERAGE ANALYZER

The set of tools that measures the coverage of test cases and assists in their preparation has been popularly termed a *test coverage analyzer*. The analyzer performs five basic functions:

1. Analysis of source code and creation of a data base.

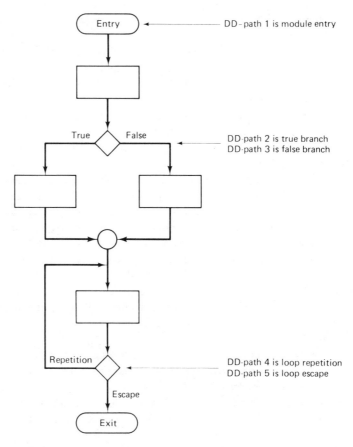

Entry ← DD-path 1 is module entry

True / False

DD-path 2 is true branch
DD-path 3 is false branch

Repetition

DD-path 4 is loop repetition
DD-path 5 is loop escape

Escape

Exit

Figure 12-13 Example of decision-to-decision path partitioning.

2. Generation of reports based on a static analysis of the source code that reveals existing or potential problems in the code and that identifies the software control and data structures.

3. Insertion of software probes into the source code that permit data collection on code segments executed.

4. Analysis of test results and generation of reports.

5. Generation of test assistance reports to aid in organizing testing and deriving input sets for particular tests.

The elements of a typical test coverage analyzer which perform these functions are diagrammed in Figure 12–14.

The static analysis module analyzes the static structure of the code without actually executing the program. Typically, such a module partitions each routine into DD-paths, providing a data base for a subsequent evaluation of the thoroughness of the testing, which is determined by measuring the number of DD-paths executed by the test cases. The static analysis module also analyzes the static invocation structure of the program—

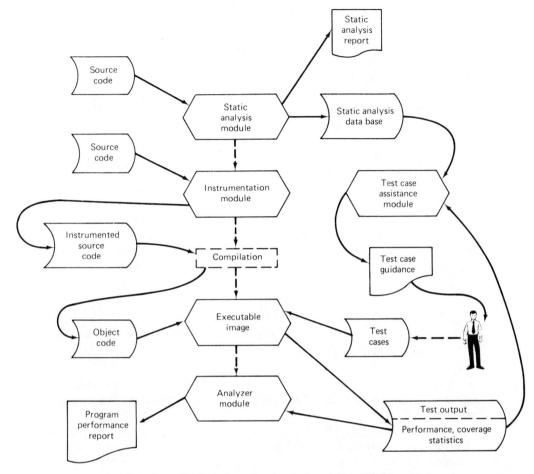

Figure 12-14 Typical elements of an automated verification system.

a tree structure of the routines that invoke and are invoked by a particular routine. This information is captured in a data base file and formatted for output in a printed report.

The instrumentation module acts as a preprocessor by inserting probes in the original source code. During execution, these probes intercept the flow of execution at key points and record program performance statistics and signals in an intermediate file. Typically, the instrumentation module permits tallies to be kept on which DD-paths are traversed how many times.

The analyzer module functions as a postprocessor after program execution. It formats and edits data recorded in an intermediate file during program execution and provides a printed report. The report furnishes information on the coverage of the testing.

The test-case assistance module aids in the selection of test inputs that will economically attain comprehensive testing goals. The module uses the static analysis data base and the coverage data recorded during the various executions of the program to guide the testers in the preparation of additional test cases. These then execute paths in the program that failed to be executed by previous test cases.

In this section, we consider a commercially available test coverage analyzer, RXVP80™, as applied to a sample problem. RXVP80™ is a tool for automated testing assistance and source program analysis. The tool was built and is marketed by General Research Corporation of Santa Barbara, California. RXVP80™ has been utilized at Hughes Aircraft Company in a production environment with generally successful results. It is used as an aid in analyzing and testing software systems by providing for syntax and structural analysis of source programs, static analysis to detect inconsistencies in program structure, automated documentation, source code instrumentation, and analysis of testing coverage. No endorsement of the product is implied in its being discussed here.

We consider the application of RXVP80™ to a part of the DC network analysis system introduced in Section 12.4. The overall configuration of this system was shown in Figure 12–10. We select a single thread, thread 12, from Figure 12–11 for demonstration of the analysis and testing capabilities of RXVP80™. The function of this thread is to print the branch currents. The thread consists of two modules:

1. *OUTPUT.* This module outputs the circuit quantities and controls the computation of certain optional data sets.

2. *IBCALC.* This module computes and outputs the branch currents, one of the optional output data sets.

Since thread 12 is the final thread of the DC network analysis system, its test configuration is that of the entire DC network analysis system architecture. No stubs or drivers are required.

If the OUTPUT and IBCALC modules have been compiled and statically analyzed, and if all errors thus far discovered have been removed from them, then a number of documentation reports based on an analysis of the source text, FORTRAN in this case, can be produced. Two typical and useful reports are the I/O statements and common matrices reports.

The I/O statements report (Figure 12–15) delineates all the input/output statements and formats contained in each module of the library. In effect, it pinpoints all the locations where data are input to and output from the system.

The common matrices report (Figure 12–16) provides an overview of the usage of each common block and each symbol within the common block. These data items are cross-referenced to each module with the type of usage (set, used, equivalenced) annotated. The common matrices report is also useful in identifying potentially affected data and modules when changes are made to the system.

After the thread has been debugged and corrected such that proper results have been obtained with a set of functional test cases, the next objective is to instrument the test target modules, OUTPUT and IBCALC, in order to determine the DD-path coverage that has been achieved with the functional test-case set. OUTPUT and IBCALC are so instrumented by running RXVP80™ with the instrumentation option. RXVP80™ performs a structural analysis of the subject modules and produces a source text listing for each module with the DD-paths identified. This listing is shown for IBCALC in Figure 12–

THE FOLLOWING MODULES CONTAIN I/O STATEMENTS

```
CNTRL
MODEQ
SOLVE
VBCALC
VECALC
TECALC
OUTPUT
IBCALC
FORM
R
GR
C
L
ESORCE
JSORCE
TC
TF
TP
TR
NODAL
INVERT
NCM
ECV
```

I/O STATEMENTS AND ASSOCIATED FORMATS

--- CNTRL ---

STMT	NEST	LINE	SOURCE . . .	. . . SOURCE TAB
8		47	READ (LUNIN,900) NODES,BRNCHS,MISC,SHORT,OPEN	
		48	C	
		49	C -----------------------------	
		50	C DETERMINE ANALYSIS OUTPUTS REQUIRED	
		51	C -----------------------------	
9		52	READ (LUNIN,910) OUT	
11		54	WRITE (LUNOUT,920) NODES,BRNCHS,OUT	
14		58	900 FORMAT (3I5,2F10.0)	
15		59	910 FORMAT (5L10)	
16		60	920 FORMAT (5X,11HEXIT CNTRL.,5X,I3,I3,2X,5L1)	

Figure 12-15 I/O statements report.

239

SUBROUTINE VBCALC (NODES,BRNCHS,A,VN,VB,VBOUT)

STMT NEST	LINE	SOURCE . . .	. . . SOURCE TAB
27	57	1 5X,15BRANCH VALUE./	
27	58	2 5X,15B -----	
28	59	920 FORMAT(7X,I2,2X,1PE12.5)	
29	60	930 FORMAT(5X,11HEXIT VBCALC)	

--- VECALC ---

STMT NEST	LINE	SOURCE . . .	. . . SOURCE TAB
8	27	WRITE (LUNOUT,900) VECUT	
25	57	WRITE (LUNOUT,910)	
27	59	WRITE (LUNOUT,920) I,VE(I)	
31	64	WRITE (LUNOUT,930)	
34	68	900 FORMAT(5X,22HENTER VECALC. VEOUT - ,I1)	
35	69	910 FORMAT(5X,16HELEMENT VOLTAGES .//	
35	70	1 5X,16HELEMENT VALUE./	
35	71	1 5X,16H -----)	
36	72	920 FORMAT(8X,I2,2X,1PE12.5)	
37	73	930 FORMAT(5X,11HEXIT VECALC)	

--- IECALC ---

STMT NEST	LINE	SOURCE . . .	. . . SOURCE TAB
9	26	WRITE (LUNOUT,900) IEOUT	
15	42	WRITE (LUNOUT,910)	
17	44	WRITE (LUNOUT,920) I,IE(I)	
21	49	WRITE (LUNOUT,930)	
24	53	900 FORMAT(5X,22HENTER IECALC. IEOUT - ,I1)	
25	54	910 FORMAT(5X,16HELEMENT CURRENTS .//	
25	55	1 5X,16HELEMENT VALUE./	
25	56	1 5X,16H -----)	
26	57	920 FORMAT(8X,I2,2X,1PE12.5)	
27	58	930 FORMAT(5X,11HEXIT IECALC)	

--- IBCALC ---

STMT NEST	LINE	SOURCE . . .	. . . SOURCE TAB
10	33	WRITE (LUNOUT,900) IBOUT	
28	66	WRITE (LUNOUT,910)	
30	68	WRITE (LUNOUT,920) I,IB(I)	
33	76	WRITE (LUNOUT,930) ERRTOT	
35	78	WRITE (LUNOUT,950)	
36	79	WRITE (LUNOUT,960) (I,ERROR(I),I=1,NODES)	
39	83	WRITE (LUNOUT,940)	

LEGEND (C=FIRST USED IN A CALL, E=EQUIVALENCED, S=SET, U=USED, X=SET AND USED

```
--------------------------------------------------------------------------------------
-------------------------------- •--------- •--------- •--------- •---------
    **           *                •          •          •          •
    * *  MODULE  * C C E EF •G I  I I J •LN NNN •OR S T T •T T V V *
    * *          * N C SO •RB ENS •  C E OO •U  O CF •PRB E *
    *   *        * T VOR • C CVO •  MT DD •T  L  •   C C *
    *    *       * R  RM•  A AER •   WAE •P  V  •   A A *
    *     *      * L  C  • L LRC •   RLQ •U  E  •   L L *
    *      *     *   E   • C CTE •    K  •T     •   C C *
    *       * *  *                •          •          •          •
COMMON * SYMBOL * *               •          •          •          •   *
    *       **                    •          •          •          •
-------------------------------- •--------- •--------- •--------- •---------
DEBUG  * MISC     * U X U U U •U U U U U •U U  U U •U U U U U •U U U U *
-------------------------------- •--------- •--------- •--------- •---------


-------------------------------- •------
    **           *                •
    * *  MODULE  * C C F GL •N R *
    * *          * N OR •E   *
    *   *        * T R •T   *
    *    *       * R M •W   *
    *     *      * L  •R   *
    *      * *   *     •K   *
    *       * *  *     •    *
COMMON * SYMBOL * *    •    *
    *       **         •
-------------------------------- •------
LIMITS * OPEN   * U S   U • U *
       * SHORT  * S   U U• U *
-------------------------------- •------


-------------------------------- •--------- •--------- •--------- •---------
    **           *                •          •          •          •
    * *  MODULE  * C C E EF •G I  I I J •LN NNN •OR S T T •T T V V *
    * *          * N C SO •RB ENS •  C E OO •U  O CF •PRB E *
    *   *        * T VOR • C CVO •  MT DD •T  L  •   C C *
    *    *       * R  RM•  A AER •   WAE •P  V  •   A A *
    *     *      * L  C  • L LRC •   RLQ •U  E  •   L L *
    *      *     *   E   • C CTE •    K  •T     ,  •   C C *
    *       * *  *                •          •          •          •
COMMON * SYMBOL * *               •          •          •          •   *
    *       **                    •          •          •          •
-------------------------------- •--------- •--------- •--------- •---------
UNITS  * LUNIN   *  U   U •          • S      •          •        *
       * LUNOUT  * U U U  U •U U U U U •U U S U U •U U  U U U •U U U U *
-------------------------------- •--------- •--------- •--------- •---------
```

Figure 12-16 Common matrices report.

17. Each statement is printed, indented in accordance with nesting level, and then, for each statement that starts a DD-path, the path numbers are annotated. The printout identifies the DD-paths that are referred to in test coverage analysis reports.

Collection of the program flow statistics is facilitated by the instrumentation of the program control structure. RXVP80™ examines the code and automatically inserts a call to a data collection routine that is invoked each time a control branch is taken. When the instrumented code is executed, the collection routine notes which module and code section are executed and builds up a data file from which the test analyzer generates its reports, for evaluation of the testing goals. The following paragraphs describe test analysis reports for the thread that consists of the modules OUTPUT and IBCALC.

SUBROUTINE IBCALC (G,VE,JS,NODES,BRNCHS,IB,A,IBOUT)

```
STMT NEST    LINE  SOURCE . . .                                                                    . . . SOURCE TAB
-----------------------------------------------------------------------------------------------------------------------
   1            1    SUBROUTINE IBCALC (G,VE,JS,NODES,BRNCHS,IB,A,IBOUT)
                2  C ROUTINE TO CALCULATE NETWORK BRANCH CURRENTS AND OUTPUT
                3  C RESULTS IF REQUESTED.
                4  C ROUTINE ALSO CALCULATES NODAL CURRENT UNBALANCES TO VALIDATE
                5  C SOLUTION ACCURACY.
                6  C
                7  C DESCRIPTION OF VARIABLES
                8  C      G        - BRANCH CONDUCTANCE MATRIX
                9  C      VE       - ELEMENT VOLTAGE VECTOR
               10  C      JS       - INDEPENDENT CURRENT SOURCE VECTOR
               11  C      BRNCHS   - NUMBER OF CIRCUIT BRANCHES
               12  C      IB       - BRANCH CURRENT VECTOR
               13  C      IBOUT    - BRANCH CURRENT OUTPUT FLAG
               14  C      A        - NODAL INCIDENCE MATRIX
               15  C      MISC     - DEBUG OUTPUT FLAG
               16  C      LUNIN    - LOGICAL INPUT UNIT
               17  C      LUNOUT   - LOGICAL OUTPUT UNIT
               18  C      ERROR    - CURRENT UNBALANCE VECTOR
               19  C      ERRTOT   - TOTAL CURRENT UNBALANCE
               20  C
               21  C-----------------------------------------------------------------
               22  C
                                                             ** DDPATH   1 IS PROCEDURE ENTRY
   2           23    INTEGER A,BRNCHS
   3           24    REAL JS,IB
   4           25    LOGICAL IBOUT
   5           26    COMMON /UNITS/ LUNIN,LUNOUT
   6           27    COMMON /DEBUG/ MISC
               28  C
   7           29    DIMENSION A(20,50), G(50,50), VE(50), JS(50), IB(50)
   8           30    DIMENSION ERROR (20)
               31  C
   9           32    IF (MISC.EQ.3)
                                                             ** DDPATH   2 IS TRUE BRANCH
                                                             ** DDPATH   3 IS FALSE BRANCH
  10     1     33    •      WRITE (LUNOUT,900) IBOUT
  11           34    END IF
               35  C
               36  C------------------------------------------------------------
               37  C CALCULATE BRANCH CURRENTS      IB = G*VE-JS
               38  C------------------------------------------------------------
               39  C
  12           40    DO (I=1,BRNCHS)
  13     1     41    •      IB(I) = 0.0
  14     1     42    •      DO (J=1,BRNCHS)
  15     2     43    •  •      IB(I) = IB(I)+G(I,J)*VE(J)
  16     1     44    •      END DO
                                                             ** DDPATH   4 IS LOOP ESCAPE
                                                             ** DDPATH   5 IS LOOP AGAIN
-----------------------------------------------------------------------------------------------------------------------
```

Figure 12-17 Module text with DD-path definitions.

STMT	NEST	LINE	SOURCE . . .	. . . SOURCE TAB
17	1	45	• IB(I) = IB(K)-JS(I)	
18		46	END DO	
		47	C	
		48	C--	
		49	C CALCULATE NODAL CURRENT UNBALANCE ER = A*IB	
		50	C--	
		51	C	

				** DDPATH 6 IS LOOP ESCAPE
				** DDPATH 7 IS LOOP AGAIN

19		52	ERROT = 0 0	
20		53	DO (I=1,NODES)	
21	1	54	• ERROR(I) = 0.0	
22	1	55	• DO (J=1,BRNCHS)	
23	2	56	• • ERROR(I) = ERROR(I)-A(I,J)*IB(J)	
24	1	57	• END DO	

				** DDPATH 8 IS LOOP ESCAPE
				** DDPATH 9 IS LOOP AGAIN

25	1	58	• ERRTOT = ERRTOT + ABS(ERROR(I))	
26		59	END DO	
		60	C	
		61	C--	
		62	C OUTPUT BRANCH CURRENTS	
		63	C--	
		64	C	

				** DDPATH 10 IS LOOP ESCAPE
				** DDPATH 11 IS LOOP AGAIN

| 27 | | 65 | IF (IBOUT) | |

				** DDPATH 12 IS TRUE BRANCH
				** DDPATH 13 IS FALSE BRANCH

28	1	66	• WRITE (LUNOUT,910)	
29	1	67	• DO (I=1,BRNCHS)	
30	2	68	• • WRITE (LUNOUT,920) I,IB(I)	
31	1	69	• END DO	

				** DDPATH 14 IS LOOP ESCAPE
				** DDPATH 15 IS LOOP AGAIN

32		70	END IF	
		71	C	
		72	C--	
		73	C OUTPUT NODAL CURRENT UNBALANCE	
		74	C--	
		75	C	
33		76	WRITE (LUNOUT,930) ERRTOT	
34		77	IF (ERRTOT.GT.0.001)	

				** DDPATH 16 IS TRUE BRANCH
				** DDPATH 17 IS FALSE BRANCH

35	1	78	• WRITE (LUNOUT,950)	
36	1	79	• WRITE (LUNOUT,960) (I,ERROR(I),I=1,NODES)	
37		80	END IF	
		81	C	

Figure 12-17   (Continued)

STMT NEST   LINE SOURCE . . .   . . . SOURCE TAB
----
   38   82   IF (MISC.EQ.3)

                                                                                                         ** DDPATH   18 IS TRUE BRANCH
                                                                                                         ** DDPATH   19 IS FALSE BRANCH

   39   1   83   •   WRITE (LUNOUT,940)
   40   84   END IF
   41   85   RETURN
                 86 C---
   42   87   900 FORMAT (5X,22HENTER IBCALC. IBOUT = ,L1)
   43   88   910 FORMAT (1H0,4X,15HBRANCH CURRENTS , / /
   43   89   1   5X,15HBRANCH   VALUE , /
   43   90   1   5X,15H ------   -----)
   44   91   920 FORMAT (7X,I2,2X,1PE12.5)
   45   92   930 FORMAT (/ / / 5X,26HNODAL CURRENT UNBALANCE = ,1PE12.5)
   46   93   940 FORMAT (5X,11HEXIT IBCALC)
   47   94   950 FORMAT (1H0,4X,30HINDIVIDUAL CURRENT UNBALANCES   / /
   47   95   1   5X,30H   NODE   VALUE   /
   47   96   2   5X,30H   ----   -----   )
   48   97   960 FORMAT (10X,IW,2X,1PE12.5)
   49   98   END

Figure 12-17   (Continued)

The coverage summary (Figure 12–18) shows the top-level view of testing progress. For each test case, and for the aggregate of all tests, the table lists the following:

- *Test case.* Sequential test number.
- *Module name.* Name of all instrumented and invoked modules in the test.
- *Number of DD-paths.* Total number of DD-paths in the module.

Under SUMMARY—THIS TEST, the table lists:

- *Number of invocations.* Total number of times the module was invoked in the single test.
- *DD-paths traversed.* Number of distinct DD-paths executed by the given test case.
- *Percent coverage.* Number of distinct DD-paths executed by the given test case as a percent of the total number of DD-paths in the module.

The data under CUMULATIVE SUMMARY essentially duplicates the preceding data for the aggregate of all test cases. At the point reached in the figure, only one test case has been run, yielding a coverage of 69.44 percent. Thus, the cumulative summary provides no additional information.

The report on DD-paths not hit (Figure 12–19) indicates which DD-paths were not executed by each test case and which remain untested after all the tests have been run.

The coverage summary report discloses the testing status: from Figure 12–17, only 69.44 percent of the DD-paths have been traversed by the set of functional test cases. But the testing goal is full coverage of all DD-paths. So the next step is to generate additional structurally oriented test cases that will extend the percentage of DD-path coverage. The process of generating new test cases focuses attention on the source code of the program and frequently reveals errors that would go undetected if execution results alone were examined.

We will now arbitrarily focus on the module IBCALC as the target for improved testing coverage. The untested DD-paths of IBCALC have been denoted on the report shown in Figure 12–18. DD-path 19 is selected as the target for the next test case because it may be at the end of a sequence of DD-paths which could provide additional incidental or collateral testing coverage. In consulting the IBCALC listing shown in Figure 12–19, we find that DD-path 19 is the false branch of a predicate controlled by the variable MISC. This DD-path will be traversed if MISC acquires a value other than 3.

By examining the IBCALC module listing in Figure 12–16, we see that MISC enters IBCALC through the common block DEBUG. Accordingly, it would be helpful to determine where this single-member common block is set. From the common matrices documentation report (Figure 12–15), we discover that the variable MISC of the common block DEBUG is set by the module CNTRL. On the possibility that MISC could be an external input to this module, the input/output statement report of Figure 12–15 is scanned for an I/O statement that involves MISC. We find that line 47 of CNTRL is a READ statement which includes MISC as the third element of the first record read by CNTRL.

TEST CASE	MODULE NAME	NUMBER OF D-D PATHS	SUMMARY--THIS TEST			CUMULATIVE SUMMARY			
			NUMBER OF INVOCATIONS	D-D PATHS TRAVERSED	PER CENT COVERAGE	NUMBER OF TESTS	INVOCATIONS	TRAVERSED	COVERAGE
2	OUTPUT	17	1	10	58.82	1	1	10	58.82
	IBCALC	19	1	15	78.95	1	1	15	78.95
	$$ALL$$	36		25	69.44	1		25	69.44

Figure 12-18 Coverage summary for one test case.

MODULE NAME	TEST NUMBER	PATHS NOT HIT	LIST OF DECISION TO DECISION PATHS NOT EXECUTED						
OUTPUT	1	7	3	5	9	11	13	15	17
	CUMUL	7	3	5	9	11	13	15	17
IBCALC	1	4	3	13	16	19			
	CUMUL	4	3	13	16	19			

Figure 12-19 DD-paths not hit for one test case.

Thus, the input source that controls the predicate associated with DD-path 19 has been located. This record will be modified so that MISC contains a value of 2 instead of 3. The change will cause the decision element in question to be evaluated as false, and hence DD-path number 19 will be executed.

Figures 12–20 and 12–21 respectively show the cumulative summary report and the report on DD-paths not hit after adding the new test case to the testing set. Note that the cumulative DD-path coverage has increased from 69.44 to 80.56 percent. The coverage achieved individually by the second test case is coincidentally identical to that of the first case. Obviously, this identical coverage was attained as a result of traversing several new DD-paths previously unexecuted, because the overall coverage has increased. It can be seen from the report on DD-paths not hit that several new DD-paths have been hit as a result of executing the second test case: DD-paths 3 and 17 in module OUTPUT, and DD-paths 3 and 19 in module IBCALC. Additional test cases may be contrived by using the methodology just described until the testing goals are attained.

Test coverage analyzers are attaining recognition as cost-effective devices that provide the ability to exhaustively test software to a level that would be prohibitive when using manual methods. The realization of the benefits that can be derived from this approach is contingent upon the scope of application of the tool. When applied to large amounts of code, the procedure can become overly involved and probably wind up neutralizing any potential positive effects. Recent experience indicates that maximum advantage is attained when testing is applied at the individual thread level, where reasonably small chunks of code (100 to 300 source lines) are involved. Indeed, this scope of application is consistent with the overall objective of uncovering as many errors as possible early in the implementation period rather than risking encountering these errors at higher levels of integration.

12.5.4 EFFECT ON LIFE-CYCLE COSTS

The expected benefits to software life-cycle costs that result from the preceding test strategy may be modeled on the basis of (1) an accounting of additional errors detected from a recent software project at Hughes Aircraft Company which utilized this approach, and (2) a profile of the escalating relative cost of correcting errors as a function of point of discovery in the life cycle.

The general effect of this exhaustive testing strategy and its projected effect on the life-cycle costs of the Hughes project are depicted in Figure 12–22. The figure compares the testing approach that utilized the automatic tool with the standard test approach, which does not. The use of the automatic testing tool results in higher error detection rates during the system construction period. During subsequent periods, however, including the operational period of the system, the detection rate of latent errors remains higher in the situation in which the testing tool is not used. The areas under both curves, that is, the total numbers of errors, are thus approximately equal, but the cost of rectifying the same error later in the life cycle is higher than it would have been were it detected earlier.

The exhaustive testing approach on the Hughes software project began with a checkout of each thread, using a set of functionally oriented test cases. At this point,

Figure 12-20 Cumulative summary after two test cases.

			SUMMARY -- THIS TEST			CUMULATIVE SUMMARY			
TEST CASE	MODULE NAME	NUMBER OF D-D PATHS	NUMBER OF INVOCATIONS	D-D PATHS TRAVERSED	PER CENT COVERAGE	NUMBER OF TESTS	INVOCATIONS	TRAVERSED	COVERAGE
2	OUTPUT	17	1	10	58.82	2	2	12	70.59
	IBCALC	19	1	15	78.95	2	2	17	89.47
	$$ALL$$	36		25	69.44	2		29	80.56

Figure 12-21 DD-paths not hit for two test cases.

MODULE NAME	TEST NUMBER	PATHS NOT HIT	LIST OF DECISION TO DECISION PATHS NOT EXECUTED
OUTPUT	1	7	3 5 9 11 13 15 17
	2	7	2 5 9 11 13 15 16
	CUMUL	5	5 9 11 13 15
IBCALC	1	4	3 13 16 19
	2	4	2 13 16 18
	CUMUL	2	13 16

248

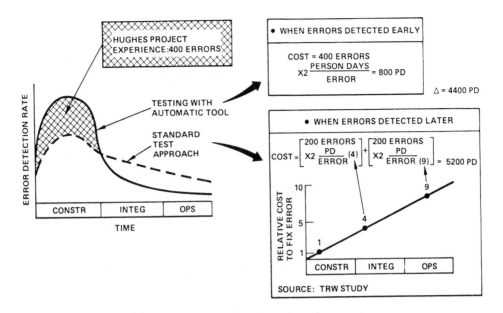

Figure 12-22 Automatic tool cost effectiveness in life cycle.

the traditional brand of testing would have concluded. Instead, additional test cases were contrived in order to achieve a DD-path coverage of close to 100 percent. The expectation was that this extra testing effort would expose additional errors.

Actual experience on the project supported this hypothesis. Because of the clearly demarcated testing phases, it was a simple matter to maintain a count of the errors detected by the extended testing. The count showed that an average of one additional error per thread was uncovered. The cost, in schedule time, of performing the extended testing ranged from a half day to three days per thread, with an average close to one day per thread. Normally, two persons were involved with the testing of the thread; hence, the incremental cost of the exhaustive testing effort was an average of two person-days per thread.

The project consisted of about 400 threads. Thus, the incremental cost of finding and correcting the 400 additional errors exposed was 800 person-days (400 errors × 2 person-days/error).

In a survey performed at TRW which seems to have become an industry standard, a profile was composed that depicted the relative cost of fixing errors as a function of the life-cycle stage in which the errors are discovered. The profile was compiled from a number of software projects at TRW, IBM, and General Telephone and Electronics. Some of the pertinent data extracted from it are that

1. The average relative cost to fix an error during integration as opposed to during construction is 4.

2. The average relative cost to fix an error during operation of the system as against construction is 9.

In order to model the life-cycle cost benefits, we will assume that the discovery of the 400 errors would otherwise have been evenly distributed over the integration and operational periods of the system; this is probably a conservative assumption because the type of errors overlooked during construction are more likely to reappear during operation of the system, where the software would undergo its first thorough execution. The 200 errors found during integration would cost 1,600 person-days (200 errors $\times$ 2 person-days/error $\times$ 4) to correct under this model, and the 200 errors found during operations would cost 3,600 person-days (200 errors $\times$ 2 person days/error $\times$ 9) to correct. Thus, the differential life-cycle cost avoidance achieved by the exhaustive testing strategy would be 4,400 person-days (3,600 + 1,600 = 5,200 person-days, less 800 person-days) for the Hughes project.

The specific quantitative cost advantage accrued on this project or any other as a result of the testing strategy discussed is undoubtedly speculative. None of us are clairvoyant, and we have no means of precisely detemining what would have occurred on a project had we done things differently. We are forced to rely on models in these circumstances, a course of action that is open to controversy. The form of the model that has been used, together with its parameters, may be arguable. But it is not the exact magnitude of the life-cycle cost benefit that is the issue here. Rather, the key thesis is that the use of this exhaustive testing approach should reveal more errors earlier in the development cycle, and this phenomenon has been observed in actual practice. Thus, the evidence shows that the approach provides a positive contribution to the software project, albeit quantitatively inexact.

Integration and Testing
of Larger Systems

13.1
Philosophy

To some extent, the description of the threads approach in the previous chapter has understated the complexity of modern software development projects by addressing a software system as a single development entity. Actually, many software projects are too large and the schedule too short to manage in this fashion. The software system is decomposed into structural elements that are developed in parallel and are eventually integrated together to recompose the system. We will refer to each of these structural elements as a *component*. On military standard software development projects, a component is known as a *computer software configuration item* (CSCI). A technique known as the *builds* approach, similar to the threads technique, is an effective means of managing the integration of the major components of the system.

The testing emphasis during component development is to remove as many functional defects from the software as possible. The emphasis on integration-level testing is to demonstrate the operation of the interfaces of the system and the overall functionality and performance as delineated in the system-level requirements specification. The success of the integration effort is very much dependent upon effective removal of most of the defects during the component-level thread testing.

Like the threads technique, the builds approach is founded upon the demonstration of a functional stimulus-response scenario. Each build may be thought of as constituting one or more system-level threads. Each system-level thread in turn is made up of a number of lower level component threads, all integrated together.

13.2
Integration Strategies

Integration and testing of larger systems can present a major risk to the overall program plan. However, the same technology applicable to the threads technique can be used for higher level system integration to reduce that risk. Basically, there are two approaches to the integration of systems: (1) the phased approach, and (2) the incremental approach.

The phased approach entails allocating a dedicated phase of the development cycle to the integration process. The software components are built in previous phases of the development cycle and then integrated to recompose the system in a single phase. Essentially, all of the integration is done in a "big bang," i.e., in one activity. Overall, phased integration is simply described as "build the software components all at once, throw it all together, and hope that it works." It almost always doesn't. Besides the obvious unmanageable aspects of this approach, it is unlikely that all the software components will be simultaneously available to allow integration to proceed. The phased technique of integration was probably tried just once in software history—or, more precisely, once in the history of every software development organization.

The incremental approach to integrating system components involves (1) coding and testing each software element by itself, (2) adding a single element to the previous baseline, (3) testing the combination, and (4) repeating steps 1, 2, and 3, until the last element is integrated. It is illustrated in Figure 13–1. Note how each integration step is focused on adding a single element of software and its associated interfaces at a time to an evolving baseline. This makes the process much more manageable and reliable than the phased approach.

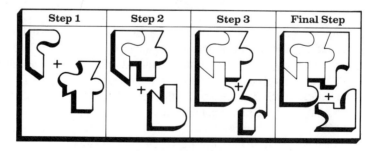

Figure 13-1 Incremental approach to integration.

In addition to providing overall manageability, incremental integration offers a number of more subtle advantages. First, it minimizes the need for separate testing beds: the testing bed for each software element is the previously evolved integrated set of elements. Also, incremental integration is reasonably self-focusing on the source of any problems that may develop: in most cases, when a problem appears, the source is in either the new element being added or the interface between that element and the baseline of previously integrated elements. Thus, a systematic investigation into error sources is facilitated. Yet another characteristic of the incremental approach is its flexibility. If major problems develop in any single integration step, it is possible to regress easily to the previous step. Indeed, it is usually even feasible to leapfrog ahead, as the schedule permits, and continue integrating with the next software element while the problem is being investigated.

13.3
Using the Builds Approach

A specific incremental integration strategy is the builds technique. Used judiciously, it can demonstrate the early viability of the overall system and its major interfaces.

The builds approach is illustrated from a planning standpoint in Figure 13–2. Build 1 constitutes an initial capability, build 2 augments this with an increased capability, and build 3 and subsequent builds incrementally increase the capability and eventually establish the total system at the final build. Each build is individually tested, with each test thought of as a partial dress rehearsal for the final system acceptance test. The system acceptance test then becomes merely the natural concluding event of the series. The overall objectives of the strategy are (1) to eliminate the risk inherent in the final system acceptance test, and (2) to establish a logically complete system as early as possible in the build sequence.

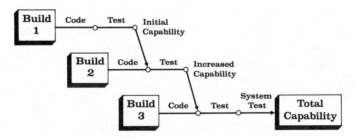

Figure 13-2   Segmenting a system using the builds approach.

The logically complete system demonstrates the essential viability of the system. The logically complete system is generally built around the major interfaces of the system, the overall planning of which should occur during the first several builds. In most large software systems, as well as in embedded applications, the major sources of risk of the system usually have something to do with the interfaces. Thus, by building the interfaces early in the integration cycle, the most risky aspects of the system are addressed first. Then, if major problems exist in the system concept, there is more time to deal with them than might be possible under more traditional integration strategies.

Each build consists of a number of system-level threads derived from the system-level specification and the system operations concept as mapped into the component structure of the physical architecture of the system. Again, this is similar to the threads approach. (See Figure 13–3.) In fact, the builds technique for integration involves the coordination of a system-level integration plan based upon system-level threads with that of component-level development plans based upon component-level threads. The infrastructure of each component development, as shown in the figure, is coordinated with the system integration plan. Each build adds one or more new threads to an evolving baseline, and each build test not only tests the new capabilities but also regressively tests previous builds.

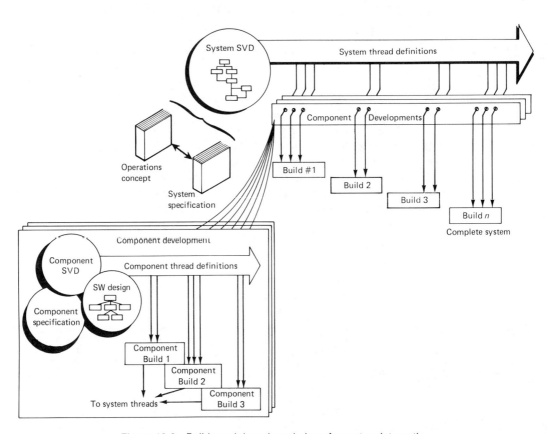

Figure 13-3 Builds and threads technique for system integration.

A simple example of the order in which builds occur is illustrated in Figure 13–4. The physical architecture of the system shown consists of two processors, machine A and machine B. The software architecture is a single hierarchically arranged component resident in each machine. We suppose that the flow of data, or the overall operations

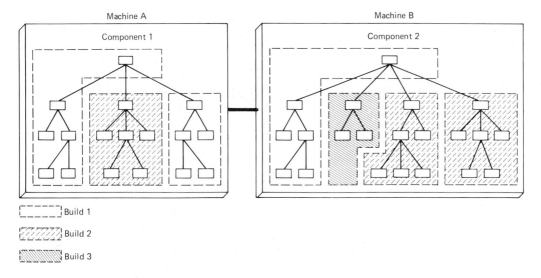

Machine A

Machine B

Component 1

Component 2

Build 1

Build 2

Build 3

Figure 13-4 Build development.

concept, is such that data enters machine A from the left and is preprocessed by software component number 1, with residual data being transferred into machine B for postprocessing by software component 2.

In considering the partitioning of this system between builds, it is necessary to assess the risk inherent in the system. Although this will depend upon the particular application involved, we can make certain general observations. Probably, the most risky aspect of the system is in the interface between machine A and machine B having to do with the data flow between software components 1 and 2.

With an eye toward this risk, a build plan is formulated to demonstrate the said interface early in the integration cycle of the system. Build 1 would then include the acceptance function at the front end of component 1, the intermachine data transmission function at the back end of component 1, and the acceptance function at the front end of component 2. Each of these functions is shown in Figure 13–4 as a "vertical slice" through the hierarchical software architectures of the two components, to be regarded as a component-level thread. The three threads are integrated to form build 1 of the system; build 1 would then constitute the major interfaces of the system—the data acceptance function and the intermachine transmission function—and would also demonstrate and mitigate the probable risk of the system.

Build 2 further adds to the skeleton set up by build 1. The final vertical slice or thread of software component 1 completes the preprocessing subsystem, which is integrated with two additional threads of software component 2 to complete build 2. Build 3 then simply adds the last thread of component 2 to finish the integration of the system. Note that each succeeding build becomes successively less risky as the initial skeleton is incrementally extended.

Now contrast the build approach with the more traditional method of integrating this type of system. The traditional method would involve two development teams, each developing its own machine-independent subsystems consisting of components 1 and 2, respectively. The last step of the development would then be to integrate these components. However, in view of the high risk inherent in the interface between the two independent subsystems, does the traditional method make sense? Of course not, for it leaves the system area with the most risk to the last integration step. By comparison, the builds approach addresses this risk area as the first step. Thus, if an interface problem is present, it will be discovered much earlier than it would using the traditional method.

3.4
Advantages of the Builds Approach

The builds technique is basically a risk-reduction strategy. Its key risk-reducing aspects are:

- It provides an early demonstration of the major interfaces of the system by the construction of a system skeleton, or logically complete system, as its primary goal.
- Each build test not only tests newly added capabilities but also regressively tests previous capabilities.
- Complete traceability to requirements is maintained by the network of threads that formally correlates stimulus-response scenarios with the requirements specification and design elements.

The builds strategy also provides schedule slippage protection: at any point in time, a partial working system will exist. This enables the customer to exercise options other than extending the schedule and nourishing the project with more money. For example, the customer might be able to accept a partial system consisting of a subset of the requirements on the original delivery date. Or the customer might be willing to accept and put into operation the partial system on the original date and then receive additional incremental deliveries at later dates to complete the system. Clearly, neither of these options is as pleasing to the customer as on-time performance, but they are preferable to an outright schedule slip with nothing to demonstrate on the original delivery date.

There is one other noteworthy advantage of the builds approach: the early integrated partial versions of the system demonstrate progress and achievement on a regular basis that is visible not only to management and the customer, but also to the development personnel. This early visible evidence of achievement acts as a morale booster to the developers, adding incentive to continue the diligent, hard work needed to successfully finish the system development and integration.

Management Aspects
of Software Quality

Analyzing the Economics
of Software Quality

14.1
Introduction

The key goal of quality engineering is to enable acquisition managers to specify the levels and types of qualities desired in a software product. A major ingredient of the approach is to introduce a deliberation of quality versus cost into the early system engineering process. Quality requirements will then be specified in light of the corresponding costs and schedule. And this is as it should be: just as functional and performance requirements are continually reviewed against required project resources, quality requirements should also be subject to the same deliberate trade-off against projected costs and schedule factors.

Because software quality engineering is a relatively new discipline, very little useful analysis is presently available to assist a manager who must ponder the cost versus quality trade-off. This chapter presents and analyzes a framework for macroestimating the relative costs of software development as a function of the desired quality level to assist in this fundamental decision. Two models are utilized, together with relative cost and schedule requirements that derive from the three tier quality model (engineering, reviews, and testing). Also included is an analysis of potential life-cycle costs and benefits. The framework, though somewhat general, is representative of the analysis that would be performed for a specific project.

14.2
Cost and Schedule Models

Historically, cost-estimating models have removed a bias toward optimistic results. Neither of the two most popular models, the Jensen and COCOMO models, (or any others for that matter) are straightforwardly aligned with the quality parameters of the software development scenarios that have been presented in this text. However, with some analysis, interpretation, and supplementation, these models provide reasonable vehicles for investigating the relative cost and schedule resources required for varying levels of quality.

14.2.1 ACQUISITION COST AND SCHEDULE

Modeling of the system acquisition requires nesting together two submodels—a developer model and an IV&V model—with a multiplicative relationship to each other to form the larger acquisition model. An overall view of an acquisition model, together with some of its more salient characteristics, is presented in Figure 14–1. The developer component of the model is driven by four quality-related parameters whose ranges of effort are noted at the right of the diagram. The level of verification and validation represents the review and testing activities; the Jensen model, chosen for purposes of example, rates the relative cost for this parameter in the range 1 to 1.98, depending upon the level of quality desired in the product. The use of modern practices and the use of automated tools represent the engineering activities. The Jensen model depicts the relative cost range of both parameters as approximately 1.5 to 1; note the opposite direction of

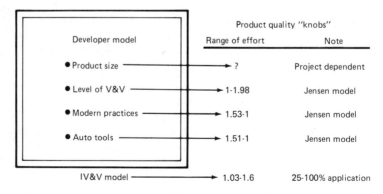

Figure 14-1 Macro quality cost analysis model.

the cost of engineering as against that of the review and testing activities; that is, more extensive use of modern practices and tools costs less, not more.

Another aspect of the developer model is the increased product size that may result from a consideration of such required quality attributes as fault tolerance and operability: because of dependencies of these attributes on specific project parameters, it is not possible to assess the product size in any general manner. On the other hand, the IV&V effort is modeled as an additional percentage of the development costs varying as a function of the desired quality and the portion of the product to be independently verified. The COCOMO, Jensen, and IV&V models are summarized in the following paragraphs.

COCOMO MODEL[1]. The Constructive Cost Model (COCOMO) operates on (1) organic, (2) embedded, and (3) semidetached software projects. Each of these has its distinct mathematical formulation.

The organic development mode usually entails a small to medium-sized project developed in a familiar, stable, in-house data processing environment. Constraints are few and relaxed. The organic mode is modeled by the equations

$$E_d = 3.2S^{1.05} \prod_{i=1}^{16} e_{ci} \text{ person-months}$$

$$t_d = 2.5E_d^{0.38} \text{ months}$$

where

E_d = product development effort
t_d = product development time
S = software product size
e_{ci} = development effort multiplier (environmental factor), to be described shortly

The embedded mode of development is associated with tight constraints. Here, the software system is generally part of an interdependent complex of hardware, software, and procedures, and the embedded project is usually larger and more complicated and involves a larger staff than an organic project. The analogous equations are

$$E_d = 2.8S^{1.20} \prod_{i=1}^{16} e_{ci}$$

and

$$t_d = 2.5E_d^{0.32}$$

The semidetached mode is a mixture of the features of the organic and embedded modes. Its equations are

$$E_d = 3.0S^{1.12} \prod_{i=1}^{16} e_{ci}$$

[1] Barry W. Boehm, *Software Engineering Economics* (Englewood Cliffs, N.J.: Prentice-Hall, 1981).

and

$$t_d = 2.5 E_d^{0.35}$$

JENSEN MODEL[2]. The Jensen cost and schedule estimation model treats all projects alike in a single pair of equations; it accounts for differences in project characteristics by means of its variable environmental factors. The Jensen equations are

$$E_d = 0.4 S^{1.4} D^{0.4} C_{tb}^{-1.2} \prod_{i=1}^{13} f_i^{1.2} \text{ person-years}$$
$$t_d = a E_d^{0.333} \text{ months}$$

where

E_d = development effort
S = software product size
C_{tb} = basic technology constant (includes some environmental factors)
D = system complexity
f = adjustment factors (other environmental factors)
a = 2.29 to 4.48, depending on system complexity

The environmental factors connected with both the COCOMO and Jensen models are listed in Table 14–1. Each factor is normalized to show the linear effect on cost, i.e., the worst-case increase in effort for each factor. The subset of these environmental factors that directly affect the cost of quality is the following:

Modern practices: Jensen range 1.53
                        COCOMO range 1.51
Software tools: Jensen range 1.51
                        COCOMO range 1.49
Required reliability: Jensen range 1.98
                        COCOMO range 1.87

The modern practices and software tools in combination model the engineering practices. The required reliability, which determines the level of verification and validation that must be applied in the development of a project, models the combination of review and testing activities in that development.

The ranges of these factors are remarkably similar. However, the actual absolute cost and schedule estimates of the two models differ considerably for the same project characteristics. This is interesting, but irrelevant to our immediate concern with the relative costs for levels of quality that are unaffected by absolute differences in the estimates produced by the models.

[2]Randall W. Jensen, "A Comparison of the Jensen and COCOMO Schedule and Cost Estimation Models," *Proceedings of International Society of Parametric Analysts*, Vol. 3, No. 1, pp. 98–99.

TABLE 14-1 ENVIRONMENTAL FACTOR SENSITIVITY COMPARISONS

Group	Factor	Jensen	COCOMO
Organization attribute	Application experience	1.59	1.57
	Language experience	1.46	1.20
	Modern practices	1.53	1.51
	Personnel capability		
	Analyst	2.09	2.06
	Programmer	2.06	2.03
	Resource access	1.96	1.32
	Software tools	1.51	1.49
	Virtual machine experience	1.92	1.34
Program attributes	Complexity	2.22	2.36
	Data-base size	—	1.23
	Real-time operation	1.33	—
	Required reliability	1.98	1.87
	Special display requirements	1.20	—
Computer attributes	Virtual machine volatility	1.67	1.49
	Memory constraint	1.50	1.56
	CPU time constraint	1.70	1.66
Project attributes	Multiple development sites	1.25	—
	Rehosting	2.22	—
	Operational site	1.39	—
	Remote support and facilities	1.43	—
	Requirements definition/volatility	1.71	1.78
	Required development schedule	—	1.23

IV&V MODEL. Here, the cost of IV&V is prescribed as a percentage of the development costs. The latter, amplified by an IV&V multiplier, constitute the acquisition cost of the system. The multiplier depends upon both the required quality level and the portion of the product that is submitted for IV&V. The gradations of IV&V percentage are delineated in Table 14–2. The actual IV&V multiplier for the three higher quality levels is expressed as an envelope resulting from the product of the development cost percentage and the product percentage. For example, the IV&V multiplier envelope for a product of good quality is 1.06 to 1.25. The full range of the IV&V multiplier over all quality levels is 1.00 to 1.60.

TABLE 14-2 INDEPENDENT VERIFICATION AND VALIDATION MODEL

Quality level	% Development costs	% Product applied to
Not an issue	0	—
Average	10	25 to 100
Good	25	25 to 100
Excellent	60	25 to 100

The IV&V development cost percentages were extracted from an empirical curve of IV&V costs accumulated by the U.S. Air Force Space Division[3] depicted in Figure 14-2. Average quality on this curve was correlated with an IV&V score of approximately 3, good quality with about 5, and excellent quality with 9. These scores, in the methodology described by the Air Force, result from an IV&V need determination based on system criticality.

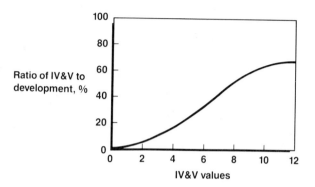

Figure 14-2 IV&V/development relative effort.

14.2.2 LIFE-CYCLE COST

The COCOMO model prescribes a maintenance mode based upon maintenance data from 24 software development projects. In general, there is a paucity of life-cycle cost data that can be mapped into software quality parameters. The COCOMO maintenance model is basically the same as the development model, except for the ratings of two environmental factors—the use of modern practices and required reliability.

The COCOMO maintenance model, supplemented by IV&V multipliers, is utilized to analyze life-cycle costs. The key aspects of the life-cycle model are:

- Modified COCOMO multipliers
  —Modern practices range of 2.07
  —Required reliability range of 1.38
- The same COCOMO software tool multipliers as for development
- The same IV&V multipliers as for development

It is important to note that the modern practices multiplier refers to the degree that these practices were used during *development;* thus, this life-cycle model reasons that the use of modern practices during development has a considerable positive impact on conserving maintenance costs. (The development range was 1.51 by comparison.)

[3]*Management Guide for Independent Verification and Validation* (Los Angeles, Ca.: U.S. Air Force Space Division, 1980).

Observe, in this model, that by and large the reliability range of 1.38 operates inversely on maintenance costs. That is, maintenance effort decreases as reliability increases, up to a point equivalent to about good quality; it then increases slightly to maintain excellent quality. Boehm points out, as an explanation for this phenomenon, that there are two overlapping influences present:

1. It costs more to maintain a higher level of reliability.

2. Latent errors are rectified less expensively for a system built to a higher reliability standard. It would appear that the crossover point where the first influence becomes dominant is just before the excellent quality level.

The model just described is used to calculate relative maintenance costs for the four levels of quality, as well as to estimate the payback periods over which increased development costs are amortized for incremental levels of quality. These periods are a function of the annual change traffic and show the crossover points where life-cycle costs become less for a higher quality level.

14.3
Relative Acquisition Cost and Schedule Analysis

Using the acquisition cost and schedule models of the previous section, we can estimate the relative costs and schedule for each of the four quality levels. For comparison, we will develop estimates from both the supplemented Jensen model and the supplemented COCOMO model. The figures are referenced to the lowest level of quality, i.e., where it is not an issue.

The supplemented Jensen model relative costs for each of the four quality levels are displayed in Table 14–3, where they are expressed as a range. Two component ranges contribute to this net range: engineering costs and IV&V costs. The IV&V range,

TABLE 14-3 SUPPLEMENTED JENSEN MODEL RELATIVE COSTS

Quality level	Engineering activities	Review/ testing	IV&V	Net
Not an issue	0.55 to 1.00	1.00	1.00	0.55 to 1.00
	0.68 to 1.00	1.00	1.00	0.68 to 1.00
Average	0.55 to 0.82	1.31	1.03 to 1.10	0.74 to 1.18
	0.68 to 0.82	1.31	1.03 to 1.10	0.92 to 1.18
Good	0.55 to 0.68	1.56	1.06 to 1.25	0.91 to 1.33
	0.68	1.56	1.06 to 1.25	1.12 to 1.33
Excellent	0.55	1.98	1.15 to 1.60	1.25 to 1.74
	0.68	1.98	1.15 to 1.60	1.55 to 2.15

Unconstrained   Realistic

as previously explained, occurs because of the assumption that anywhere from 25 to 100 percent of the product will be independently verified. The engineering costs comprise the combined effect of the modern practices and software tool environmental factor multipliers; from Table 14-1, the sensitivity ranges for these are 1.53 and 1.51, respectively, and 2.31 collectively. In practice, something less than these full ranges applies. At the low end of the scale, some minimal use of modern practices and tools is required even when quality is not an issue (and by this late date, even a minimally competent software organization can provide this level of technology). This truncates the potential range of 2.31 down to 1.82 to become 1.00 to 0.55, normalized to the "not an issue" quality level. Now, even though only a 1.00 degree of "smartness" is required for this level of quality, it is theoretically possible to offer anything up to an unconstrained excellent level of engineering. Hence, a range for engineering costs of 0.55–1.00, 0.55–0.82, 0.55–0.68, and 0.55 is shown for each of the four quality levels in the unconstrained case.

A more realistic assessment also places a constraint at the "smart" end of the scale. It is believed that no large-scale software development organization possesses, at this time, a staff that is both large and fully proficient in all modern practices in a highly automated tool environment. Therefore, an engineering relative cost of 0.68 represents the maximum realistic proficiency in engineering costs. In this case, the engineering cost ranges shown are 0.68–1.00, 0.68–0.82, 0.68, and 0.68 for each of the four quality levels. This "floor" for engineering costs is diagrammed in Figure 14-3, together with the envelope of IV&V costs and the review and testing costs as a function of quality level.

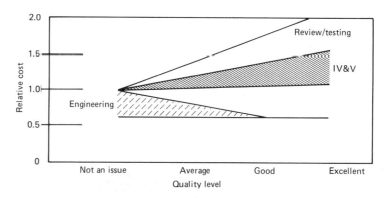

Figure 14-3 Components of the cost of quality.

An identical analysis of relative acquisition cost using the supplemented COCOMO model is contained in Table 14-4. The full range of the relative acquisition cost over the four quality levels is 2.06, close to the Jensen model range of 2.15. This slight difference is accounted for by the small variations in the multipliers for the engineering activities (modern practices and software tools) and the review and testing activities (required reliability; see Table 14-1).

TABLE 14-4 SUPPLEMENTED COCOMO MODEL RELATIVE COSTS

Quality level	Engineering activities	Review/ testing	IV&V	Net
Not an issue	0.56 to 1.00	1.00	1.00	0.56 to 1.00
	0.69 to 1.00	1.00	1.00	0.69 to 1.00
Average	0.56 to 0.83	1.27	1.03 to 1.10	0.73 to 1.16
	0.69 to 0.83	1.27	1.03 to 1.10	0.90 to 1.16
Good	0.56 to 0.69	1.51	1.06 to 1.25	0.90 to 1.30
	0.69	1.51	1.06 to 1.25	1.10 to 1.30
Excellent	0.56	1.87	1.15 to 1.60	1.20 to 1.68
	0.69	1.87	1.15 to 1.60	1.48 to 2.06

Unconstrained   Realistic

The variation in schedule over the range of quality is charted in Table 14–5. The analysis shows that, over the four levels of quality, the relative schedule will increase up to 30 percent as predicted by the supplemented Jensen model, and up to 26 percent as determined by the supplemented COCOMO model. These variations derive from the schedule formulations for each of the two models presented in Section 14.2. As the development times are dependent upon the relative effort, the ranges in the engineering activities and IV&V influence the relative schedule estimates proportionally.

TABLE 14-5 RELATIVE SCHEDULE ANALYSIS

Quality level	Relative Jensen schedule	Relative COCOMO schedule
Not an issue	0.88 to 1.00	0.89 to 1.00
Average	0.97 to 1.06	0.97 to 1.05
Good	1.04 to 1.10	1.03 to 1.09
Excellent	1.16 to 1.30	1.13 to 1.26

In both relative schedule and cost, the sensitivities of the supplemented COCOMO and Jensen models to required levels of quality are remarkably similar—all the more noteworthy in view of the fact that the two models were derived from completely independent data bases of software projects. For a specific set of project characteristics, however, it is likely that the absolute estimates of effort and schedule will be significantly different.

14.4
Life-Cycle Cost Analysis

The COCOMO maintenance model offers representative data for gaining insight into the life-cycle aspects of quality. Recall from Section 14.2 that the key aspects of the life-cycle projection model using the COCOMO maintenance mode as its base are as follows:

- The cost multiplier range for the engineering activities is different from that for the usage of modern practices during development.
- The higher the quality standard desired during acquisition, the lower the cost for maintenance of the software, up to the "good" level of quality, where the relationship reverses itself.
- All other aspects of the life-cycle mode are the same as in the acquisition model.

The relative maintenance costs for each of the four levels of quality are presented in Table 14–6. The data are specified for two sizes of software product, 512,000 source lines of code (LOC) and 32,000 source lines of code. The engineering muliplier for the larger sized product represents a more efficient maintenance process than for a smaller product. The net maintenance costs decrease for each increment of built-in higher quality up to the good level; the cost of maintenance for an excellent product is comparatively greater, becoming dominant over efficiency in rectifying latent defects at this level of quality.

TABLE 14-6 SUPPLEMENTED COCOMO MODEL RELATIVE MAINTENANCE COSTS

Quality level	Engineering activities	Review/ testing	IV&V	Net
Not an issue	1.00	1.00	1.00	1.00
	1.00	1.00	1.00	1.00
Average	0.76	0.79	1.03 to 1.10	0.62 to 0.66
	0.86	0.79	1.03 to 1.10	0.70 to 0.75
Good	0.58	0.72	1.06 to 1.25	0.44 to 0.52
	0.74	0.72	1.06 to 1.25	0.56 to 0.67
Excellent	0.58	0.81	1.15 to 1.60	0.54 to 0.75
	0.74	0.81	1.15 to 1.60	0.70 to 0.96

512K LOC product   32K LOC product

One of the issues that exist early in the acquisition process when quality levels are specified is the determination of any life-cycle cost advantages that may be present in selecting a higher quality level. Included in this determination is the expected lifetime of the system and the rate at which the system will be modified. These are parameters that are difficult to predict when a system is in its infant stages. Nonetheless, an educated estimate must be made if we are to intelligently decide whether or not an additional investment of development funds for a higher level of quality is to be repaid in lower long-term costs over the life of the system. A representative analysis of this issue is displayed graphically in Figure 14–4. The figure shows the period required to pay back the incremental development costs for each level of quality as a function of the annual percent of change traffic; the payback or amortization period is based upon a comparison of the average, good, and excellent quality levels with the basic level where quality is

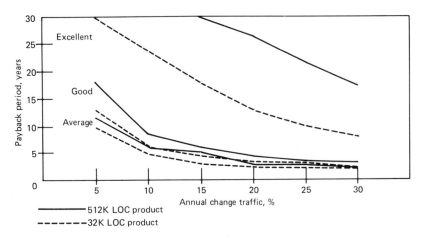

Figure 14-4 Life-cycle payback analysis (minimal quality baseline).

not an issue. The analysis was performed for both the large sized product and the smaller product. The figure thus represents the number of years required to equalize the extra costs associated with acquiring a higher level of quality with the lesser costs associated with maintaining the same quality level.

A similar analysis is presented in Figure 14–5, except that here the comparison is based upon the quality level that is one increment lower. Since the maintenance cost for excellent quality is higher than that for good quality, there is no real amortization period for the excellent quality level, at least as far as the model portrayed is concerned. The same general conclusion is thus apparent from the two analyses: long-lived and frequently changed systems may merit an additional investment during acquisition because they are

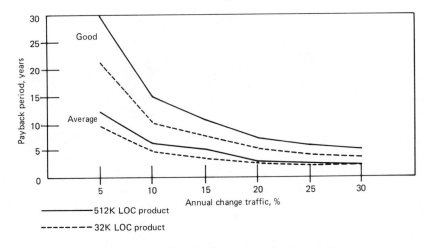

Figure 14-5 Marginal life-cycle payback analysis.

likely to accrue a reduction in costs over the life cycle of the system. Referring back to Figure 14–4, it would appear difficult nonetheless to justify an excellent-quality-level system on purely economic grounds based on these data because of the very long payback periods. However, for any specific project, the technical needs for quality could supersede the economic factors.

14.5
Conclusions

The sensitivity of both acquisition and life-cycle costs to quality level appear to be in the intuitively reasonable range. However, the analyses presented should not necessarily be regarded as templates for general application. It would be more proper to regard the information as a starting point or framework for establishing the trade-offs more precisely for a specific project. What is promising is that the analysis yields results that are consistent with intuition.

Of considerable concern is the paucity of published life-cycle cost data. While the COCOMO data are useful, greater confidence would be achieved if other independent data sources were available for analysis. Certainly, a more systematic vehicle for data collection and distribution would be immensely valuable and well received.

Finally, we should not overlook the fact that people are the most important ingredient in the eventual cost of quality. The quality of a product is a function of its history, which, in the final analysis, comes down to how well people have been prepared and what effort has been invested in careful plans for developing the product.

Management Aspects of Software Quality Engineering

As with any complex activity, the technical aspects of software quality engineering must be planned, organized, monitored, and constantly readjusted to be successful. This chapter discusses the management of software quality engineering, underlying which are the following key points:

1. Software quality engineering is accomplished by software engineers; there are no special quality organizations needed. Therefore, other than the team techniques to be discussed in Chapter 16, there is no need for reorganizing for software quality engineering.

2. If you agree with the principles that this book proposes, ''quality'' is defined by documented software quality requirements. (See Chapter 4.) Therefore, measuring quality means measuring how completely those requirements have been implemented.

3. We assume that, in general, engineers want to do a high-quality job. Given this assumption and the absence of roadblocks that stand in the engineer's way, the goal is not to motivate but to educate.

15.1
What is Required for Software Quality Engineering?

Effectively planning for software quality engineering requires being aware of all of the activities, products, people, etc., needed to achieve it. The following checklist itemizes these needs.

Quality requirements Has "high quality" been defined by an agreed-upon set of software quality requirements? The remainder of this checklist will be practically useless if the answer to this question is no.

Effective plans Do plans for software development emphasize review and rework? Are the plans realistic? (Are they achievable or just wish lists?) Will you be able to provide staff under the plan? Or should functional requirements be narrowed in scope?

Organization Is your organization being built with achievement of quality in mind? Are serious goals for quality set and promulgated? Are capable designers and programmers being recruited? Is quality in the product being emphasized to the same extent as (or even more than) meeting production milestones? Is there aware-ness and communication within the organization?

Training Are there plans for training engineers, or is training just catch as catch can? You can't expect engineers to be effective in methods, if they don't know what standards or software quality requirements are in place.

Standards Have all required standards been identified? If not, is there a plan to identify them? Is there a plan to decide on and develop the standards? Are they included in the training plan?

Reviews Have in-process reviews been included in the planning? Are rework and re-review included in the planning? Have procedures for the reviews been developed? Are there objective completion criteria defined as a precondition for review? Are the reviews serious or just milestones to be met? Do the reviews include design, process, and document reviews?

Testing Is planning for tests on par with planning for software development? Is test-ability a part of the requirements review, design review, and code review? Do you have a separate staff dedicated to testing? Are they involved from the start (during requirements analysis)?

People Are designers and programmers aware of the importance of quality? Are they motivated? Are they prepared through training? Has communication of organiza-tional goals reached everyone on the staff? Are people capable of doing the job?

Procedures Has a set of defined procedures to back up the planned methodology been selected and specified? Are they tried and true? Do the procedures support achieve-ment of the software quality requirements? Are the designers and programmers experienced in the procedures? Are the procedures appropriate for the problem to be solved? Are there tools to help implement the procedures?

Tools Has a set of tools to back up the planned procedures been selected and specified? Are they tried and true? Are the designers and programmers experienced in the tools? Do the tools support achievement of the quality requirements? Do the tools support the specified standards?

Facilities Are there enough resources (computers, terminals, response time, etc.) to meet all of the designers' and programmers' needs?

Configuration Control Are there specified procedures for controlling changes to designs and programs during development? Are the software standards and procedures controlled? How are software changes controlled during testing?

Subcontractor Control What plans, procedures, tools, and configuration control will be in place to manage the quality of subcontractors developing software for your organization? What procedures will be used to certify whether their product complies with your organization's standards? Are they responsible for the same organizational goals, procedures, tools, standards, and configuration control as your organization is?

Measurement and Feedback Does your organization have a plan for measuring incremental achievement of quality? Have quality metrics been decided upon and specified? Are the metrics part of the review procedures? Are there plans for corrective action to resolve any defects found? Will there be an analytical effort to identify endemic problems? Does your organization audit itself?

Although not specifically oriented to software quality engineering, the interested reader will find a comprehensive checklist for quality software engineering in the following report: W. S. Humphrey, et al., *A Method for Assessing the Software Engineering Capability of Contractors*, Software Engineering Institute, Carnegie-Mellon University, Pittsburgh, Pa., Technical Report CMU/SEI-87-TR-23, September 1987.

15.2
Who Is Responsible for Software Quality Engineering?

After a major defense contractor's Tucson manufacturing facility was shut down because of poor quality, a tiger team was sent in to investigate the cause of the problem. The major outcome of the investigation was that "quality" was centered in a large quality assurance organization that inspected parts after they were built. Accordingly, no one on the production line felt responsible for quality; everyone felt it was quality assurance's job. But the quality assurance people functioned too late in the production cycle and were too overworked to find all the defects that eventually led to the shutdown.

The outcome of this investigation is a lesson we can learn from to help us manage software quality. The solution to the serious problem that existed in the Tucson firm was to decentralize quality down to all of the first-line supervisors. They and their employees were made responsible for the quality of the products that they built, and the quality assurance organization was disbanded.

No one person or organization is responsible for quality; instead, everyone is responsible for quality in some way or another. As Figure 15-1 illustrates, there are at least seven functions that come together to achieve software quality. They are all pieces of the same puzzle; remove any one of them, and a hole is left. If any one person doesn't carry his or her own weight, all the others suffer.

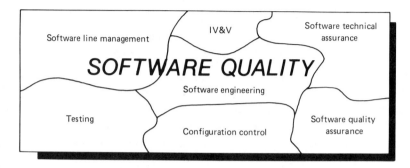

Figure 15-1 The software quality puzzle.

Following is a brief description of the seven functions and what they are responsible for:

SOFTWARE TECHNICAL ASSURANCE.   The software technical assurance function is responsible for quality planning, quality preparation, quality specification, and validating that quality requirements are being implemented into the designs. (This may be a new role for your organization; see the next section for more details.)

SOFTWARE LINE MANAGEMENT.   This traditional function is responsible for implementing the software quality plans, monitoring and measuring the software development process, and removing roadblocks to quality.

SOFTWARE ENGINEERING.   Software engineers are responsible for adding quality into the software. They are the most important part of the quality "puzzle," for they leave a hole that is impossible to fill without their contribution. Software engineering is the only function that can add quality to the product during development. It is also responsible for reviewing software to uncover defects.

TESTING.   Software testing validates whether the implemented software meets its specification in an error-free manner, i.e., whether the software quality requirements have been unerroneously incorporated into the finished product. In a sense, software testing can also add quality to the software: better testing will uncover more errors, which adds to the reliability of the software.

SOFTWARE QUALITY ASSURANCE.   This traditional function is responsible for uncovering bottlenecks to the achievement of quality and uncovering product and process defects. Software quality assurance is an importnat role because it can provide an independent auditor's viewpoint and oftentimes it uncovers problems that are not apparent to the developers.

CONFIGURATION CONTROL. The traditional function of configuration control is responsible for ensuring the integrity of the evolving software product. The absence of integrity results in chaos and a lack of control over the achievement of quality attributes.

IV&V. IV&V is a highly concentrated, more technical form of software quality assurance.

15.3
Introducing Software Technical Assurance

Earlier, we stated that there is a need in software quality engineering for activities and products that have not traditionally been a part of software development—for example, products like a quality needs data base, a level-of-quality matrix, and software quality requirements. But who is responsible for these products and activities?

```
ROLES AND RESPONSIBILITIES OF STA

SUBGOALS
     1. Define quality in such a way that it is achievable
     2. Select software engineering standards, procedures, and tools that
        make achievement of quality possible
     3. Prepare staff to achieve quality
     4. Help staff achieve quality in their work (i.e engineer in quality)
RESPONSIBILITIES
     1. Define quality in such a way that it is achievable
        a. Specify software quality requirements
        b. Set quantifiable quality goals
     2. Select standards, procedures, and tools
        a. Interpret customer's required standards
        b. Establish notebook index of standards and procedures
        c. Review and approve candidate standards, procedures, and tools
     3. Prepare staff to achieve quality
        a. Help establish awareness of quality
        b. Establish training plan
        c. Help motivate
     4. Help staff achieve quality in their work
        a. Get involved in the engineering process
        b. Find and help remove bottlenecks to achieving quality
        c. Verify that designs meet quality requirements
        d. Validate that code meets quality requirements
        e. Assist in software quality assurance (SQA)
        f. Review and approve software deliverables
PRODUCTS OF STA
     1. Software quality requirements specification
     2. Total quality plan
     3. Notebook index for standards and procedures
     4. Quality performance status report
     5. Training plan
```

Figure 15-2   Roles and responsibilities of STA.

TABLE 15-1 ALLOCATION OF RESPONSIBILITIES AMONG STA, SQA, AND ENGINEERS

	SQA			STA			ENG		
	R	A	C*	R	A	C	R	A	C
STANDARDS AND PROCEDURES									
Interpret customer requirements			x	x			x		
Specify standards/procedures			x	x				x	
Develop standards/procedures			x		x		x		
Use standards/procedures							x		
Monitor use of standards/procedures	x					x			x
Subcontractor control of standards/procedures	x					x			
QUALITY REQUIREMENTS									
Specify software quality requirements			x	x					x
Implement requirements						x	x		
Find and remove bottlenecks to achieving quality	x			x					
REVIEW DESIGNS TO VERIFY QUALITY									
Internal design/code reviews		x				x	x		
Quality requirements reviews			x	x					
Trend data analysis	x					x			
Formal (customer) reviews			x			x	x		
Assure action on closure of item	x					x			
TEST CODE TO VALIDATE QUALITY									
Prepare test plans/procedures						x	x		
Review test plans/procedures		x		x					
Conduct unit/CSC tests		x					x		
Validate quality requirements exhibited in SW		x		x					
CSCI-level test witnessing	x					x			x
QUALITY OF DOCUMENTS									
Develop quality documentation of designs							x		
Review for adherence to standards	x								
Review for quality requirements			x	x					

TABLE 15-1 (cont.)

	SQA			STA			ENG		
	R	A	C*	R	A	C	R	A	C
SOFTWARE CONTROL Configuration management control		x				x	x		
Software and document impoundment and release	x								
System-level certification	x								

*LEGEND:
R: responsible for; either does or delegates the work
A: approval/rejection authority
C: consultant; no authority, no responsibility

One approach is to train existing engineers to undertake the added responsibilities. Another approach is to define a new role in software development to focus on the specialized expertise needed to perform the specialized tasks. In either case, we define this role as *software technical assurance*, or STA. Figure 15-2 shows the roles and responsibilities of STA.

As the figure shows, STA is responsible not for achieving quality, but, instead, for acting as a catalyst in engineers' attempts to achieve quality. STA does not engineer in quality, review for defects, or test for errors; engineers do that. Rather, STA helps engineers perform these quality-enhancing activities through the development of understandable quality specifications, quality planning, training, and coaching.

Software technical assurance may be contrasted with software quality assurance in its relationship to software development. Although both functions have the same goal— a quality software product—STA works with engineers to engineer in quality, while SQA audits the processes and products of engineers to validate that quality has in fact been engineered in. The key difference is that STA is part of the engineering, whereas SQA is independent of it. A sample allocation of responsibilities for quality among STA, SQA, and software engineers (ENG) is given in Table 15-1.

15.4
Measuring Software Quality

Figure 15-3 is an interesting introduction to the topic of software quality measurement. It illustrates one of the ways that the software quality assurance organization at Hitachi's Software Works in Yokohama, Japan, measures and reports on software quality. For any given software component, a goal regarding the number of defects allowed is determined (as a function of complexity, experience, and the like), management risk boundaries are drawn (based on experience), and cumulative defects found in the software component are plotted over time. When the actual number of defects found exceeds the risk boundaries, or when predicted defects fall short of the goal, an alert is established for required corrective action.

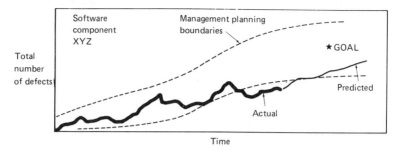

Figure 15-3 Measuring software process quality.

One question to ask is whether it is software *product* quality or software *process* quality that is measured by this technique? The answer is that since this type of data collection and reporting is meant to motivate an organization to spend enough time reviewing its products to ensure that as many defects as possible have been eliminated, it is software process quality that is measured by the technique. This does not, however, mean that high quality products will result from such a measurement approach. High quality products are our goal.

15.4.1 MEASURING SOFTWARE PRODUCT QUALITY

The objective of measuring software product quality is to determine the extent to which a software product exhibits required software quality requirements. In most cases nowadays, these are contained in developer-derived checklists for design and coding reviews. Consequently, measuring software product quality by using this checklist is inconclusive and open to interpretation from an end user's viewpoint. However, if software quality requirements have been developed as suggested in Chapters 3 and 4, then there exist objective and well-defined requirements which can serve as a checklist for measuring quality. Moreover, if an agreement with the end user has been negotiated on these requirements, then the interpretation problem is circumvented: there is a well-defined contract regarding the criteria of high quality between the developer and the user.

Under these assumptions, to measure software product quality means to hold the applicable requirements up against the product to see how many of them have been implemented. When we finish checking, we can call those unimplemented requirements defects. A measure of the progress in achieving quality can then be determined by dividing the number of defects by the total number of requirements. Measurement of software product quality is shown in Figure 15–4 in a set of curves analogous to those of Figure 15–3 which measure software process quality.

This treatment may seem overly simplistic to those who have experience in measuring software product quality. However, its simplicity derives from (1) the

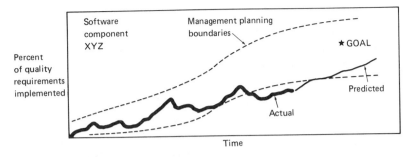

Figure 15-4 Measuring software product quality.

existence of the software quality requirements, and (2) the purposeful omission of some complexities. On the latter score, we have assumed, for example, that we are dealing only with static quality requirements, i.e., attributes of designs, code, and documents that are exhibited without executing the software. When dynamic requirements are included we enter another realm of measurement altogether. For instance, we may need to collect data on the occurrence of failures during software execution, apply reliability models to the data, plot the MTBF over time, and show achievement of some required reliability value. This would obviously complicate matters considerably.

Indeed, even determining whether a given product does or does not meet a quality requirement is not always as easy as it sounds. For example, a quality requirement may be that the so-called software science difficulty metric[1] be less than some value x for all program units. To apply this metric to 20,000 program units is not a trivial task! Nonetheless, well-defined, objective static software quality requirements will make measuring software product quality simpler, in general, than it otherwise would be.

15.4.2 MEASURING SOFTWARE PROCESS QUALITY

The objective of measuring software process quality is to detect roadblocks in the software development environment that interfere with achieving software product quality. As illustrated in Figure 15–3, cumulative defects persistently found in a product give us an indication of the extent to which the product is being reviewed. Falling short of the review goal could indicate a roadblock in the software development environment. The roadblock may be lack of motivation, lack of time to perform the reviews, inadequate tools or resources, ineffective review procedures, or lack of training in the procedures.

The following list presents some examples of metrics used to measure software process quality based on the discussion in the next section of the kind of software

[1]See M. H. Halstead, "Elements of Software Science," in P. J. Denning (ed.), Operating and Programming System Series (New York: Elsevier North Holland, 1977).

engineering environment and attributes that lead to good process quality (more examples can be found in Draft IEEE Standard P982):

> Number of reviews per unit
>
> Number of defects per unit
>
> Number of compilations per unit
>
> Effort to integrate per unit
>
> Training class hours per employee
>
> Facility downtime (percent of total time)
>
> Number of quality assurance deficiency reports per person
>
> Percent of staff familiar with software development plan
>
> Employee turnover rate (percent)
>
> Percent of milestones met

$$\text{Quality Effectiveness} = 1 - \frac{\text{Rework Effort}}{\text{Total Effort}}$$

15.5
Avoiding Roadblocks to Achieving Quality

Figure 15–5, written in big bold letters, is a good chart to hang on your wall at work.

> **TWO FUNDAMENTALS OF QUALITY:**
>
> 1. In general, people want to do a high-quality job
>
> 2. Crisis management and quality cannot coexist

Figure 15-5 Two fundamentals of quality.

Most people agree with the first principle—that engineers, in general, want to do high-quality work. However, as soon as one admits that this is true, a dilemma exists, namely, that if people want to do a high-quality job, then why is there such a problem turning out high-quality software products? The answer is twofold: (1) lack of training, and (2) lack of time.

We will assume that motivation for training is not a big problem; after all, you are reading this book. Therefore, the second reason is the one that is more problematic: quality-minded engineers do not turn out high-quality products because they don't have enough time to do so—time to be trained in software quality engineering techniques, time to learn what software quality is, time to proceed iteratively through a design to ensure that quality has been engineered in, time for good reviews, time for rework, time for thorough testing, and so forth. In effect, crisis management takes over and the second principle of Figure 15–5 comes to the fore: crisis management and quality cannot coexist.

There are other roadblocks to achieving quality besides crisis management—lack of specification of software quality requirements and selection of good engineering techniques to achieve the quality requirements, to name just two that have already been examined. In general, it is important in this regard to consider the efficiency of the software engineering environment as a whole. Figure 15–6 presents a useful way to view the software engineering environment for purposes of efficiency.

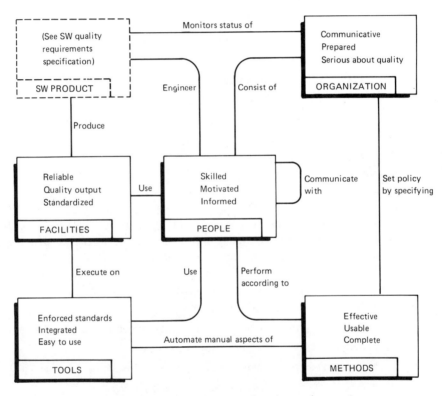

Figure 15-6   The software engineering environment.

The model shown is a simplification of a very complex system. The system has several parts: people, organizations, tools, methods, and facilities. Each part consists of components; for example, the people part represents all of the employees in the organization. In this scheme, parts interact with other parts to produce software products (e.g., a person *uses* tools to *perform engineering according to* some method). The annotated lines connecting the parts of the network are the primary interactions.

A sample scenario will be helpful in clarifying the model. An organization consists of a two-person design team which sets policy by deciding to use the peer review method for evaluating designs. The design review is performed according to a documented procedure on design reviews whereby each person communicates with every other person regarding each other's design. The reviewers use an automated tool to record and collect data on the results of the design review. The tool executes on a personal computer to produce the final report.

It takes people, organizations, methods, tools, and facilities all working together as a whole to produce quality software products. Like an automobile engine, any part that isn't working right or isn't tuned will cause the whole engine to "run rough." Roadblocks to achieving quality can occur between many different parts of the system, for example,

- People who are not aware of available tools.
- People who are not skilled in the use of certain methods.
- People who are uninformed because of a breakdown in communication.
- Inadequate facilities to run the required tools.
- Planning that doesn't allow enough time for preparation.
- Methods that nobody understands.
- Poor-quality printers.

Attributes of each part listed are shown inside each box. For example, we would read the attributes for people as "people who are skilled, motivated, and informed." The attributes shown are those which are most important to the efficiency of achieving software quality in the software engineering environment. That is, to avoid roadblocks to achieving quality, we avoid the negations of these attributes, for example,

- An immediate supervisor who accepts sloppy work.
- A lack of organizational goals.
- A company slogan that emphasizes merely getting the product out on time.
- People who work by unrealistic schedules.
- Equal rewards for poor as well as high quality.
- A lack of recognition of superior quality work.
- People who ask for quality but don't define it.

In an engineering environment characterized by the preceding attributes, can employees be expected to achieve high-quality products? Not at all, and the same can be said for the negations of all of the other attributes of all of the other parts of the software engineering environment.

Remember, no matter how good the software quality requirements, the techniques, and the tools are, they are rendered useless by roadblocks in the software engineering environment.

Utilizing Team Techniques

16.1
Advantages of Team Techniques

The organization of personnel into small teams permits the concentration of collective mental resources on the product being developed or the activity being performed. This collaboration is intended to produce a higher quality product with the same expenditure of labor as if the team members worked separately. Most team techniques are described in terms of the ''lean and mean'' philosophy: an intense effort by a highly cooperative and dedicated small group of people with strong leadership. The degree to which these attributes can be achieved in practice is highly dependent on the availability of skilled people.

Team practices address the need to establish simpler communication patterns within the software development organization. The team approach permits the focusing of several minds on the product of the effort. The expectation is that products of higher quality will be produced under this method than what would result from the conventional one-to-one assignments of individuals to tasks. The key features that distinguish team practices from the conventional organization are (1) continuous verification and validation, and (2) better integration of individual efforts. These features come about largely as a result of a continuous communication pattern. Fuller communication generally yields a fuller understanding of the problem by each team member and also results in a continuous walk-through environment that fosters the removal of errors closer to their sources.

The initial formal team concept was that of IBM's chief programmer team. Since the inception of this team approach in the early 1970s, other team concepts have emerged, some of which may even have chronologically preceded IBM's. Regardless of the historical circumstances, the notion of a chief programmer team can be pointed to as a milestone in the awareness of the positive contributions that team practices have made to quality. Practically any task can be organized as a team activity; some have been so utilized with successful results, while some remain unproven. The following team techniques have some basis in actual practice and are explained in the rest of this chapter:

- The chief programmer team
- The dual-person design team
- The thread integration team
- Test teams

16.2
Chief Programmer Team

The chief programmer team is a prime instance of the ''lean and mean'' theme. It usually consists of not more than ten people organized around a single problem solver, the chief programmer. The chief programmer performs the core creative and policy-making work on all the technical aspects of the project—requirements definition, design, some of the coding, and testing. The approach is centered around the superior problem-solving abilities of the chief programmer, who must indeed be a highly skilled individual.

The configuration of the chief programmer team is outlined in Figure 16-1. The chief programmer is assisted by a less experienced backup programmer, as well as additional coders who further amplify the role of the chief programmer in a production-line environment during the coding phase. Other functional specialists, including documenters, testers, and possibly a tool expert, are also members of the team. The

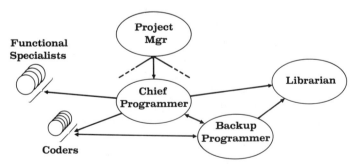

Figure 16-1 Chief programmer team.

actual membership of the team will vary as a function of the development phase, and each phase will require the support of different types of specialists.

Configuration management for the entire team effort is provided by a computer program librarian, who asserts baseline control over documents, code products, test cases, and reports. All activity on the team radiates from the exemplary lead work done by the chief programmer, who essentially leads by example. The major efficiencies that result from the work of the chief programmer team are derived from its centralized decision-making and associated abilities to cut across functional lines. All technical functions are under the control of the chief programmer, and unnecessary formalism is avoided by the direct communications afforded by the small-team environment.

When the chief programmer team was first popularized, it appeared to be a major breakthrough in software development practices. The concept is very appealing and does work well on small projects of perhaps twenty person-years or less. The size of the team can be constrained to ten persons or less for projects of this size. There are, however, a couple of major fallacies to consider if it is desired to extend the chief programmer team concept to larger projects. The first is the addition of more people to a team to meet the demand for a larger volume of work. In fact, this dilutes and eventually destroys the simple and precise communication paths present on a small team. Moreover, additional people also extend the chief programmer's span of control: the influence of the chief programmer's superior ability is reduced as he or she must spend more time managing people rather than performing the hard-core lead technical work that was essential to the original concept. In the final analysis, adding more staff simply causes a degeneration back to traditional organization practices.

The second fallacy is that the first fallacy can be avoided by proliferating the number of chief programmer teams. However, this places an extra burden on the next higher level manager to integrate the work of the various teams. By itself, this does not do violence to the benefits of chief programmer teams. Rather, the problem inheres in the availability of chief programmers. Consider again the job description of the chief programmer delineated in the first paragraph of this section. How many super problem solvers that fit this mold are there in any given company or organization? Undoubtedly, very few. In fact, if the description of the chief programmer's duties are interpreted literally, there may not be any "real" chief programmers in existence at all. Even on a liberal interpretation, there are too few highly skilled personnel that can fill the job, thus limiting the number of teams that can be mobilized concurrently.

The chief programmer team can be a very risky development approach. Since all activities center around the chief programmer, and since work is geared to his or her intellect, what happens if the chief programmer becomes unavailable to the project? What can happen is that because his or hers is a highly skilled technical talent, the departure of the chief programmer becomes an extreme setback for the project.

16.3
Dual-Member Design Team

The dual-member design team is employed during the software design phases of a project. Figure 16–2 shows the structure of a development organization during design activities.

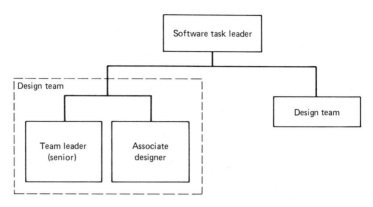

Figure 16-2 Development organization during design activities.

Improved productivity and quality are accomplished by attacking the problem at two levels:

1. The number of elements controlled by any leader is limited to avoid the inefficiencies caused by overloading.
2. The basic element is a two-person design team, which reduces the likelihood of incorrectly interpreting requirements, hidden design flaws, and poor communciations.

The design team consists of a team leader and his or her associate. Ideally, the team leader is the senior member. The concept has shown itself to be workable, however, when both members function on a coequal basis. The two members of the design team function as a unit through the design activities to provide

- More effective use of human resources (the augmented super-designer).
- Better design due to an effective, *continuous* design walkthrough environment.
- Continuity in case of loss of a team member.
- Fewer design errors.
- Faster response to changes in requirements.
- An improved training atmosphere for junior designers.

The mechanics of the dual-member approach do not dictate that both members meet continuously. Initially, the designers chart out together the top level of the design structure and partition the next lower-level design elements between them. Then each design member individually makes a first-cut design of the assigned elements. The team then reconvenes, perhaps the next day, to review and evaluate the individual efforts. Design flaws may be corrected collectively during the meeting, or an individual may accept a request to make certain design changes before the next meeting. The process repeats itself until all the identified design flaws are removed and the necessary level of detail is achieved. The final design represents the collective intellectual investment of both team members.

The contrast with the traditional utilization of personnel resources is depicted in Figure 16-3. The traditional approach involves each designer working individually on a task in parallel with one or more other designers. The collaborative team concept replaces the parallel approach with a serial effort. The same tasks are addressed in sequence by the team. Although it would be desirable in most circumstances to generate a design as a series of sequential tasks, realism demands that several design teams function in parallel in order to generate the required design within the constraints of the schedule.

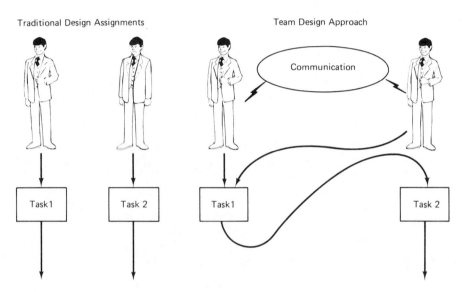

Figure 16-3   Team design approach contrasted with traditional method.

16.4
Thread Integration Team

The thread integration team replaces the dual-member design team for the software construction activity. The thread integration team fulfills the same objectives as the dual-member design team, including providing

- Continuous verification and validation.
- Simpler communication paths.
- A limited number of elements controlled by any leader.
- A continuous walkthrough environment.
- Better integration of individual efforts.
- Insurance against the loss of a team member.

The thread integration team consists of two to five members at the software construction stage of the life cycle. Preferably the number of thread integration teams should be limited to two, as experience has shown that the management of three parallel efforts within a major component development effort is difficult.

A small integration team (two to three members) is composed of a senior programmer complemented by junior members. Each programmer is assigned a module of the thread to code, and code walkthroughs are organized by the senior member to expose the code to the team immediately after an informal checkout. The code walkthroughs allow each member to see the "big picture," minimizing the specialist mentality. The senior programmer is responsible for the integration of the modules into a cohesive function. As with the dual-member design team, the emphasis is on a sequential approach: each thread is integrated into the evolving whole before initiating activity on the next thread.

The mechanics of a larger integration team (four to five members) are similar, but more complex. The larger team contains two senior members, permitting the intitiation of action on a succeeding thread before complete integration of the predecessor thread occurs. A typical scenario is illustrated in Figure 16–4. The thread developments are still largely sequential, with some overlap in time. Responsibility for thread integration alternates between the two senior programmers.

The larger thread integration team can be especially productive if the human resources involved are properly managed. This, of course, places more of a burden on the component task leader and senior programmers. But that is exactly where such a burden should reside in order to insulate the junior programmers from being distracted from their technical efforts.

16.5
Test Teams

The (independent) test team is a suborganization of the independent test organization (ITO). The test team is dedicated to the planning, conduct, and reporting of a single formal test. The ITO may consist of several test teams and is responsible for all of the project's formal testing and integration activities.

On contemporary software projects of significant size and complexity, the organization responsible for formal test activities is independent of the development organizations. Both the testing and development organizations may report to the same program manager. Where testing is part of an IV&V effort, the ITO is responsible to the customer or sponsoring organization. Reasons for establishing the test function as an independent entity are that (1) the engineering of a test program is a major task, and (2) an ITO preserves objectivity.

Planning and execution of testing requires an investment of time and effort which can exceed that of the software construction on a project. In order to assure that testing represents more than an afterthought to the construction, a parallel effort is necessary to properly engineer the test program. A group of people not involved with the software implementation is more likely to do a more thorough and objective job of planning the tests. The developers would be more likely to plan a trivial series of test cases. Devel-

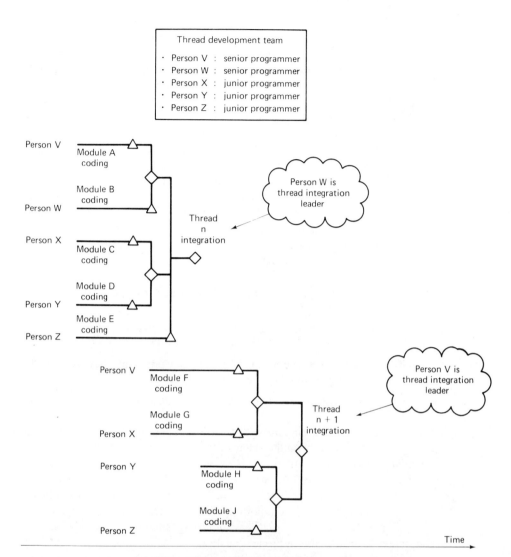

Figure 16-4 Thread development scenario.

opers can and do participate in the actual conduct of the testing (not the test planning!), but usually only in a supporting role.

A test team will design, execute, and report on an individual test, documenting the test design in a written plan and procedure. The team can consist of from one to, say, ten persons. The actual size and composition of the team will vary according to the scope of the test. There is no strict upper limit on the size of the team; more than ten members, however, will likely present inordinate communications and managerial complications. The key player of the team is the test director, who is assigned by the manager of the ITO as the individual singularly responsible for all aspects of the test. The test director is assisted by several other test engineers assigned to the team. Besides designing the overall testing and test cases, the test team generates the test case inputs and/or test data base. These may involve the use of simulation and other data-generation tools. The size of the team varies in response to the scope and complexity of the testing. For a simple test, the test director may be able to individually perform the preparatory activities.

During testing and during evaluation of the results, the original team of test engineers may be assisted by representatives of other interested organizations, including a system engineer, key software developers, and/or users. The system engineer participates to interpret and assure satisfaction of the requirements. The developers are involved to help diagnose and isolate problems, and to make controlled software modifications when necessary to allow the test to continue. Users participate to evaluate the functioning and performance of the software from an operational perspective and, in doing so, may even occupy operational positions to simulate the operational environment during a test.

The test director controls the conduct of the test by means of a number of meetings. A typical sequence of these meetings is the following:

1. A first pretest meeting to acquaint all test participants with the test objectives and the status of the test materials.
2. A pretest meeting for each test run to identify the specific objectives for the upcoming run.
3. A posttest meeting after each run to review problems just encountered and assign actions in pursuit of resolving the problems.
4. A final posttest meeting to affirm that all test objectives have been met.

It is common practice during a lengthy test for the test director to brief the customer and management periodically on the status of the test. The subjects discussed would include accomplishments, the current status, near term goals, long-term goals, and major problems.

The test team is composed of a small number of persons who can focus intensely on the planning, conduct, and reporting of a test without having to endure the complexities of large organizations. This streamlining simplifies communication paths and contributes to an increase in product quality.

The overall features of team development approaches include a continuous verification and validation atmosphere that is intrinsic to the basic development tasks and to keeping team members in touch with one another through simpler lines of communication. These features result in better integration of human resources than is attained under the conventional one-person-per-task approach.

Sample Software Quality Requirements Specification

The following is a sample of a software quality requirements specification documented in accordance with DOD-STD-2167's data item description for software requirements specifications (DI-MCCR-80025). Some deviations from the standard that were taken are:

- Consecutive numbering of paragraphs from 3.6.1 to 3.6.15
- Addition of survivability, expandability, and safety factors

In this specification, references are made to the following software components:

CSCI Computer software configuration item; consists of CSCs and units.

CSC Computer software component; consists of other CSCs and units.

Unit The physical software elements implemented in code.

This specification is applicable to one CSCI.

Special attention should be given to the use of the words "will" and "shall." The word "will" denotes an untestable goal of the design or a duplication of a requirement given elsewhere in this requirements specification. Verification of these requirements is accomplished by showing intent. The word "shall" denotes a testable, binding requirement verified by a formal test or inspection.

3.6
Quality Factors

The following paragraphs specify the quality requirements for this CSCI. These requirements specify static attributes of designs, code, and tests that can be observed during the development process.

Table 3.6–1 is a mapping from quality factors (paragraphs 3.6.1 to 3.6.14) to quality criteria. For each quality factor, there is at least one quality criterion that is applicable. For each quality criterion, there is at least one quality requirement listed in the subparagraphs of section 3.6.15.

The quantitative requirement for each quality factor is that all (100%) of the requirements applicable to the factor according to Table 3.6–1 will be implemented in the completed CSCI.

3.6.1 CORRECTNESS REQUIREMENTS.   Correctness is the degree to which the CSCI satisfies the specified requirements. The CSCI will meet the quality criteria identified in Table 3.6–1 and specified in the subparagraphs of Section 3.6.15.

3.6.2 RELIABILITY REQUIREMENTS.   Reliability is the extent to which the CSCI consistently performs the functions specified in Section 3.4 of the text and any associated interface documents. The CSCI will meet the quality criteria identified in Table 3.6–1 and specified in the subparagraphs of Section 3.6.15.

3.6.3 EFFICIENCY REQUIREMENTS.   Efficiency is the ratio of actual versus budgeted resource utilization by the CSCI. Resources include processor time, memory size, and communication bandwidth. The CSCI will meet the quality criteria identified in Table 3.6–1 and specified in the subparagraphs of Section 3.6.15.

3.6.4 INTEGRITY REQUIREMENTS.   Integrity is the extent to which the CSCI controls access to system resources. Resources include data-base items, functions, and software-controlled hardware. The CSCI will meet the quality criteria identified in Table 3.6–1 and specified in the subparagraphs of Section 3.6.15.

3.6.5 USABILITY REQUIREMENTS.   Usability is the time and effort required to learn the human interface with the CSCI, prepare input, and interpret the output of the CSCI. The CSCI will meet the quality criteria identified in Table 3.6–1 and specified in the subparagraphs of Section 3.6.15.

TABLE 3.6-1 QUALITY FACTOR/QUALITY CRITERIA CROSS REFERENCE

FACTOR / CRITERIA	Correctness	Reliability	Efficiency	Integrity	Usability	Testability	Flexibility	Portability	Reusability	Interoperability	Survivability	Expandability	Safety
3.6.15.1 Accuracy		x											x
3.6.15.2 Anomaly management		x									x		x
3.6.15.3 Application independence									x				
3.6.15.4 Augmentability												x	
3.6.15.5 Commonality									x				
3.6.15.6 Completeness	x												
3.6.15.7 Consistency	x					x							
3.6.15.8 Distributivity											x		x
3.6.15.9 Efficiency of communication			x										
3.6.15.10 Efficiency of processing			x										
3.6.15.11 Efficiency of storage			x										
3.6.15.12 Functional overlap										x			
3.6.15.13 Functional scope									x				
3.6.15.14 Generality							x		x			x	
3.6.15.15 Independence							x	x	x				
3.6.15.16 Modularity						x	x	x	x	x	x	x	x
3.6.15.17 Operability					x								
3.6.15.18 Reconfigurability											x		x
3.6.15.19 Safety management													x
3.6.15.20 Self-descriptiveness						x	x	x	x	x		x	
3.6.15.21 Simplicity		x				x	x	x	x			x	
3.6.15.22 System accessibility				x									
3.6.15.23 System clarity									x				
3.6.15.24 System compatibility										x			
3.6.15.25 Traceability	x												
3.6.15.26 Training					x								
3.6.15.27 Visibility						x	x						

3.6.6 MAINTAINABILITY REQUIREMENTS.   Maintainability is the extent of effort required to find and fix errors in the CSCI. The CSCI will meet the quality criteria identified in Table 3.6–1 and specified in the subparagraphs of Section 3.6.15.

3.6.7 TESTABILITY REQUIREMENTS.   Testability is the extent of effort required to verify software operation and performance. This CSCI will meet the quality criteria identified in Table 3.6–1 and specified in the subparagraphs of Section 3.6.15.

3.6.8 FLEXIBILITY REQUIREMENTS.   Flexibility is the extent of effort required to change (modify existing) software to accommodate changes in requirements. This CSCI will meet the quality criteria identified in Table 3.6–1 and specified in the subparagraphs of Section 3.6.15.

3.6.9 PORTABILITY REQUIREMENTS.   Portability is the extent of effort required to transfer this CSCI from one hardware or software system environment to another. This CSCI will meet the quality criteria identified in Table 3.6–1 and specified in the subparagraphs of Section 3.6.15.

3.6.10 REUSABILITY REQUIREMENTS.   Reusability is the extent of effort required to convert a portion of this CSCI for use in another application. This CSCI will meet the quality criteria identified in Table 3.6–1 and specified in the subparagraphs of Section 3.6.15.

3.6.11 INTEROPERABILITY REQUIREMENTS.   Interoperability is the extent of effort required to facilitate the interface of this CSCI with other systems or CSCIs. This CSCI will meet the quality criteria identified in Table 3.6–1 and specified in the subparagraphs of Section 3.6.15.

3.6.12 SURVIVABILITY REQUIREMENTS.   Survivability is the extent to which the CSCI continues to perform its required functions even when a portion of the system has failed. The CSCI will meet the quality criteria identified in Table 3.6–1 and specified in the subparagraphs of Section 3.6.15.

3.6.13 EXPANDABILITY REQUIREMENTS.   Expandability is the extent of effort required to expand (add new) software capabilities or performance. The CSCI will meet the quality criteria identified in Table 3.6–1 and specified in the subparagraphs of Section 3.6.15.

3.6.14 SAFETY REQUIREMENTS.   Safety is the absence of hazardous conditions. Software that can prevent a hazard from occurring is defined to be critical. The CSCI will meet the quality criteria identified in Table 3.6–1 and specified in the subparagraphs of Section 3.6.15.

3.6.15   CRITERIA REQUIREMENTS

3.6.15.1 ACCURACY.   Accuracy is the software characteristic that provides the required precision in calculations and outputs.

a. The specified accuracy requirements for individual functions shall be allocated to CSCs and units.

b. The specified quantitative accuracy requirements for outputs from functions will be implemented.

c. The outputs associated with CSCs and units shall have enough precision to meet the specified accuracy requirements.

d. Existing (i.e., off-the-shelf) mathematical library CSCs and units planned for use shall be implemented with enough precision to meet the specified accuracy requirements.

e. Numerical techniques used in implementing CSCs and units shall provide enough precision to meet the specified accuracy requirements.

*Fault tolerance comparison mechanisms shall be implemented with sufficient precision to meet specified accuracy requirements for the presented data values, and they shall operate upon the presented data values with no more precision than actually exists.

3.6.15.2 ANOMALY MANAGEMENT. Anomaly management is the software characteristic that ensures continuity of operations under and recovery from abnormal conditions.

a. Concurrent tasks that require synchronization shall be centrally controlled.

b. Critical inputs from interfacing CSCIs and external systems shall be checked with respect to their specified range prior to their use.

c. Critical inputs from interfacing CSCIs and external systems shall be checked with respect to specified conflicts prior to their use.

d. Critical inputs from interfacing CSCIs and external systems shall be checked with respect to specified reasonableness criteria prior to their use.

e. Critical inputs from interfacing CSCIs and external systems shall be checked with respect to specified invalid combinations prior to their use.

f. The design of the CSCI shall include fault-tolerance mechanisms which establish alternative means for continued error-free system operation within response-time requirements in the presence of detected software errors.

g. The design of the CSCI shall include fault containment mechanisms that prevent the propagation of failures resulting from individually or multiply detected software errors.

h. Detection of and recovery from computational errors in units will be provided.

i. Central control shall be used for concurrent or redundant processing of tasks which are required to execute more than once for comparison purposes.

j. The design of the CSCI shall include fault-tolerance mechanisms which provide uninterrupted service in the presence of individually or multiply detected software errors.

k. The design of the CSCI shall include recovery from detected hardware and software errors (i.e., arithmetic faults, hardware failures, clock interrupts, I/O device errors, and communication transmission errors).

l. The design of the CSCI shall include recovery from detected failures to communicate with interfacing CSCIs or external systems.

m. External systems and CSCIs that interface with a given CSCI will be periodically checked for operational status.

n. For all detected errors the time of occurrence, the unit in which the error occurred and its calling unit, and the data elements associated with the error shall be recorded when detected.

o. When an error condition is detected within a called unit, resolution of the error shall be determined by the calling unit.

p. Transmission retries between a given CSCI and interfacing CSCIs or external systems shall be parametrically defined for each interface.

q. For processing that is dependent on data received from interfacing CSCIs or external systems, a check shall be performed before the processing begins to determine that the data are available.

r. Critical data output to interfacing CSCIs and external systems shall be checked for reasonable values prior to outputting.

s. Error-checking information will be computed and transmitted with critical data output to interfacing CSCIs and external systems (except where precluded by existing interface specifications).

t. The specified error checking for inputs received from interfacing CSCIs and external systems shall be allocated to CSCs and units.

u. For critical units, all control variables and array indices shall be checked for out-of-range values prior to their use.

v. The design of the CSCI shall include alternative routing of messages when a communication error is detected and an alternative communication path exists.

w. The design of the CSCI shall utilize automatic fault isolation and recovery mechanisms for critical functions.

x. The design of the CSCI will assure that the CSCI is initialized to a correct state upon recovery from a detected fault and that processing is continued after recovery.

y. The design of the CSCI will include detecting when a task has exceeded predetermined execution time limits and taking remedial action.

z. All detected errors shall be reported to the operator.

3.6.15.3 APPLICATION INDEPENDENCE.   Application independence is the software characteristic that ensures that the software is not dependent on any data-base system, microcode, computer architecture, or algorithms.

a. Application software shall be unaware of the fault tolerant approach being used.

b. Interfaces to computer devices and peripherals shall be localized to the operating system or specific CSCs designated for that purpose.

c. Data calls for global data-base information shall be processed externally to the calling unit and the calls shall be free from specific knowledge of the data-base management scheme (i.e., storage and navigation details).

d. Software and firmware shall be separated into different CSCs (i.e., don't mix software and firmware in one CSC).

e. Units which are not part of the operating system CSC shall be free from specific references to the hardware architecture.

f. Data shall be symbolically defined and referenced in CSCs and units.

3.6.15.4 AUGMENTABILITY. Augmentability is the software characteristic that ensures expansion of capability for functions and data.

a. CSCs shall be partitioned to be logically complete and self-contained (i.e., functionally cohesive).

b. The specified spare memory requirements shall be met or exceeded.

c. The specified spare auxiliary storage requirements shall be met or exceeded.

d. The specified spare CPU utilization requirements shall be met or exceeded.

e. The specified spare I/O channel utilization requirements shall be met or exceeded.

f. The specified spare communication channel utilization requirements shall be met or exceeded.

g. The specified accuracy, convergence, timing attributes, and timing limitations shall be implemented parametrically.

h. Where practical, commercial or reusable software will be utilized to meet the requirements of the CSCI.

i. Provision will be made in unit source code to accommodate additional functions and new equipment.

j. Provision will be made in the physical data base to accommodate additional functions, new equipment, and new data.

k. The design of the CSCI shall include software that tests the operating system and the communication links, memory devices, and peripheral devices.

l. The number of units performing physical layer protocol processing for a hardware device interface shall not exceed two (one for input and one for output).

m. CSCs and units that handle hardware and device interface protocol shall not include unrelated processing.

n. Variable dimensions and sizes of dynamic arrays shall be defined parametrically.

o. Data-base references by units shall be symbolic.

p. Application software shall be independent of the specific details of the underlying data-base structure.

3.6.15.5 COMMONALITY. Commonality is the software characteristic that ensures the use of interface standards for protocols, routines, and data representations.

a. Data representations and translations for communication with external systems will comply with established standards.

b. A common technical glossary shall be used with equivalent definitions for use with the CSCI and for interfacing CSCIs.

c. Inputs shall be received by a single CSC for any single CSCI or external system interface.

d. Outputs shall be transmitted by a single CSC for any single CSCI or external system interface.

e. Translations of data shall be performed by a single CSC for any single CSCI or external system interface.

f. Input data received from interfacing CSCIs shall utilize a common format for the position of the data in message, data packing, and block transmission.

g. Output data transmitted to interfacing CSCIs shall utilize a common format for the position of the data in message, data packing, and block transmission.

h. Messages transmitted to interfacing CSCIs shall contain message labels identifying the type of data they contain.

i. The design of the CSCI shall comply with the specified LAN protocol standard.

j. The design of the CSCI shall comply with the specified LAN network monitor and control protocol standard.

k. The design of the CSCI shall comply with the specified LAN user session protocol standard.

l. The design of the CSCI shall comply with the specified LAN communication routing protocol standard.

m. The design of the CSCI shall comply with the specified LAN message-handling protocol standard.

3.6.15.6 COMPLETENESS. Completeness is the software characteristic that ensures full implementation of the functions required.

a. All specified requirements of the CSCI shall be allocated to CSCs of the CSCI.

b. Input, processing, and output requirements of each CSC and unit shall be defined in accordance with specified standards.

c. Each defined data item in each CSC and unit shall be set or used.

d. Global and local data shall bear comments in CSCI design documentation with regard to purpose and format.

e. The top-level and detailed designs of the CSCI shall be complete in themselves.

f. Conditions and alternative processing options shall be defined and documented for each decision point for all units.

g. A complete flow of data and execution control within each CSC down to the unit level shall be determined in the detailed design.

h. The detailed design shall include the logic to be employed and the algorithms and interrupt capabilities to be implemented in each unit.

i. All developed units shall be tested in at least one CSC integration test.

3.6.15.7 CONSISTENCY. Consistency is the software characteristic that ensures uniform design and implementation techniques and notations.

a. References to the same CSC shall use a single unique name, the CSC designator.

b. The naming of global and local data bases and formal parameters within CSCs and units shall comply with specified standards.

c. References to the same data files or items within CSCs and units shall use a single unique name.

d. Data representation in CSCs and units shall comply with a specified standard.

e. The peripheral I/O protocol and format shall comply with a specified standard.

f. The handling of detected error conditions shall comply with a specified standard (e.g., formats for error messages and diagnostic messages).

g. The definition and use of global data-base items shall be in accordance with a specified standard.

h. The calling sequence protocol between CSCs and between units shall comply with a specified standard.

i. The data-base management design shall provide a common and controlled approach to adding new data and to modifying and retrieving existing data from the global data bases.

j. References to a unit shall use the unit name or its assigned abbreviation.

k. The design of the CSCI shall be implementable in the specified programming language and its associated programming tools.

l. The unit design representation shall include unit specifications.

m. Units shall be implemented in accordance with specified programming standards.

n. Comments associated with executable source code shall be uniformly indented.

o. A single program design language (PDL) shall be used in all unit design representations.

3.6.15.8 DISTRIBUTIVITY. Distributivity is the degree to which software functions are geographically or logically separated within the system.

a. Critical application software shall be distributed redundantly over redundant processing elements.

b. Control of critical CSCs and units shall be distributed over different redundant processing elements (so as to ensure that there is no single point of failure).

c. A processing element shall contain complete CSCs (i.e., don't split CSCs among processors).

d. A processing element and storage device shall contain complete logical files (i.e., don't split logical files among processors or storage devices).

3.6.15.9 EFFICIENCY OF COMMUNICATION. Efficiency of communication is the software characteristic that ensures minimum utilization of communication resources in performing functions.

a. Utilization of communication resources shall not be minimized at the expense of fault tolerance.

b. The specified performance requirements and limitations for CSCI communications for each CSCI function will be implemented.

c. Local data will be separated from global data in the design of the CSCI.

3.6.15.10 EFFICIENCY OF PROCESSING. Efficiency of processing is the characteristic of software that ensures minimum utilization of processing resources in performing functions.

a. Utilization of processing resources shall not be minimized at the expense of fault tolerance.

b. The specified performance requirements and limitations for processor efficiency for each CSCI function will be implemented.

c. The storage implementation of files, code, arrays, and buffers will be organized for minimum search time.

d. Overlays will be avoided in the implementation of the CSCI.

e. The specified processing optimization requirements for the compiler shall be implemented.

f. Loops in the unit shall be free from non-loop-dependent statements (i.e., initializing a non-loop-dependent variable).

g. Loops within a unit will be free from unnecessary instances of bit and byte packing and unpacking.

h. Arithmetic expressions in a unit will avoid mixed data types in the same expression (i.e., conversion to the same data type will be explicit).

i. The data structure used for relating similar data items in a unit will be chosen to facilitate efficient processing (e.g., arrays, doubly linked lists, directories).

j. Arithmetic expressions in a unit will avoid different-size data items in the same expression (i.e., bytes, words, double words, and quad words should not coexist in a given expression).

k. Data items will be initialized in units when declared, when static initialization is appropriate.

l. Unnecessary assignment of a constant value to a variable in a unit (especially within a loop) will not be made.

m. Data packing will be minimized.

3.6.15.11 EFFICIENCY OF STORAGE.   Efficiency of storage is the software characteristic that ensures minimum utilization of storage resources.

a. Utilization of storage resources shall not be minimized at the expense of fault tolerance.

b. Data will efficiently utilize main and auxiliary storage for the CSCI (e.g., memory management should incorporate dynamic reallocation of physical memory space during execution).

c. Global data-base items shall not be referenced by more than one name in CSCs and units.

d. The CSCI will not store duplicate copies of files on the same storage device.

e. The specified storage optimizing requirements for the compiler shall be implemented.

f. The separation of the CSCI into segments (i.e., load modules) will efficiently utilize the memory space available.

3.6.15.12 FUNCTIONAL OVERLAP.   Functional overlap is the commonality of functions between CSCIs.

a. Except for fault tolerant software, CSCs and units which are duplicated in interfacing CSCIs will require neither redundancy management techniques nor logic to enable CSCI interoperability.

b. Except for fault tolerant software, CSCs and units which are duplicated in interfacing CSCIs will not require synchronization.

c. Functions which are duplicated in more than one CSCI will consist of common CSCs and units where appropriate.

d. The design and implementation of the software shall be identical for each site in which it is installed, varying only in adaptation to the operational configuration of the site.

e. The design of the CSCI will maximize the use of common CSCs and units, consistent with minimization of overall life-cycle costs.

3.6.15.13 FUNCTIONAL SCOPE.   Functional scope is the commonality of functions within a CSCI.

a. CSC and unit inputs shall be documented in the design as to the specific meaning and limitations of the data.

b. A description of the function(s) of a unit shall be provided in the unit's comments.

3.6.15.14 GENERALITY.   Generality is the characteristic of software that ensures the breadth of the functions performed with respect to the application.

    a. Units will be designed to be common units where practical.

    b. Common subprograms shall not mix any of the following processing categories: CSCI input, CSCI output, algorithmic processing.

    c. Common units will be free from strict limitations on the number of data items processed (e.g., the data number limits should be parametrized).

    d. Common units will be free from strict limitations on the values of input data (e.g., error tolerances, range tests, and reasonableness checks should be parametrized).

3.6.15.15 INDEPENDENCE.   Independence is the characteristic of software that ensures that it does not depend on its environment (the computing system, operating system, utilities, I/O routines, and libraries).

    a. Application software shall not rely on specific architectural details of lower level software and hardware.

    b. Developed code shall be regenerative and maintainable using only existing or delivered support software.

    c. The CSCI design shall provide logical and physical data independence for global data.

    d. Implementation of data structures for CSCI adaptation data will be distinct from data structures for unadaptable data.

    e. The number of units containing operations dependent on word or character size will be minimized.

    f. The number of units containing data item representations that are machine dependent will be minimized.

    g. Unit code constructs shall use specified coding standards (i.e., code will be free from nonstandard constructs of the specified programming language).

    h. Unit references to services unique to the operating system or language implementation (e.g., environment-dependent library routines and utilities) will be minimized.

    i. Assembly language shall be used only when specified memory or processing performance requirements cannot be met with the use of the specified programming language, and each such use shall be justified in a waiver request.

3.6.15.16 MODULARITY.   Modularity is the characteristic of software that ensures a highly cohesive component structure with optimum coupling.

    a. The design of the CSCI will minimize the use of control variables as formal parameters.

    b. The design of the CSCI will result in CSC and unit interfaces that exhibit the following types of coupling in the following order: data, stamp, control, external, common (with data being the most desirable).

c. The design of the CSCI shall be partitioned into one or more CSCs which, in turn, shall be partitioned into one or more units.

d. The CSCI design representation and structure shall be based on a formally defined, unambiguous syntax.

e. The CSCI design representation will be comprised of successive independent levels of abstraction, i.e., each level will be complete and independent, and each level will contain complete definitions of data and operations on those data.

f. Items in each logical file of the data-base design shall be functionally dependent at the identifier level (functional cohesion).

g. The design of the CSCI will result in CSCs and units that exhibit the following types of cohesion in the following order: functional, informational, communicational, procedural, classical, logical, coincidental (with functional being the most desirable).

h. Unit interfaces will be implemented in such manner as to minimize coupling (i.e., interfaces will be parsimonius.

i. Commercial and reusable software will be separated from developed software in the top-level design.

j. Data input to a called unit shall be passed to the unit through formal parameters or through the unit's access to global data items.

k. Data output from a called unit shall be passed back to the calling unit through formal parameters or through updates to global data items.

l. A subprogram shall consist of not more than 200 executable HOL statements.

m. When (either normal or exceptional) execution is completed, a called unit will return control to the calling unit.

n. Each unit shall be separately compilable.

o. Each unit shall consist of a specification, data declarations, and a sequence of executable statements.

3.6.15.17 OPERABILITY. Operability is the ease by which a person can use the software.

a. Operator inputs will be recorded.

b. Implementation of the data-entry functional requirements of the CSCI will be transparent to the operator.

c. All operator input data will be terminated by explicitly defined logical ends of input.

d. The operator shall be given a uniform interface to data regardless of the data's physical location in the system.

e. The operator shall be able to select from among available nodes for different types of processing or for retrieval of information.

f. User input parameters will have default values.

g. The number of different format types used for operator messages and responses will be minimized.

h. The number of different input formats with which the user must be familiar will be minimized.

i. The number of different default formats output to the user (e.g., CRT display arrangements and printer outputs) will be minimized.

j. The number of operator inputs/responses for a typical mission or job will be minimized.

k. The user shall be able to review and modify all input data prior to execution.

l. Capability will be provided for optional operator response to all reported errors.

m. The user shall be able to select from among the specified options for input media.

n. The user shall be able to select from among specified outputs, output media, output formats, and amounts of output.

o. The operator will be able to obtain specific system or network resource status information and reallocate resources.

p. Users will be able to quickly and easily "pop" to the top of the stack any partially obscured viewport, and/or "reshuffle" the stack or viewports in any desired order.

q. Form entries which are optional will be distinguishable from those which are mandatory.

r. All specified error conditions shall be reported to the operator in such manner that the nature of the error and any response required by the operator are identified and described in the error message.

s. Operator messages and responses will be simple and consistent.

3.6.15.18 RECONFIGURABILITY. Reconfigurability is the characteristic of software that ensures continuity of system operation when one or more processors, storage units, or communication links fail.

a. Modification of data bases shall be performed using transactions that are atomic, consistent, have integrity, and are durable.

b. CSCI processing shall continue without interruption when an interfacing CSCI is added to the LAN or when a redundant interfacing CSCI is removed from the LAN.

c. The integrity of the data base shall be restored following recovery from detected error conditions.

d. Critical CSCI data shall be recoverable.

e. The CSCI will be designed to avoid single points of failure and to minimize the operational effects of individual hardware or software failures.

f. CSCs and tasks will be partitioned to provide for differences in priority of execution.

g. Redundant data shall be consistent.

3.6.15.19 SAFETY MANAGEMENT. Safety management is the characteristic of software that separates critical and non-critical software to prevent unsafe conditions from occurring.

a. Where practical, critical functional requirements and data will not be mixed with noncritical requirements and data in the same CSC or unit.

b. Where practical, coupling between critical CSCs and units and noncritical CSCs and units will be of the data type only.

c. For critical units, the code for recovery from detected errors or undesirable events shall be lexically separate from the remaining code.

d. Where practical, critical functional requirements and data which are likely to change will be allocated to CSCs and units which are isolated from other CSCs and units. ("Isolated" means using at most the data coupling type.)

e. Code for critical units shall comply with a specified coding standard for critical units only.

f. Run-time scheduling of critical software shall avoid nondeterminism (e.g., by using pre-run-time scheduling decisions).

g. Fault tolerance mechanisms shall be utilized such that specified unsafe conditions shall be tested for, and when such conditions are detected, the software shall be restored to safe operation.

h. Communication of critical data between any two software components residing on different devices shall use a fault-tolerant protocol (e.g., two-phase commit, Byzantine generals protocols) to ensure validity of the data.

3.6.15.20 SELF-DESCRIPTIVENESS. Self-descriptiveness is the characteristic of software that ensures explanation of the implementation of functions.

a. The CSCI design representation will explicitly document the results of design decisions.

b. The design description of a CSC shall identify interfacing CSCs, CSCIs, and external systems.

c. A standard method shall be utilized for comments accompanying global data within a unit. Such comments shall include both meaning (i.e., what the item is) and limitations.

d. A standard method shall be used for comments accompanying parameter input and output, and local variables within a unit. Such comments shall include both meaning (i.e., what the item is) and limitations.

e. Unit prologue comments which contain all information in accordance with an established standard shall exist.

f. The identification and placement of comments within a unit shall be in accordance with an established standard.

g. Machine-dependent code in a unit shall bear comments to the effect that it is machine dependent.

h. HOL statements within a unit that do not comply with an established standard shall bear comments.

i. Comments related to a unit's operations shall describe the purpose or intent of those operations.

j. The unit shall be coded using the specified programming language.

k. Unit programming language keywords shall be used only with their predefined meanings (i.e., no keywords shall be used as variable names).

l. The prologue, specification, data and type declarations, program statements, comments, and exception handlers for any unit shall be structured in an established standard format.

m. Unit variable names will be descriptive of the physical or functional property they represent.

n. The attributes (i.e., usage, properties, and units of measure) of declared variables within a unit shall be described by comments.

o. The range of values and the default conditions associated with unit input parameters shall be described within each unit.

p. Source code within a unit, excluding comments, will be free from continuation lines.

q. The unit design representation shall be composed of a specification part and an execution part.

r. Source code shall be blocked and indented to denote logical levels of constructs.

s. Source code shall have comments to explain inputs, outputs, branches, conditional statements, case statements, loop statements, and other features that are not obvious in the code.

t. Data names and labels within units will be meaningful.

3.6.15.21 SIMPLICITY. Simplicity is the characteristic of software that ensures definition and implementation of functions in the most direct and understandable way.

a. The number of unit accesses (i.e., the utilization) of common data blocks and global data items will be minimized.

b. The ratio of unique items in common data blocks to unique common data blocks will be minimized within units.

c. The unit design shall permit only internal procedures to access a unit's data, while restricting other units to formal interface access.

d. Macros, procedures, functions, and other such reusability packages will be used to avoid repeated and redundant code within CSCs and units.

e. Units shall be implemented according to an established programming standard.

f. Unit implementation will minimize the Halstead difficulty measure (i.e., $D = (n_1/n_2)\,(N_2/2)$, where n_1 is the number of unique operators, n_2 is the number of unique operands, and N_2 is the total number of operands).

g. The flow of control within a unit will be from top (i.e., point of entry) to bottom.

h. The use of negative Boolean and compound Boolean expressions in unit source code will be minimized.

i. Unnatural exits (e.g., jumps and returns) from loops will be minimized.

j. Block nesting levels in the unit source code beyond three (3) levels will be avoided; nesting beyond five (5) levels shall be avoided.

k. The number of conditional and unconditional branches in unit source code will be minimized.

l. The number of statement labels within units will be minimized.

m. The design descriptions of units shall identify interfacing units, CSCIs, HWCIs, and external systems.

n. The unit design description and prologue shall include input, output, processing, limitations, and exceptions that are raised or handled by this unit.

o. The total number of data items in a unit's source code will be minimized.

p. The number of data declaration statements and data manipulation statements in a unit's source code will be minimized.

q. The unit implementation will be independent of the source of the inputs and the destination of the outputs (i.e., the principles of information hiding and scope of effect/control will be used).

r. Each data item in unit source code shall be used in accordance with its description in an accompanying comment (i.e., the item serves only one purpose).

s. Units will be implemented independently of any knowledge of prior processing outside of them.

t. Units shall be implemented using only the following constructs or their equivalents: sequence, if . . . then . . . else, do . . . while, do . . . until, and case.

u. Except for comment statements, nonexecutable statements shall be grouped in one area in each unit.

v. Unit data declarations will be grouped and arranged in a meaningful order in the source code (e.g., in a columnar arrangement rather than horizontally).

w. Except for data declarations, each line of source code shall contain at most one executable language statement.

x. Iteration loop indices will not be explicitly modified in the source code within the loop.

y. The unit will be free from self-modifying code.

z. Except for exit points for exception handling, units shall have a single entry point and a single exit point.

3.6.15.22 SYSTEM ACCESSIBILITY. System accessibility is the characteristic of software that ensures control and auditing of access to the software and data.

a. The CSCI will ensure a valid data base. Key CSCI parameters will be monitored by the software to ensure their specified validity.

b. Data-base access will be controlled by access authorization and privacy locks.

c. All access to the system (i.e., sign-on) will be recorded.

d. The capability of disabling or disconnecting any or all of the interfacing systems will be provided.

e. The design of the CSCI will ensure that files associated with controlling access to the system will not be accessible to user programs or any system program operated under user control.

f. The design of the CSCI will provide protection against unauthorized access and modification to the data base.

g. The design of the CSCI will provide protection against unauthorized modification to the implemented CSCI.

h. The design of the CSCI will provide protection against loss of CSCI services by inadvertent or unauthorized operator input.

i. The design of the CSCI will provide protection against unauthorized modification or bypass of any operating system or application function security logic.

j. The design of the CSCI will alert personnel and provide identification of the source of attempts to defeat security features.

k. The design of the CSCI will perform checks periodically and at random to ensure that necessary software is in the system and has not been modified.

l. The design of the CSCI will ascertain user authorization for system entry and ensure that unauthorized users are precluded.

m. The design of the CSCI will ensure that there is no opportunity for the operator to accidentally injure either the system, the data with which the operator is working, or any processing transactions that are under way.

n. A security protection capability will be provided to assure that only valid users are permitted access to functions which only they are authorized to use.

o. Unsuccessful access attempts will be routed to the supervisory position for display.

p. The design of the CSCI will provide protection against any inadvertent or erroneous actions that cause the CSCI to operate in a degraded mode.

q. The design of the CSCI will require positive operator confirmation before executing a command to cause the CSCI to operate in a degraded mode.

r. The scope of task operations during execution will be controlled (e.g., invoke other tasks, access system registers, or use privileged commands).

3.6.15.23 SYSTEM CLARITY. System clarity is the characteristic of software that ensures the clear description of program structure in a direct, understandable manner.

a. The same functional requirement shall not be performed within different CSCs if it can be restricted to a single CSC.

b. I/O and I/O translation requirements shall be isolated from computational requirements in the allocation of requirements to units.

c. The documentation for a unit shall specify the units called by the given unit.

d. Units shall not include unreachable source code.

e. The number of conditional branch statements within a unit will be minimized.

f. The number of iteration loops in the unit will be minimized.

g. Interface data items in any unit shall be free from negative qualification logic (i.e., they shall not have Boolean values that return "TRUE" upon failure rather than success).

h. The design of a unit will not intentionally modify the internal code or data of other units.

i. Except for transaction centers, the number of other units called by a given unit (fan-out) will be limited to seven (7).

j. For reusable (i.e., common) units, communication with interfacing units shall be only via data parameters (i.e., there shall be no control or exception parameters).

k. For reusable (i.e., common) units, the unit interface will be established only by arguments in the calling sequence parameter list (i.e., no interface via global data item references).

l. Global data items in a given unit's interface shall bear comments regarding the purpose, type, and limitations of the data items.

m. The design of the CSCI will be represented in a manner which facilitates ease of understanding and ease of implementation.

n. Units shall not share temporary storage locations of variables with other units.

o. Each unit shall be uniquely identified in the design documentation.

p. Unit implementation will avoid complicated expressions (e.g., negative Boolean expressions).

3.6.15.24 SYSTEM COMPATIBILITY. System compatibility is the characteristic of software that ensures the hardware, software, and communication compatibility of two CSCIs.

a. The CSCI interface design will be compatible with the interface design of the interfacing CSCIs with which it communicates.

b. The CSCI implementation will use the same programming language as the interfacing CSCIs.

c. The CSCI will use an operating system which is compatible with the operating system(s) of its interfacing CSCIs.

d. The CSCI shall utilize the same support software as interfacing CSCIs.

e. The interface design of the CSCI shall use the same data type, data representation, and data units as interfacing CSCIs.

f. The design of the CSCI will be compatible with the data-base design of interfacing CSCIs.

g. The design of the CSCI shall include data-base access techniques which are compatible with interfacing CSCIs.

h. The design of the CSCI shall include the use of interrupt structures which are compatible with those of interfacing CSCIs.

i. The implementation of the CSCI will make use of an instruction set which is compatible with the instruction set used in the implementation of interfacing CSCIs.

j. The CSCI will use the same structure and sequence for the contents of messages as do the interfacing CSCIs (i.e., all real variables will be the same bit length, and all real coordinates will be in the same order).

3.6.15.25 TRACEABILITY.   Traceability is the software characteristic that provides a thread of origin from the implementation to the requirements with respect to the specified development envelope and operational environment.

a. The design of the CSCI will be represented in a manner which facilitates traceability to its specification.

b. The CSCI implementation shall conform functionally and structurally to the software design as specified in the design documentation.

3.6.15.26 TRAINING.   Training ensures initial familiarization with and subsequent transition from the current operation of the software.

a. Realistic training exercises will be provided to familiarize the user with the functionality of the CSCI.

b. Faults in on-line training exercises shall not affect mission operations.

3.6.15.27 VISIBILITY.   Visibility is the software characteristic that provides monitoring of the development and operation of the software.

a. The CSCI will include rapid and positive detection and reporting of hardware and software malfunctions, intermittent errors, and marginal performance of the software.

b. The CSCI will isolate defective components and tasks to facilitate both recovery and repair.

Index

Completeness, 14, 54, 77, 110, 116, 298 (*See also* Quality criteria)
Consistency, 55, 77, 299 (*See also* Quality criteria)
Correctness, 48, 116, 292 (*See also* Quality factors)
Correctness proofs, 194–195
Cost of quality
    acquisition cost, 8, 11, 17, 48, 79, 88–90
    acquisition cost analysis, 265–267
    acquisition cost and schedule model, 260–264
    acquisition schedule analysis, 267
    IV&V contribution, 263
    life-cycle cost analysis, 267–270
    life cycle cost model, 264–265
    maintenance effects, 265
    models of, 260–265
    payback period analysis, 268–270
Cost/schedule estimating models
    COCOMO, 261–262, 264
    Jensen, 262
    sensitivity factor comparisons, 263
Coupling, 63, 303
Crisis management, 17, 109, 280
Criteria (*See* Quality criteria)
Critical quality factors, 56, 64, 65, 96, 102, 104, 116, 295, 299, 304, 305

D

Decision-to-decision path
    definition, 235, 242–244
    use as test coverage measure, 242–248
Defect, 15, 16, 17, 18, 21, 280
Design iteration, 106, 116
Design reviews
    acceptability criteria, 128–129, 130
    concepts, 27, 128
    critical design reviews, 134
    formal qualification review, 135–136

Design reviews (*Contd.*)
    functional and physical configuration audit, 135
    mechanics, 129–130
    preliminary design review, 133
    sequence of, 130–131
    strengths and weaknesses, 136
    system design review, 131–133
    system requirements review, 130–131
    test readiness review, 134–135
Design validation
    case study, functional requirements, 161–172
    case study, prototyping, 176–181
    empirical rules for, 162–165
    using threads, 162, 169–172
Distributivity, 56, 77, 114, 299 (*See also* Quality criteria)
Documentation quality, 13, 57, 77 (*See also* Quality criteria)
Dual member design team, 285–287

E

Efficiency, 48, 292 (*See also* Quality factors)
Efficiency of communication, 58, 77, 300 (*See also* Quality criteria)
Efficiency of processing, 58, 77, 300 (*See also* Quality criteria)
Efficiency of storage, 59, 77, 300 (*See also* Quality criteria)
Errors, 11, 15–18, 21, 51, 57, 74, 295–296, 299
Expandability, 48, 294 (*See also* Quality factors)

F

Factors (*See* Quality factors)
Failures, 14, 49, 51, 53, 56, 75, 116, 295–296

Fault tolerance, 51, 114, 116, 295–296, 300–301, 305
Fault tree analysis, 199–200
Fitness for use (*See* Quality, definition of)
Flexibility, 48, 294 (*See also* Quality factors)
Formal design reviews, 27, 128–136
Full coverage testing
    application case study, 238–248
    based on decision-to-decision paths, 235
    cost to discover error, 249
    coverage report examples, 246, 248
    definitions, 234–235
    life cycle cost effectiveness, 247, 249–250
    using RSVP80™ tool, 238–248
    using test coverage analyzer tools, 235–237
Functional scope, 60, 77, 301 (*See also* Quality criteria)

G

Generality, 61, 77, 302 (*See also* Quality criteria)

I

IEEE standard, 4, 9, 98, 101, 280
"Ilities" (*See* Quality factors)
Implement to schedule strategy, 222
Independence, 61, 77, 302 (*See also* Quality criteria)
Independent test organization, 184, 207–210
Independent verification and validation (IV&V)
    activity allocation, 187–188
    background and origins, 183–184
    case study, unsuccessful application, 191–192
    contribution to cost of quality, 263

Independent verification and validation (IV&V) (*Contd.*)
    costs of, 190–191
    customer performance of, 184
    independent contractor approach, 184–192
    independent test organization, 184
    levels of activities, 185–186
    need determination, 188–190
    organization profile, 186–187
    overview, 31, 33
    types of, 184
    use of small companies, 187
Inspections
    advantages over walkthroughs, 139–140, 145
    benefits and disadvantages, 146
    concepts, 28, 140
    cost of, 146
    error recording, 142–143
    members of team, 140
    procedure, 141
    quality evaluation, use in, 140–141
    reports, 142–144
Integration
    alternate strategies, 252–253
    builds versus traditional method, 255–256
    logically complete system goal, 253, 256
    philosophy of, 251–252
    risk reduction strategy, 256
    using builds, 253–256
    using threads, 180, 254–255
Integrity, 48, 292 (*See also* Quality factors)
Internal review cycle
    advantages and disadvantages, 137–138
    concept, 27–28, 136
Interoperability, 48, 54, 70, 94, 294 (*See also* Quality factors)

J

Jensen cost estimating model, 262

T

U

V